THE DEVELOPMENT OF ISLAMIC JURISPRUDENCE

Prof. AHMED HASAN

Adam Publishers & Distributors
New Delhi -2 (India)

Adam Publishers & Distributors
(Exporters & Importers)
1542, Pataudi House, Darya Ganj,
New Delhi-110002
Ph.: (O) 23282550, 23284740,
Fax.: 23267510
E-mail: apd@bol.net.in,
syedsajid_ali@rediffmail.com
website: www.adambooks.com

Edition- **2013**
ISBN : 81-7435-009-8
Price :

Printed & Bound in India
Published by :
S. Sajid Ali, for
Adam Publishers & Distributors
1542, Pataudi House, Darya Ganj,
New Delhi-110002, India

FOREWORD *

Alongside of economic blueprints and five-year plans the Muslims all over the world are now refreshingly devoting their attention to a reinterpretation of Islam in the context of modern times. Generally speaking, the desire for religious reconstruction and moral regeneration in the light of fundamental principles of Islam has, throughout their historical destiny, been deeply rooted among the Muslims—progressivists as well as traditionalists. Both the sections seem conscious of the fact that the only way for the Muslims of today, for an active and honourable participation in world affairs, is the reformulation of positive lines of conduct suitable to contemporary needs in the light of social and moral guidance offered by Islam. This, however, entails a great and heavy responsibility for all those engaged in the onerous task of reconstruction. Theirs is the endeavour to strike a happy balance between the divergent views of the traditionalists and the modernists, or, in standard language, between conservatism and progressivism.

It was indeed unfortunately considered during the preceding centuries that Muslims closed the door of *Ijtihād*, resulting in stagnation and lack of dynamism. Resurgence of the new spirit for a re-evaluation of their religious and moral attitudes towards the ever-emerging problems of life in a changing world has been spasmodic and relatively fruitless. Though thwarted, the spirit remained alive and was never wholly stifled. We find its periodic effulgence in the emergence of various reformist movements that convulsed the world of Islam from time to time. The Indo-Pakistan sub-continent was no exception. The lamp lit by Shāh Waliy Allāh al-Dihlawī continued to burn and shed its light. The Islamic Research Institute may be regarded as a link in that long-drawn-out process. It was established by the Government of Pakistan with the specific purpose of enabling

* First Edition (1970)

the Muslims of Pakistan to lead their lives in accordance with the dictates of the Qur'ān and the *Sunnah*, in the light of modern developments and commensurate with the challenge of the time. By its very nature, however, the work of the Institute cannot remain confined to the geographical limits of Pakistan but will serve the *Ummah* in general. The people entrusted with this heavy responsibility are, therefore, required to have a clear and well-defined conception of their objectives with a view to their institutional implementation in the wider fabric of state organisation and national development. This is exactly what the members of the Institute are endeavouring to accomplish.

Conscious as we are of the fact that Islamic scholarship, during the past few centuries, has been more or less mechanical and semantic rather than interpretative or scientific, our efforts, howsoever humble and small, are directed towards breaking the thaw in Islamic thinking—both religious and moral. With these objectives in view, the Institute has decided to launch a series of publications, covering a wide and diverse field of Islamic studies, prepared mostly by its own members. The Institute has a definite direction and a cohesive ideology, although honest and academic difference of opinion is naturally allowed. We hope that the Muslims, living under the stress and strain of modern times, will find enough food for thought in these publications resulting ultimately in rekindling in them the burning desire, nay, the longing, for exercising *Ijtihād*, the only prerequisite for recapturing the pristine glory of Islam and for ensuring an honourable place for the Muslim *Ummah* in the comity of progressive, dynamic and living nations of the world. We also hope that these works will equally provide sound and solid scholarship for the non-Muslim Islamists.

M. ṢAGHĪR ḤASAN MAʿṢŪMĪ
Professor-in-Charge
Islamic Research Institute, Pakistan

Islamabad
11 June 1970

PREFACE*

The Islamic Research Institute has launched a training programme which "aims at producing scholars of Islamic sciences who would also be familiar with the modern methods of research and scholarship and who could understand and present the teachings of Islam in the light of present-day problems". The training course culminates in the preparation of doctoral dissertations. The present work is the first dissertation in this training programme.

The early history of Islamic jurisprudence, especially up to the time of al-Shāfi'ī (d. 204 A.H.), is vitally important for a student of Islamic jurisprudence because it throws light on the origins and evolution of this subject in its most formative stage. A most original, comprehensive and detailed study of the subject to date is "*The Origins of Muhammadan Jurisprudence*" by Prof. Joseph Schacht. This early period has also been partly covered by Prof. N. J. Coulson in his work "*A History of Islamic Law*". Prof. Schacht has attempted to establish that Islamic jurisprudence originated from the popular Umayyad practice, rather than taking its threads from the Qur'ān and the *Sunnah* of the Prophet directly. Norms derived from the Qur'ān, according to him, were introduced in Islamic law almost at a secondary stage. The concept '*Sunnah* of the Prophet', he thinks, appeared in Islam in connection with the assassination of 'Uthmān, the third Caliph, in a political context for the first time; subsequently it developed a theological connotation and, lastly, after one full century it took its place in Islamic law through the 'Irāqī jurists. Besides, he presumes that *Sunnah* of the Prophet in Islam is another name of the *Sunnah* of the pre-Islamic Arabs. He has tried to establish that the 'living tradition' of the early Muslims was attributed to the Prophet, and thus he has come to hold the view that the entire corpus of *Ḥadīth* is apocryphal.

* First Edition (1970)

His thesis centres around the 'back-projection' of legal opinions to the Prophet and the early authorities. *Qiyās*, he holds, has been taken from Judaism and *Ijmā'* of the learned from Roman law. Such are the conclusions reached by Prof. Schacht on the basis of his detailed analysis of the early legal material.

These are some of the problems which moved the present writer to study the subject in greater detail, of which the present thesis is the result. The writer has come to the conclusion that the content of Islamic jurisprudence was based on the Qur'ān and the *Sunnah* of the Prophet from the very beginning, although this does not exclude the fact that the materials were largely supplied by the popular Umayyad practice and administration. It discusses the historical evolution of the theory of the basic principles of Islamic jurisprudence, namely, the Qur'ān, the *Sunnah*, *Qiyās* and *Ijmā'*. The thesis studies in detail the application of these principles by the early jurists. It also traces the origins of the early schools, and presents an analysis of al-Shāfi'ī's contribution to Islamic jurisprudence.

Arabic words have been transliterated according to the standard introduced by the Institute. The geographical names like Mecca, Medina, Basra, Kufa and others, however, have been spelt according to the common practice.

References in the text to the Qur'ānic verses are from the English translation of the Qur'ān by Mohammad Marmaduke Pickthall, *The Meaning of the Glorious Koran*, New York, 1954, with some changes in the translation where these were found necessary.

The author acknowledges his debt of gratitude to Dr. Fazlur Rahman, the former Director, Islamic Research Institute, who guided him in this task ; he also read the manuscript from the beginning to the end, and improved the language, despite his heavy preoccupations. The author is also indebted to Dr. S. M. Yusuf,

Professor and Head of the Department of Arabic, University of Karachi, who presented to him a copy of his article "The *Sunnah*—its transmission, development and revision", published in the *Islamic Culture*, which profoundly benefited him. The author is further grateful to 'Abd al-Ras͟hīd Nu'mānī for providing him with his MS. of al-S͟haybānī's *Kitāb al-Ḥujaj*.

The author is also grateful to the authorities of the University of Karachi for according permission to get this thesis published through the Institute. This thesis was submitted to the Department of Arabic, University of Karachi, in 1967 under the title '*Jurisprudence in the Early Phase of Islam*'.

Most of the chapters of this thesis were published in the Institute's Journal, *Islamic Studies*. The author is obliged to Messrs. S. Q. Fatimi and Mazheruddin Siddiqi, editors of the Journal, for initial editing of these chapters at the time of their publication in the Journal.

Islamabad: AHMAD HASAN
10th May, 1970.

NOTE ON TRANSLITERATION

The system of transliteration of Arabic words adopted in this book is the same as has been employed by the editors of the *Encyclopaedia of Islam*, new edition, with the following exceptions: *q* has been used for *ḳ* and *j* for *dj*, as these are more convenient to follow for English-knowing reader than the international signs. The use of *c̲h̲*, *d̲h̲*, *g̲h̲*, *s̲h̲*, *t̲h̲*, and *z̲h̲* with a subscript dash, although it may appear pedantic, has been considered necessary for the sake of accuracy and clear pronunciation of the letters peculiar to Arabic and Persian. As against the Encyclopaedia, *tā murbūṭa* has throughout been retained and shown by *ḵ* or *t*, as the case may be. This was also found necessary in order to avoid any confusion.

CONTENTS

INTRODUCTION

Law in every society aims at the maintenance of social control. It is a system which is primarily established to protect the rights of individuals as well as of society. The legal system in every society has its own nature, character and scope. Similarly, Islam has its own legal system known as *Fiqh.* Islamic law is not purely legal, in the strict sense of the term; rather it embraces all the spheres of life—ethical, religious, political and economic. It has its origin in the Divine Revelation. The Revelation determined the norms and basic concepts of Islamic Law and in many respects initiated a break with the customs and the tribal legal system of pre-Islamic Arabia.

It should be noted that there are certain basic differences between the purpose and scope of law in the modern sense and in the sense of the Qur'ān. Laws in the modern sense are specific rules governing the social, economic, and political affairs of a nation made by a competent authority and enforced by the sanctions of a state. Rules of individual moral behaviour are not covered by modern laws, although they do exist in the form of customs, social manners and mores, and are enforced to some extent by morality squads or local police, and by the sheer force of public opinion. But in case public opinion accepts certain immoral individual actions, moral laxity is bound to prevail with change in the very concept of morality as may be noticed in the case of most of the highly industrialised nations of Western Europe and North America.

The scope of Qur'ānic laws encompasses rules of human conduct in all spheres of life, ensuring man's well-being in his mundane life as well as in the Hereafter. The enforcement of Islamic laws contained in the Qur'ān is the duty of an Islamic state. The application of the individual's rules of moral conduct is governed by two important factors, namely, the Muslim society's collective responsibility to observe Islamic teachings, and the individual's relationship with his Creator as well as with society. Muslim society is supposed to be under the obligation, according to the Qur'ān, to enforce the application of rules of moral behaviour as divine commandments. The Qur'ān repeatedly appeals to human conscience to follow the teachings of the Revelation for its own welfare as well as for the well-being of fellow human beings. Thus, the Qur'ān, by making the observance of the rules of the *Sharī'ah* a matter of human conscience, has dignified the concept of law and the ethical values of its teachings, which constitute the noblest and most perfect basis of universal laws.

Jurisprudence is the science of the first principles of law which may concern itself with law in its various aspects, namely, with its traditional analysis, with its historical origin and development, and with its ideal character. The starting-point of jurisprudence, in the history of the development of law, is a phase in which law is developed from its rudimentary form and begins to be systematically constructed. At this stage, questions about the authority of law-making, the source of law and the method of reasoning arise. Therefore, law is followed by jurisprudence. A particular legal theory springs from a legal system which already exists in a society. The theory of law in Islam must have existed in its nebulous form during the time of the Companions when they were faced with new conditions. They must have thought about the source of law, and the method of reasoning for solving fresh problems. In certain cases they gave their own rulings and violated the existing practice. The classical legal theory, however, was not given its technical and systematic form by the Companions, but developed and was formalized during the second and the third generation. The principles of law were derived from the law itself which was in the process of developing since the earliest days of Islam. Thus Islamic jurisprudence is an afterthought which evolved as a result of the formalization of law as its justification. The first available systematic work on the theory of Islamic law is al-Shāfi'ī's *Risālah.*

The present dissertation is an attempt at showing the historical development of Islamic jurisprudence in the first two centuries of the Hijrah. It is based mainly on the works of Mālik, Abūf Yūsuf, al-Shaybānī, and al-Shāfi'ī. We have avoided, as far as possible, reliance on the late sources which rather present the subsequent medieval picture of Islamic jurisprudence. History is a continuous developing phenomenon. It changes its course at different stages, but even when it seems to be a continuous smooth process, imperceptible changes occur as a result of various historical factors. Therefore, neither a formal description of events nor a mere presentation of the conventional picture as recorded in the classical literature will do justice to the writing of history. The picture of Islamic jurisprudence of the earlier period which emerges from the late works is, in fact, itself the result of a historical development. Therefore, the correct method is to make a critical analysis of the problems themselves as they are discussed in the early legal manuals and to derive conclusions from them. In writing the history of this period one is unfortunately faced with paucity of sources and comparative lack of information. The manuals of *Fiqh* were first written during the second century of the Hijrah; we have no source going back to the first century. While these second-century works have been mostly relied upon in this thesis, certain later works nevertheless have also been consulted in view of the overall scarcity of sources for this period.

After making a closer study of the early legal material, whereas one is forced to differ on a number of important points from the classical theory and standpoint on the basis of evidence, one is equally forced to disagree with several of the theses put forward by Professor Schacht. The present study, in fact, poses a number of problems for the holders of the medieval view and shows a line for further investigation and research into the early history of this subject.

Chapter I

MEANING OF THE TERM *FIQH* AND OTHER ALLIED TERMS

The original meaning of *fiqh* is the understanding and knowledge of something. In this sense, *fiqh* and *fahm* are synonyms. An Arabic idiom goes: فلان لا يفقه و لا ينقه ("So-and-so neither understands nor comprehends"[1]). The word *fiqh* was originally used by the Arabs for a camel expert in covering; he who distinguishes the she-camels that are lusting from those that are pregnant. Accordingly, the expression فحل فقيه was current among them.[2] From this expression, it is believed, the meaning of deep knowledge and understanding of anything has been derived. Hence, *Fiqh al-Lughah* (understanding of the science of language) is the title of a work produced by al-Tha'ālibī (d. 429 A.H.). This work has nothing to do with law; instead, it deals with the rules and regulations the mastery of which enables a person to acquire command over the Arabic language. In pre-Islamic days the term *Faqīh al-'Arab* was an appellation given to al-Ḥārith b. Kaladah who was also called *Ṭabīb al-'Arab*, this latter expression being synonymous with the former term.[3]

In more than one place the Qur'ān has used the word *fiqh* in its general sense of "understanding". The Qur'ānic expression ليتفقهوا فى الدين ('that they may gain understanding in religion') shows that in the Prophet's time the term *fiqh* was not applied in the legal sense alone but carried a wider meaning covering all aspects of Islam, namely, theological, political, economic, and legal. In the following paragraphs we shall discuss in greater detail how this developed from its original meaning into its technical sense.

In the early period we find a number of terms like *fiqh*, *'ilm*, *īmān*, *tawḥīd*, *tadhkīr* and *ḥikmah*[4] that were used in a broader sense; but later on their original meanings changed and became more narrow and specific. The reason for this change is obvious. The Muslim society during the Prophet's lifetime was not so much diversified and complex as it became later. The association of the Muslims with the non-Muslims of conquered territories, the emergence of several legal and theological schools in Islam, and the development of Islamic learning were the major factors that caused a change in the simple and unsophisticated meanings of several Islamic terms as understood by the Muslims of the Prophet's time. It will take us far afield if we discuss how each of the aforesaid terms shifted its meaning from the original. We shall discuss the term '*fiqh*' alone with which we are concerned here. It may be noted that in the early days of Islam the terms '*ilm* and *fiqh* were frequently used for an understanding of Islam in general. The Prophet is reported to have blessed Ibn 'Abbās (d. 68 A.H.) saying: "O God, give him understanding in religion (اللهم فقهه فى الدين)"[5]! It is quite obvious that the Prophet could not have meant exclusively knowledge of the law; but rather a deeper understanding of Islam in general. In the times of the Prophet some bedouins are reported to have requested him to depute someone to their tribe to instruct them in religion (يفقهو نا فى الدين)[6]. These examples show that the term *fiqh* was used in its broader sense extending to the tenets as well as the law of Islam. The bedouins obviously did not intend to be taught exclusively the legal rules leaving aside other essentials of religion.

In its broader sense, the term *fiqh* could perhaps even cover the meaning of asceticism in the early period. It is reported that the Ṣūfī Farqad (d. ca. 131 A.H.), while discussing certain questions, said to al-Ḥasan al-Baṣrī (d. 110 A.H.), that the *fuqahā'* would oppose him on this. Al-Ḥasan replied that a real *faqīh*, as a matter of fact, was a person who despised the world, was interested in the hereafter, possessed a deeper knowledge of religion, was regular in his prayers, pious in his dealings, refrained from disparaging Muslims and was the well-wisher of the community.[7] (This sort of report, however, does not prove that this term *was not applied* to the legal issues). The reason for its generic use in the early days of Islam appears to be that primarily the fundamentals of religion were emphasised. People were not engaged in the *minutiae*. Hence, this term signified, besides the purely intellectual understanding, also *the depth and intensity of faith*, knowledge of the Qur'ān, laws relating to rituals and other general injunctions of Islam.

It is to be noted that *Kalām* and *Fiqh* were not separated till the time of al-Ma'mūn (d. 218 A.H.). It appears that *fiqh* embraced the theological problems as well as the legal issues till the second century of the Hijrah. A book known as *al-Fiqh al-Akbar* and attributed to Abū Ḥanīfah (d. 150 A.H.) against the beliefs of *Ahl al-Qadar* deals with the basic tenets of Islam like faith, unity of God, His attributes, the life hereafter, prophethood, etc. These are problems that are dealt with in *Kalām* and not in the science of law. The name of this book, therefore, suggests that *Kalām*, too, was covered by the term *fiqh* in the early stages. Due to its comprehensive and generic meaning Abū Ḥanīfah is reported to have defined *Fiqh* as 'a soul's knowledge of its rights and obligations'.[8] When theological problems arose among the Muslims and the *Ummah* was divided into several sects, considerable importance came to be attached to the veracity of beliefs. At this time Abū Ḥanīfah is said to have declared that obtaining the knowledge of *dīn* was better than that of *aḥkām*. By *dīn* he obviously meant the basic beliefs of Islam, because he calls the knowledge of the unity of God and other allied beliefs '*al-fiqh al-akbar* (the greater understanding).'[9] *Kalām* was introduced for the first time by the *Mu'tazilah* as an independent science, when Greek works on philosophy were rendered into Arabic during the time of al-Ma'mūn.[10] This indicates that prior to the existence of *kalām* as an independent science, *fiqh* covered the problems of this science.

Like the term *fiqh* the word *'ilm* also had a comprehensive meaning in the early period. On the occasion of the death of 'Umar, the second Caliph, in the year 24 A.H., Ibn Mas'ūd (d. 32 A.H.) is said to have remarked that nine-tenths of *'ilm* had gone away with him.[11] It may be noted that 'Umar had not only legislated and settled points of theology, but possessed a comprehensive knowledge of Islam. It seems, therefore, that Ibn Mas'ūd used the term *'ilm* not for a specific branch of knowledge but in a broader sense. After the lifetime of the Prophet, the Muslims were confronted with new problems, and had to exercise their personal judgement. At this stage the term *fiqh* came to be frequently used for the exercise of intelligence. At the same time, people endeavoured to collect and record the traditions coming through the chains of narrators. Thus, the knowledge resulting from the exercise of intelligence and personal opinion was termed as *fiqh*, and the knowledge that came through the reporters was described as *'ilm*. The term *'ilm* came generally to be used in the sense of the knowledge of the Tradition, *i.e.* *Ḥadīth* and *Āthār*, when the movement of collecting *Ḥadīth* towards the end of the first century of the Hijrah started. Simultaneously, the term *fiqh* came to be used exclusively for the knowledge based on the exercise of intelligence and independent judgement. Roughly, in this period these two terms began to separate from each other. The year 94 A.H. is known as "*sanat al-fuqahā*' (the year of the jurists)", because a number of the celebrated jurists of Medina like Sa'īd b. al-Musayyib and Abū Bakr b. 'Abd al-Raḥmān died in that year.[12] It seems, therefore, reasonable to assume that the terms *'ilm* and *fiqh* were separated when jurists and specialists in *Ḥadīth* came into existence towards the end of the first century. In the Qur'ān the derivatives of the word *fiqh* have been frequently used denoting understanding of any matter. We do not find this word in the Qur'ān used in the sense of learning. On the other hand, the word *'ilm* has been used in the Qur'ān for learning. A Qur'ānic passage reads: "And hasten not with the Qur'ān ere its revelation hath been perfected unto thee, and say: My Lord! Increase me in knowledge (*'ilm.*)"[13] In this passage, *'ilm* refers to the revelation that came to the Prophet. This revelation in the form of the Qur'ān was learnt and read by the Muslims. Now *fiqh* was not learnt and read like *'ilm*, *i.e.* Qur'ān or *Ḥadīth*. But with the passage of time, a body of laws came into existence, and this whole corpus came to be known as *Fiqh*—now a systematic science of law that was *learnt* and *acquired* like *'ilm.*

It is a point to be noted that *'ilm* from the beginning carried the sense of the knowledge which came through an authority—it may be God or the Prophet (*i.e.* the Qur'ān and *Ḥadīth*)—while *fiqh*, by its very definition, involved the exercise of one's intelligence and personal thinking. We have earlier shown its usage in the pre-Islamic days. In this sense, *fiqh* always remained distinct from *'ilm*. Although both these terms were used in their broader meanings and were more or less interchangeable, yet *fiqh* never lost its intellectual character. The Companions of the Prophet who gave legal judgements and were noted for exercising intelligence in their decisions were known as *fuqahā'*. A report indicates that the *fuqahā'* in the presence of 'Umar, the second Caliph, dared not speak, as he dominated them by virtue of his *fiqh* (intelligence) and *'ilm* (knowledge).[14] Here the term *fuqahā'* appears to signify those persons who were distinguished for employing their reason and intelligence in solving legal and administrative problems. 'Umar b. al-Khaṭṭāb, in his speech at Jābiyah, *inter alia*, said: "Let him who desires to seek *fiqh* go to Mu'ādh b. Jabal" (d. 18 A.H.)."[15] Since Mu'ādh had worked as a judge in the

Yemen during the time of the Prophet, 'Umar might be referring to his intelligence and legal experience. It is, however, difficult to draw a sharp distinction between the meanings of these terms especially in the early decades of Islam.

From the above analysis, it may be gathered that the scope of the term *fiqh* was gradually narrowed down, and ultimately came to be applied to the legal problems and even simply to legal literature. Similarly, the term *'ilm* lost its general meaning and was confined to *Ḥadīth* and *Āthār*. With the growth of legal activity and with the development of *Ḥadīth*, *ra'y* and *riwāyah* became synonymous with *fiqh* and *'ilm* respectively. A report indicates that when 'Aṭā' b. Abī Rabāḥ (d. 114 A.H.) gave an opinion, Ibn Jurayj (d. 150 A.H.) asked him whether he had made the statement on the basis of *'ilm* or *ra'y*.[16] Here *'ilm* is distinguished from *ra'y*, and has been used in the sense of the knowledge based on tradition. 'Umar b. 'Abd al-'Azīz (d. 101 A.H.) is reported to have advised Abū Bakr b. Muḥammad b. 'Amr b. Ḥazm (d. 120 A.H.) to collect and record *Ḥadīth*, arguing that he feared the 'extinction of knowledge' (*durūs al-'ilm*).[17]

To sum up, *'ilm* and *fiqh* had, in the beginning, a broader sense but were restricted to specific meanings subsequently. This is the reason why the chapters on *'ilm* in the collections of *Ḥadīth* consists of a number of reports that contain the word *fiqh* used in its earlier and broader sense.

Alongside of the term *fiqh*, the term *sharā'i'* (in the plural) was also current among the early Muslims. Reports indicate that the newly converted Muslims who had come to the Prophet from different parts of Arabia, requested him to depute someone to their locality to instruct them in the "*sharā'i'*" of Islam.[18] As for the term *sharī'ah*, it was hardly used in the early days of Islam. It was introduced to carry the specific meaning, *i.e.* the law of Islam, at a later date. Literally, the word *sharī'ah* means a "course to the watering-place" and a "resort of drinkers." The Arabs applied this term particularly to a course leading to a watering place, which was permanent and clearly marked out to the eye. Hence, it means the clear path or the "highway" to be followed.[19] The Qur'ān uses the words *shir'ah* and *sharī'ah*[20] in the meaning of *dīn* (religion), in the sense that it is the way ordained by God for man, or in the sense that it is the clear-cut path of God for man. The term *sharā'i'* (pl. of *sharī'ah*) was used in the Prophet's time for the essentials of Islam. The bedouins who requested the Prophet to depute someone to their tribe to teach them the *sharā'i'* of Islam, obviously meant the essentials of religion. They wanted to be acquainted with the fundamentals and obligatory duties of Islam. This presumption is supported by the tradition which states that the Prophet, when once asked about the *sharā'i'* of Islam, mentioned prayer, *zakāh*, fasting of *Ramaḍān* and *Ḥajj* pilgrimage.[21] It shows that the term *sharā'i'* meant *farā'iḍ* (obligatory duties).

Abū Ḥanīfah, if the ascription of *K. al-'Ālim wa'l-Muta'allim* to him is correct, distinguished *dīn* from *sharī'ah* on the ground that *dīn* was never changed, whereas *sharī'ah* continued to change through history. By *dīn* he meant the basic tenets of the faith like belief in the unity of God, in the prophets, in the life after death, etc., while by *sharī'ah* he meant the performatory duties. He does not recognize any difference between the *dīn* of various prophets, but differentiates between their *sharā'i'*. He holds that every prophet invited the people to his own *sharī'ah* and forbade them to follow the *sharī'ah* of earlier Prophets.[22] The term *dīn* came to be used in a restricted sense, *i.e.* tenets of Islam, in Abū Ḥanīfah's time, for the reasons given earlier. Hence, the term *Uṣūl al-Dīn* was used for *Kalām* in later ages.

Al-Shāfi'i uses the term *sharī'ah* in the sense of institution. He disagrees with Mālik who disallows *Ḥajj* by proxy (*Ḥajj badal*) in the lifetime of a person. Mālik compares *Ḥajj* with prayer and fasting which cannot be performed, according to all the jurists, on behalf of another person. Refuting Mālik's opinion al-Shāfi'ī remarks: "One *sharī'ah* (institution) should not be compared with another *sharī'ah* (institution) analogically."[23] The use of this term in the sense of institution is unique with al-Shāfi'ī, because it is not generally used in this meaning. Moreover, he uses the term *sharā'i'* in the sense of performatory duties.[24]

Today the term *sharī'ah* covers all aspects of Islam. It combines *Fiqh* and *Kalām* both. A contemporary author defines *Sharī'ah* and distinguishes it from *Fiqh* in the following words;—

> "*Sharī'at* is the wider circle, it embraces in its orbit all human actions; *fiqh* is the narrow one, and deals with what are commonly understood as legal acts. *Sharī'at* reminds us always of revelation, that *'ilm* (knowledge) which we could never have possessed but for the Koran or *Ḥadīth;* in *fiqh*, the power of reasoning is stressed, and deductions based upon *'ilm* are continuously cited with approval. The path of *sharī'at* is laid down by God and His Prophet; the edifice of *fiqh* is erected by human endeavour. In the *fiqh*, an action is either legal or illegal, *yajūzu wa mā lā yajūzu*, permissible or not permissible. In the *sharī'at* there are various grades of approval or disapproval. *Fiqh* is the term used for the law as a science; and *sharī'at*, for the law as the divinely ordained path of rectitude."[25]

It is, however, difficult to draw a sharp line of distinction between them, as they are generally used interchangeably. One difference may, however, be noted that *sharī'ah* combines law and tenets both, while *Fiqh* deals with law alone. Here it may be pointed out that neither *Fiqh* nor *Sharī'ah* corresponds to the Canon Law of Christianity or to the 'Law' in the West in its purely technical sense.

In the Prophet's time the term *qurrā'* was also current among the Muslims. As reading was not common in Arabia, it was applied to those persons who could read the Qur'ān. The seventy persons whom the Prophet had deputed to the newly converted Muslims for teaching the Qur'ān and the essentials of Islam came to be known as *qurrā'*.[26] Later, when the Arabs came in contact with new cultures and civilizations, knowledge spread among them, and they advanced in various fields of learning. Now that Islamic law was perfected and other branches of Islamic learning had developed, the Qur'ān readers, according to Ibn Khaldūn, were no longer called *qurrā'* but were known as *fuqahā'* and *'ulamā'*.[27] Among the *Successors* (*Tābi'ūn*) there were *fuqahā'* and *'ulamā'*, *i.e.* those who were authorities in law and *Ḥadīth*.[28] Among the learned men of Medina, Sa'īd b. al-Musayyib (d. 94 A.H.) figured prominently and was known as *faqīh al-fuqahā'* and *'ālim at-ulamā'*.[29] The phrase *'ahl al-'ilm'* and sometimes *'ahl al-fiqh'* was commonly used in the second generation as is obvious from *al-Muwaṭṭa'* of Mālik. It appears that these expressions were applied to those learned persons who were deeply concerned with deriving rules from the Qur'ān and the *Sunnah* and giving verdicts on legal issues.

At the time when the term *fiqh* came to be applied exclusively to the legal problems, people began to write independent works on this particular subject. 'Abd Allāh b. al-Mubārak (d. 181 A.H.) is reported to have compiled *'ilm* (i.e. *Ḥadīth*) in a book and arranged it according to the order of legal topics (*fiqh*), battles (*ghazawāt*) and asceticism (*zuhd*)[30] etc. Towards the middle of the second century of the Hijrah we find a number of books written exclusively on *Fiqh*. The works of Abū Yūsuf (d. 182 A.H.) and specially of al-Shaybānī (d. 189 A.H.) were the first systematic efforts in this field. *Al-Muwaṭṭa'* of Mālik is the first in the list of the early available literature, but it may be noted that it is a book neither exclusively on *Ḥadīth* nor on *Fiqh*. It is, in fact, the remnant of the literature of the period when *Fiqh* and *Ḥadīth* were intermingled. Henceforth, books began to be written on these two subjects separately. The result of our inquiry so far is that the generality of the term *fiqh* gradually became restricted until it began to be applied to the legal sphere alone.

NOTES

1. Al-Jawharī, *al-Ṣiḥāḥ* (s. v.).
2. Ibn Manẓūr, *Lisān al-'Arab*, Beirut, 1956, vol. XIII, p. 253.
3. Lane, Edward William, *Arabic-English Lexicon*, (s.v.); cf. al-Suyūṭī, Jalāl al-Dīn, *al-Muzhir*, Cairo, n.d., vol. I, p. 638.
4. Al-Ghazālī *Iḥyā' 'ulūm al-Dīn*, Cairo, 1939, vol. I, p. 38.
5. Ibn Sa'd, *al-Ṭabaqāt al-Kubrā*, Beirut, 1957, vol. II, p. 363.
6. Ibn-Hishām, *al-Sīrah*, Cairo, 1329 A.H., vol. III, p. 32.
7. Al-Ghazālī, *op. cit.*, vol. I, p. 39.
8. Abū Ḥanīfah, *al-Fiqh al-Absaṭ*, quoted by Kamāl al-Dīn Aḥmad al-Bayāḍī in *Ishārāt al-Marām min 'Ibārāt al-Imām*, Cairo, 1949, pp. 28-29.

معرفة النفس ما لها و ما عليها

9. *Ibid.*, pp. 28-30.

اعلم أن الفقه فى الدين أفضل من الفقه and اصل التوحيد و ما يصح الاعتقاد عليه و ما يتعلق الاعتقاد منها فى الاعتقاديات هو الفقه الاكبر.

10. Al-Shahristānī, *al-Milal wa'l-Niḥal*, Cairo, 1317 A.H., vol. I, p. 32.
11. Ibn Sa'd, *op. cit.*, vol. II, p. 336.
12. *Ibid.*, vol. V, pp. 143, 208.
13. Qur'ān, 20 : 114.
14. Ibn Sa'd, *op. cit.*, vol. II, p. 336.
15. *Ibid.*, p. 348.
16. *Ibid.*, p. 386.
17. Al-Shaybānī, *al-Muwaṭṭa'*, Deoband, n.d., p. 391.

ان عمر بن عبدالعزيز كتب إلى ابى بكر بن عمرو بن حزم أن انظر ما كان من حديث رسول الله صلى الله عليه وسلم او سنته او حديث عمر او نحو هذا ، فانى خفت دروس العلم و ذهاب العلماء.

18. Ibn Sa'd, *op. cit.*, vol. I, pp. 333, 345, 355. It appears that terms like *sharā'i'* and *farā'iḍ* were synonymous in the Prophet's time and meant performatory duties. The Prophet is reported to have written to a bedouin a letter which contained فرائض الصدقات ; and another of his letters is reported to have consisted of شرائع الاسلام (Ibn Sa'd, *op. cit.*, vol. I, pp. 307, 327).
19. Ibn Manẓūr, *Lisān al-'Arab* (s.v.),
20. *Qur'ān*, 5 : 51; 45 : 17.
21. Abū Ḥanīfah, *op. cit.*, pp. 52-56.
22. Abū Ḥanīfah, *Kitāb al-'Ālim wa'l-Muta'allim.* Hyderabad, Deccan, 1349 A.H., pp. 5-6.
23. Al-Shāfi'ī, *Kitāb al-Umm*, Cairo, 1325 A.H., vol. VII, pp. 196-97.

    لا تقاس شريعة على شريعة

24. Al-Shāfi'ī, *Jimā' al-'Ilm*, Cairo, 1940, p. 104.
25. Fayzee, Asaf A. A., *Outlines of Muhammadan Law*, London, 1960, p. 21.
26. Ibn Sa'd, *op. cit.*, vol. II, p. 52.
27. Ibn Khaldūn, *Muqaddimah*, Beirut, 1900, p. 446.

    Ibn Khaldūn's statement is supported by al-Shaybānī's remarks that in those days the people who had more knowledge of the Qur'ān had more understanding in the religion.

    انما قيل أقرأهم لكتاب الله، لأن الناس كانوا فى ذلك الزمان أقرأهم للقرآن افقههم فى الدين .

    Al-Shaybānī, *Kitāb al-Āthār*, Karachi, n.d., p. 68. It appears that the term *qurrā'*, in the time of Ibn Mas'ūd, began to have been used in its literal sense, *i.e.* reciters, and ceased to convey the meaning of 'learned'. This is implied from the following report :

    ان عبدالله بن مسعود قال لانسان : انك فى زمان كثير فقهاؤه ، قليل قراؤه تحفظ فيه حدود القران و تضيع حروفه. . . . وسياتى على الناس زمان قليل فقهاؤه، كثير قراؤه ، يحفظ فيه حروف القرآن و تضيع حدوده .

    Mālik, *al-Muwaṭṭa'*, Cairo, 1951, vol. I, p. 173.

28. Ibn Sa'd, *op. cit.*, vol. II, p. 378.
29. *Ibid.*, vol. V, p. 121.
30. Al-Dhahabī, *Tadhkirat al-Ḥuffāẓ*, Hyderabad, Deccan, n.d., vol. I, p. 250.

Chapter II

ORIGINS OF THE EARLY SCHOOLS OF LAW

The Historical Background

During the time of the Prophet, there was no such science as that of jurisprudence. The Prophet did not categorise the injunctions into *wājib* (imperative), *mandūb* (recommended), *ḥarām* (forbidden), *makrūh* (disapproved) and *mubāḥ* (indifferent) as propounded in the later legal theory. This classification of acts is the work of the jurists themselves who studied different passages of the Qur'ān, various traditions of the Prophet, the practice of the Companions and the early Muslims.[1] According to the jurists, every act must fall under one of these five categories. But this was not the case with the Companions in the Prophet's lifetime. The only 'ideal' for them was the conduct of the Prophet. They learnt ablutions, saying prayers, performing *Ḥajj* etc. by observing the Prophet's normative actions under his instructions. But they did not reflect what parts of these actions constituted *arkān* (essentials) and what constituted *ādāb* (adjuncts). On occasions, cases were brought to the Prophet for his decision. In his decisions the people around him did not ask about the particular points of law for purely theoretical purposes; they took his decisions as a model for taking similar decisions in similar cases.

There is no doubt that the Companions occasionally asked him questions relating to certain serious problems, as we learn from the Qur'ān.[2] The Prophet gave suitable replies to them. People in his lifetime were not apparently interested in unnecessary philosophical discussions or in the meticulous details of all regulations. From the Qur'ān it appears that the Companions generally asked the Prophet very few questions. On one occasion when some person put unnecessary questions to him, the Qur'ān asked the Companions to desist from doing so.[3] The result was that the *Sunnah* remained mostly a general directive, performatory in character and interpreted by the early Muslims in different ways. People did not know the details of many a problem even in the lifetime of the Prophet.[4] Of course, the Prophet laid down certain regulations, but the jurists elaborated them with more details. The reason for this further addition to the laws enunciated by the Prophet by interpretation is that he himself had made allowances in his commands. He left many things to the discretion of the community to be decided according to a given situation.

Law was neither inflexible nor so rigidly applied in the early days of Islam as one finds it in the later days. Different and even contradictory laws relating to many problems could be tolerated on the basis of argument. This is obvious from the differences of the Companions of the Prophet after his death and from the practice of the early legists. It seems that the Prophet provided a wide scope for differences by giving instructions of a general nature or, by validating two diverse actions in the same situation. Since it was a period of the evolution of a pattern of behaviour for the coming generations, the Prophet aimed at providing opportunities for the employment of human reason and common sense in diverse circumstances. Had the Prophet laid down specific and rigid rules for each problem once and for all—what was not possible for him in face of urgency of conducting the struggle for Islam—the coming generations would have been deprived of exercising reason and framing laws according to the exegencies of time. Hence, in the Prophet's time, it was possible for two persons to take different courses in one and the same situation. To illustrate our viewpoint, we may give an example. On the occasion of the battle of Banū Qurayẓah, the Prophet sent some of his companions to the enemy territory and asked them to say their *'Aṣr* prayers on arrival at their destination. But it so happened that the time of the prayers came on the way. Therefore, some of the Companions said their prayers on the way arguing that the Prophet had not meant to postpone the prayers, while others said their prayers on reaching the destination at nightfall, taking the Prophet's command literally. When the incident was reported to the Prophet, he kept silent. The Companions deemed this to be a tacit approval of the actions of both the parties.[5] Had the actions of either party been considered unlawful, it is argued, the Prophet would have pointed out and corrected it.

The above example shows that the Prophet while laying down a law, primarily considered the value and spirit of the action and not the form of the action itself. What appears significant in this case was the obedience to divine commandments. It may be noted that both the parties exhibited their allegiance to God. One of them obeyed the Prophet's command taking it literally and performed *'Aṣr* prayers at nightfall, while the other obeyed him in spirit. It is important to note that a commandment is not intended *per se*; what counts is intention and the spirit which constitutes the allegiance to God and the Prophet. This, too, implies that people can differ in the form of obedience on the basis of interpretation. Hence, differences arose in law among the jurists.

After the death of the Prophet the Companions were spread out in different parts of the Muslim world. Most of them came to occupy the positions of intellectual and religious leadership. They were approached by the people of their regions for decisions regarding various problems. They gave their decisions sometimes according to what they had learnt and retained in their memory from the commandments of the

Prophet ; at other times according to what they understood from the Qur'ān and the *Sunnah.* Often they formed an opinion by looking to the *Sharī'ah*-value which led the Prophet to take a decision. Once, for example, Ibn Mas'ūd was reportedly asked whether a woman would be entitled to dower if her husband died without fixing its amount and consummating the marriage. Ibn Mas'ūd at first replied that he had not heard anything from the Prophet on the subject. But when he was requested to make a suggestion he opined that the woman would be entitled to the average dower which a woman of her social standing might expect. He further suggested that she would receive full share from the heritage of her husband, and that there would be a period of waiting for her. Ma'qil b. Sinān (d. 63 A.H.) is reported to have stood up on the occasion and said that the Prophet had given a similar decision.[6] But Ibn 'Umar (d. 73 A.H.) and Zayd b. Thābit (d. 45 A.H.) are reported to have given a different decision in a similar case. According to them, such a widow would not receive any dower but, instead, would be entitled only to her share in the heritage. The 'Irāqīs follow the opinion of Ibn Mas'ūd and reject the decision of Ibn 'Umar and Zayd b. Thābit.[7] The reason for this preference may be that the former view is attributed to the Prophet, while the latter is not. In case each is based on traditions, neither of the two opposing views can, as a general rule, go back to the Prophet. For, if there had been a clear decision from the Prophet on such an important social institution as marriage, how could such differences of opinion, leading in opposite directions, ever arise? Further, in case only the 'Irāqī opinion claims the authority of the tradition from the Prophet, the ignorance of this *Ḥadīth* on the part of such prominent Companions like Ibn 'Umar, Zayd b. Thābit and even Ibn Mas'ūd makes its authenticity extremely doubtful, particularly when the point in question is such an important one as that of marriage. It is difficult to believe that the Prophet's decision on such an important question remained so private and isolated that it was known only to a Companion or two. Therefore, the usual way of answering such problems *viz.* that the *Ḥadīth* might not have reached other Companions, cannot be accepted.

There were occasions when some *Ḥadīth* was adduced, but rejected because it was found contrary to the Qur'ānic verses. Take, for example, the case of Fāṭimah b. Qays. She is reported to have testified before 'Umar, the second Caliph, that she was given a triple divorce by her husband, but the Prophet made no provision for her residential accommodation during the period of waiting, nor did he recommend expenses for her maintenance. 'Umar did not accept this *Ḥadīth* saying that he could not abandon the Book of Allāh for the report of a woman when he could not judge whether she was speaking the truth or telling a lie.[8] What is interesting here is that this remark of 'Umar is known only to the 'Irāqīs and reported by Abū Yūsuf alone. Mālik and al-Shāfi'ī have, therefore, followed this *Ḥadīth* providing no maintenance to a divorced woman (in the case of an irrevocable divorce) during the period of waiting. They interpret the Qur'ānic verse 65 : 6 which contains the injunction of providing maintenance to the divorce in favour of the pregnant woman alone.[9]

The interpretation of the Qur'ān also caused differences of opinion among the Companions. The points on which the Qur'ānic injunctions were either silent or ambiguous were to be explained. The result was that these verses were sometimes interpreted in the light of the traditions from the Prophet, and sometimes on the basis of the lawyers' opinion. Moreover, since the traditions themselves were diverse, the differences were natural. Al-Shāfi'ī mentions several instances on the subject.[10] A Qur'ānic verse says: "Women who are divorced shall wait, keeping themselves apart, three courses (*qurū'*).[11] In this verse, the word *qurū'* is ambiguous. It has been taken to stand for menstruation, and for the state of purity (*ṭuhr*). Thus, 'Umar, the second Caliph, 'Alī, Ibn Mas'ūd, Abū Mūsā al-Ash'arī are reported to have held that *aqrā'* (sing. *qur'*) means menstruations (*ḥiyaḍ*). This view is also said to have been held by Sa'īd b. al-Musayyib, 'Aṭā' and a group of Successors and a number of jurists. On the other hand, 'Ā'ishah, Zayd b. Thābit, and Ibn 'Umar are reported to have maintained that *aqrā'* means the periods of purity between menstruations (*aṭhār*). The result of the difference between the two views is that, according to the former, the waiting period is finished after the completion of the third course, while according to the latter it comes to an end with the beginning of the third course. Similarly, the Companions are reported to have differed in the interpretation of the verses 65 : 6 and 2 ; 226.[12] The difference of opinion among the jurists is, as a matter of fact, due to the difference among the Companions in interpreting the Qur'ān.

The same is the case with *Ḥadīth*. Differences arose in *Ḥadīth* due to several factors. Sometimes two contradictory traditions were reported from the Prophet. Some Companions followed one of them, and some followed the other. Traditions on *ribā'* provide the best illustration for contradictory *Ḥadīth*. Ibn 'Abbās reports, on the authority of Usāmah b. Zayd from the Prophet, that there is no *ribā'* except on loan. But 'Ubādah b. al-Ṣāmit, Abū Sa'īd al-Khudrī. 'Uthmān b. 'Affān and Abū Hurayrah reported the famous tradition of *ribā'* in six commodities in a hand-to-hand transaction. The former view is reported to be held by the followers of Ibn 'Abbās and the jurists of Mecca. According to this view, there is no harm in exchanging one *dirham* for two and one *dīnār* for two *dīnārs*. Ibn Mas'ūd, too, is reported to have said that he did not see any harm in the exchange of one *dirham* for two *dirhams* although, according to the report, he did not do so himself. Al-Shāfi'ī explains away this contradiction and follows the opinion of the majority.[13] In fact, such stray opinions did always exist since the first generation after the Prophet, but they were neglected on the basis of *Ijmā'* and submerged. We shall discuss the principle of *Ijmā'* in Chapter VII.

In some cases, a *Ḥadīth* was not known to a Companion; hence, he decided the problem on the basis of his own opinion. When the relevant *Ḥadīth* was brought to his notice, he withdrew his personal judgement. Al-Shāfi'ī has given several instances where 'Umar, the second Caliph, is reported to have changed his opinions.[14]

On certain occasions it so happened that the relevant *Ḥadīth* was available but the reporter himself could not understand its real import. Ibn 'Umar is reported to have narrated a *Ḥadīth* from the Prophet that a deceased is punished on account of the mourning of his relatives. When this tradition reached 'Ā'ishah, she rebutted it saying that Ibn 'Umar might have been mistaken or he might have forgotten some relevant part of the tradition. "The fact is", she remarked, "that the Prophet once heard the relatives of a deceased Jewess weeping over her death. On this occasion, he remarked that the relatives were mourning her demise, while the deceased was being punished in the grave."[15] Later works add that 'Ā'ishah also said that the *Ḥadīth* reported by Ibn 'Umar goes against the Qur'ānic verse: "No soul bears the burden of another."[16]

The contradiction of a certain *Ḥadīth* by a verse from the Qur'ān also gave rise to differences of opinion among the Companions. Earlier we have shown how 'Umar rejected the tradition reported by Fāṭimah b. Qays because it contradicted the Qur'ān.

The Companions, however, tried their best to base their decisions on the Qur'ān and the *Sunnah*. They aspired to keep their decisions and personal judgements as much close to those of the Prophet as possible. Despite their differences, they did not, in any way, deviate from the spirit of the Qur'ān and the *Sunnah*.

The Successors took their stand on the opinions expressed by the Companions. They retained in their memory, what they could, of the *Ḥadīth* of the Prophet and the opinions of his Companions. Further, at this stage attempts were made to reconcile opposite opinions held by the Companions on many problems ; nevertheless, the Successors exercised *Ijtihād* (independent interpretation) in two ways. First, they were not afraid of giving preference to the opinions of one Companion over another's and, sometimes, even the opinions of a Successor over those of a Companion. Secondly, they exercised original thinking themselves and, in fact, the real formation of Islamic law starts in a more or less professional manner at the hands of the Successors.[17] Finally, differences in legal opinion were, to no small degree, due to local and regional factors.

During the time of the second generation, *i.e.* the Successors, there emerged three great geographical divisions in the Islamic world, where independent legal activity was going on. They were Iraq, Hejaz and Syria. Iraq further had two schools, those of Basra and Kufa. We know comparatively more about the development of legal thought in Kufa than in Basra. Similarly, Hejaz also had two well-known centres of legal activity, namely, Mecca and Medina. Of these two, Medina was more prominent and took a lead in the development of law in Hejaz. The Syrian school is not so frequently mentioned in the early texts; nevertheless, the legal trend of this school is authoritatively known to us through the writings of Abū Yūsuf. We cannot include Egypt in the early schools of law as it did not develop its own legal thought. There were some lawyers in Egypt who followed the doctrines of Iraq while others followed those of Medina.[18] Al-Layth b. Sa'd (d. 175 A.H.) seems to have figured prominently in Egyptian legal circles. He had certain differences with Mālik. A letter by him to Mālik, if it is genuine,[19] shows his legal acumen and independent thinking.

Every important town had its own leader of opinion who contributed to the development of legal thought in that province. The following are reported to be the well-known early jurists of various localities.

Mecca :

'Aṭā b. Abī Rabāḥ (d. 114 A.H.)
'Amr b. Dīnar (d. 126 A.H.)

Medina:

Sa'īd b. al-Musayyib (d. ca. 94 A.H.)
'Urwah b. al-Zubayr (d. 93 or 94 A.H.)
Abū Bakr b. 'Abd al-Raḥmān (d. 94 or 95 A.H.)
'Ubayd Allah b. 'Abd Allāh (d. ca. 98 A.H.)
Kh̲ārijah b. Zayd (d. 99 A.H.)
Sulaymān b. Yasār (d. ca. 107 A.H.)
Al-Qāsim b. Muḥammad (d. 107 A.H.)[20]

These were generally included in the list of the "seven jurists of Medina". Besides, there were other celebrated names :

Sālim b. 'Abd Allāh b. 'Umar (d. 107 A.H.)
Ibn S̲hihāb al-Zuhrī (d. 124 A.H.)
Rabī'ah b. Abī 'Abd al-Raḥmān (d. 136 A.H.)
Yaḥyā b. Sa'īd (d. 143 A.H.)

Mālik (d. 179 A.H.) and his contemporary jurists were the last exponents of the Medinese school.

Basra :

Muslim b. Yasār (d. 108 A.H.)
Al-Ḥasan b. Yasār (d. 110 A.H.)
Muḥammad b. Sīrīn (d. 110 A.H.)

Kufa :

'Alqamah b. Qays (d. 62 A.H.)
Masrūq b. al-Ajda' (d. 63 A.H.)
Al-Aswad b. Yazīd (d. 75 A.H.)
Shurayḥ b. al-Ḥārith (d. 78 A.H.)

These were the celebrated companions of 'Abd Allah b. Mas'ūd.

Ibrāhīm al-Nakha'ī (d. 96 A.H.)
Al-Sha'bī (d. ca. 103 A.H.)
Ḥammād b. Abī Sulayman al-Ash'ārī (d. 120 A.H.)
Abū Ḥanīfah and his disciples.

Syria ;

Qabīṣah b. Dhuwayb (d. 86 A.H.)
'Umar b. 'Abd al-'Azīz (d. 101 A.H.)
Makḥūl (d. 113 A.H.)
Al-Awzā'ī (d. 157 A.H.), the last of the leaders of the Syrian school.

These jurists of different regions based their decisions and legal verdicts on the opinions and decisions of the Companions who lived in their respective places. The jurists of Medina derived their legal knowledge from the reports of the verdicts of 'Umar, 'Ā'ishah and Ibn 'Umar. The Kūfī jurists derived their legal doctrines from the opinions and judgements of Ibn Mas'ūd and 'Alī. This was their general trend, otherwise each of these schools also quotes several other Companions in support of its legal opinion.

Al-Shāfi'ī mentions these centres of learning in his writings. He says that every town of the Muslims was a seat of learning whose people followed the opinion of ancient jurists of their town in most cases.[22] Further, he mentions the authorities of Mecca, Medina, Kufa, Basra and Syria. In al-Shāfi'ī's time these early regional schools were engaged in an intense legal activity and controversy. He mentions differences among the jurists in each principal town. He says that some people in Mecca nearly differed from the opinion of 'Aṭā', while others followed a different opinion. Similar was the case in Medina. Most people followed the opinions of Ibn al-Musayyib, but afterwards they abandoned some of his principles for those of Mālik. Mālik in turn was treated similarly. While Ibn Abi'l-Zinād exaggerated his opposition to Mālik, Mughīrah, Ibn Ḥāzim and al-Darāwardī followed some of his opinions, but others opposed them. In Kufa, he says, some people were inclined towards Ibn Abī Laylā, and opposed the opinions of Abū Yūsuf ; but others followed Abū Yūsuf and attacked the doctrines of Ibn Abī Laylā.[23]

The local element was very powerful in the early schools. Abū Ja'far al-Manṣūr (d. 158 A.H.), the 'Abbasid Caliph, is reported to have gone for *Ḥajj*. He told Mālik that he was thinking of distributing the copies of the latter's book, *al-Muwaṭṭa'*, in the provinces with the instructions that it should be taken as the sole authority in law. Mālik advised him not to do so on the ground that people in various localities had already developed divergent opinions basing themselves on diverse traditions. He, therefore, suggested to al-Manṣūr not to interfere with the laws of these localities which they had already come to adopt.[24] Mālik's reply provides justification for the difference of opinion in the legal field. It also implies that Islamic law has, ever since its early days, remained flexible, allowing a wide margin for differences.

The reasons for differences of opinion among the prominent scholars of each province are almost the same as we have mentioned earlier in the case of the Companions. With the end of the Tābi'ūn (Successors), there began a period wherein the traditions of the Prophet, the opinions and personal decisions of the Companions as well as of the Successors were in circulation in each principal town. Besides contradictory traditions from the Prophet, there were contradictory reports from the Companions about their own opinions and practice. According to one report, Abū Bakr and 'Umar used to recite *qunūt* (imprecations) in *Fajr* prayers, but according to another they never recited it. Sometimes opinions and practices of the Companions, opposed to the traditions from the Prophet, were reported. A report indicates that Abū Bakr, 'Umar, and 'Uthmān practised *muzāra'ah* and gave their lands on one-third share. But this report goes against the traditions of the Prophet reported by Jābir and Rāfi' b. Khadīj which regard the contract of *muzāra'ah* as illegal.[26] A report states that the Prophet performed *masḥ* on socks, but 'Alī, 'Ā'ishah, Ibn 'Abbās, and Abū Hurayrah are reported to have denied it.[27] There are other numerous such examples of contradictory reports from early authorities. Thus, with the compilation of *Ḥadīth* and *Āthār*, contradictions increased day by day , and the jurists came to argue on the basis of these contradictory reports.

Another vital factor that produced differences among these jurists was the exercise of personal opinion. As a result of this more or less common procedure of personal opinions, differences were bound to arise and, indeed, contradictory legal decisions were given on the same case in different quarters of a city at the same time. In order to check this chaotic state of affairs and to protect the *Ummah* from disintegration, the institution of *Ijmā'* was introduced. Leaving aside the stray opinions, the average general opinion of each locality was taken as the local *Ijmā'*.

Another method followed by these early jurists to eliminate this chaos was that they adopted such traditions from the Prophet or from the Companions as were confirmed by the practice of the Muslims. This is the reason why we find so much emphasis on 'practice' in these early schools of law.[28] Mālik repeatedly refers to the 'agreed practice' of Medina.[29] Abū Yūsuf warns against the isolated traditions and lays stress on well-known *Sunnah,* and al-Awzā'ī frequently uses the phrase 'the practice of the past leaders of the Muslims'.[30]

Among the early schools of law we repeatedly hear the names of Abū Ḥanīfah, Abū Yūsuf, al-Shaybānī, Mālik, and al-Awzā'ī in different regions. It is usually thought that they won their fame for their independent *Ijtihād* based on pure reasoning in the sphere of Islamic Law. This apparently leads us to believe that these jurists were not influenced by the milieu in which they lived, or by the general trend of their respective regions. But this is not entirely correct. They were influenced both by the practice and thought of their respective regions. This is clearly reflected in their reasoning. In Medina, for example, a specific trend of opinion was already in existence before the appearance of Mālik on the scene. There had lived in Medina a number of persons from among the Companions as well as from the Successors who had insight in law. Ibn 'Umar, 'Ā'ishah, Ibn al-Musayyib and the rest of the seven celebrated jurists of Medina contributed much to the formation of legal opinion in Medina. These predecessors of Mālik originally exercised *Ijtihād,* and left a mass of legal opinion behind them. Mālik, undoubtedly, exercised *Ijtihād* himself in several cases; nevertheless, he did not deviate from the spirit of his predecessors. Similar was the case with Iraq. A trend of 'Irāqī opinion had already been formed before Abū Ḥanīfah. Companions like 'Alī, 'Abd Allāh b. Mas'ūd and Successors like 'Alqamah, al-Aswad, al-Sha'bī, Ibrāhīm al-Nakha'ī and others had lived in Iraq. These people left a rich heritage of legal decisions which represent 'Irāqī tradition. Abū Ḥanīfah studied these precedents, held discussions with his contemporary jurists, and arrived at some conclusions. He exercised *Ijtihād* on the lines of his predecessors but keeping alive the spirit and practice prevalent in Iraq. His influence, however, spread far and wide, and he became a symbol around which the 'Irāqī tradition crystallized. In short, these early schools of law owe their origins to a long process of independent interpretation of law, that continued in different regions from the earliest time. As time went on, people began to depend mostly on the decisions and legal opinions of these early authorities and ultimately *Ijtihād*, which was previously open to every competent Muslim, came to be restricted to the minimum.

While this process of crystallization of legal opinion in different schools was still underway, al-Shāfi'ī appeared on the scene. He studied the works of his predecessors, travelled to several towns in various regions and learnt *Ḥadīth* from a number of specialists. He held lengthy discussions with the 'Irāqī and Medinese jurists, and differed from them on a number of problems. In the system of his predecessors and contemporary jurists, he found several things which prevented him from following them. He found inconsistency in their reasoning. In other words, he saw that despite the existence of the traditions from the Prophet, these early jurists occasionally preferred the opinions of the Companions or ignored the traditions if these went against the local practice. Mālik, for instance, reports a *Ḥadīth* of *khiyār al-majlis* from the Prophet. The *Ḥadīth* gives to the parties, in a contract of sale, the right of option as long as they have not separated. After reporting this *Ḥadīth*, Mālik says: "We have no fixed limit (of time) and no established practice on that matter."[31] But in many other cases Mālik quotes *Ḥadīth* from the Prophet and follows it. Al-Shāfi'ī, however, insists that when a tradition from the Prophet is established to be genuine, it must be accepted. He says: "I have unwaveringly held, thanks be to Allāh, that if something is related from the Prophet, I do not venture to neglect it, whether we have a great or small opposition of Companions and Successors against us."[32] Moreover, he saw that most cases were decided on the basis of personal opinion. There were no strict rules to bring about uniformity in their decisions. Hence, he formulated rules for *Qiyās*. Above all, he witnessed these jurists reporting traditions from the Prophet, sometimes without the relevant chain of narrators, sometimes with a broken chain. He, therefore, emphasised the importance of narrating the chain of reporters punctiliously. This we shall discuss in the concluding chapter.

The reason of al-Shāfi'ī's emphasis on *Ḥadīth* is that in the pre-Shāfi'ī period *Ḥadīth* was not properly compiled. It was afterwards that there came forward a group of people who made it their life-work to probe into *Ḥadīth* and determined the criterion to judge the authenticity of *Ḥadīth*. They travelled throughout the Muslim world, and collected *Ḥadīth* from different places. Although the six collections of *Ḥadīth* had not yet come into existence, the movement of collecting *Ḥadīth* had already started in his time. Al-Shāfi'ī refers to the term '*Ahl al-Ḥadīth*'[33] in his writings. By this he means the specialists in *Ḥadīth*. Moreover, with the wide circulation of *Ḥadīth*, people began to accept even isolated traditions that were neglected by the early schools. This explains why al-Shāfi'ī regards *Ḥadīth* as more authoritative than the agreed practice of the Muslims in different regions. Al-Shāfi'ī, despite his best endeavours to reconcile the differences among the early jurists by establishing the principle of authentic *Ḥadīth* from the Prophet, could not put an end to this conflict of opinions rather paved the way for the rise of a new school. Besides, there could be no compromise between al-Shāfi'ī and the early schools, because the theory of law and the principles enunciated by him were mostly alien to them.

In the first two centuries of the Hijrah, there was no strict personal allegiance to one master. There did exist these geographical divisions of which we spoke previously. There were some common principles and the lawyers in each division were more or less like-minded. These early schools, however, concentrated their traditions around certain persons from whom they claimed to have acquired their knowledge. In the early texts Abū Ḥanīfah has been reported to have taken his knowledge from Ibrāhīm al-Nakha'ī through his teacher Ḥammād. Despite his sporadic differences on some points, he mostly follows Ibrāhīm. Al-Shaybānī refers to Abū Ḥanīfah in *al-Muwaṭṭa'*. He generally concludes each chapter with his formula, 'this is the opinion of Abū Ḥanīfah and our jurists in general.'[34] Abū Yūsuf often refers to 'our masters' or 'our jurists' in his writings.[35] Al-Shāfi'ī tells us that a group in Kufa followed Abū Yūsuf, while another followed Ibn Abī Laylā.[36] He calls some people in Kufa 'the followers of Abū Ḥanīfah'.[37]

Similar was the case in Medina where a group of people relied mostly on Mālik. They took his opinions as the *Ijmā'*[38] of Medina. On one occasion some of the Medinese are reported to have remarked expressly: "We follow the opinion of our master",[39] referring particularly to Mālik. Al-Shāfi'ī himself, during the course of his debates with the Medinese, calls Mālik as 'their master', and sometimes 'my master and theirs.'[40] Even Abū Yūsuf calls the Medinese 'our Companions from Hejaz'.[41] All these examples show that people had some personal attachment to Mālik. The other reason for calling Mālik as 'their master' may be that they had gained knowledge from him. Mālik had composed the first systematic work on *Fiqh* and people from far and wide, indeed, from Iraq, Africa, and Spain, flocked to him to acquire knowledge from him.

Al-Shāfi'ī is himself opposed to the personal allegiance to an individual jurist. He condemns it in his writings.[42] Nevertheless, he considers himself a member of the school of Medina. Occasionally, he refers to the Medinese as 'our Companions' and to Mālik as 'our master'.[43] Al-Shāfi'ī, however, separates himself from the Medinese when he criticizes their doctrines. On the whole he seems to be free from school bias.

The above analysis shows that the trend towards personal allegiance started roughly towards the middle of the second century of the Hijrah. Apart from these groupings in different regions, people were generally engaged in independent thinking on law. Later on, al-S͟hāfiʻī developed his own legal theory and tried to bring about strict consistency in law. After him the regional character of the early schools began to be corroded; and the influence of personal allegiance to one master and to his principles prevailed gradually.

NOTES

1. According to Prof. Schacht, the scale of 'five qualifications' (*al-aḥkām al-k͟hamsah*) was derived from Stoic Philosophy by the later jurists. Cf. Schacht, *An Introduction to Islamic Law*, Oxford, 1964, p. 20. This may be true. It should be noted, however, that the existence of a counterpart in a foreign culture does not indicate its foreign provenance unless the ideational influence from without is positively proved.
2. Qur'ān, 2 : 189, 215 and 8 : 1 etc.
3. Qur'ān, 5 : 101.
4. Abū Yūsuf quotes several instances which indicate that even 'Umar lacked detailed knowledge from the Prophet on several issues. He is, therefore, reported to have consulted the people. See *Kitāb al-K͟harāj*, Cairo, 1332 A.H. pp. 13-20, 25, 106.
5. Ibn Sa'd, *al-Ṭabaqāt al-Kubrā*, Beirut, 1957, vol. II, p. 76. Ibn Ḥazm has mentioned several examples that subtantiate this viewpoint. See Ibn Ḥazm, *al-Iḥkām fī Uṣūl al-Aḥkām*, Cairo, 1947, vol. V, p. 72 ff.
6. Abū Yūsuf, *Kitāb al-Āt͟hār*, Cairo, 1356 A.H., p. 132
7. Al-S͟haybānī, *al-Muwaṭṭa'*, Deoband, n.d. pp. 249-50.
8. Abū Yūsuf, *Kitāb al-Āt͟hār*, p. 132.

   According to 'Umar, the tradition reported by Fāṭimah b. Qays might contradict the Qur'ānic verse 65: 6.
9. Mālik, *al-Muwaṭṭa'*, Cairo, 1951, vol. II, p. 581; al-S͟hāfiʻī, *Kitāb al-Umm*, Cairo, 1322 A.H., vol. V, p. 219.
10. Al-S͟hāfiʻī, *op. cit.*, vol. VII, p. 245.
11. Qur'ān, 2 : 228.
12. Al-S͟hafiʻī, *op. cit.*, vol. VII, p. 245 .

13. Al-Shāfi'ī, *Ikhtilāf al-Ḥadīth* (on the margin of *Kitāb al-Umm*), Cairo, 1322 A.H., vol. VII, pp. 241-43; *Kitāb al-Umm*, vol. VII, p. 163; cf. al-Shāfi'ī, *al-Risālah*, Cairo, 1321 A.H., p. 40.

14. al-Shāfi'ī, *Ikhtilāf al-Ḥadīth*, *ed. cit.*, p. 140.

15. Mālik, *op. cit.*, vol. I, p. 234; cf. al-Shāfi'ī, *Ikhtilāf al-Ḥadīth*, *ed. cit.*, pp. 266-67.

16. Qur'ān 6 : 165.

17. By this we mean that the Islamic law was not systematised during the time of the Prophet and the Companions. Since the Successors' time it began to take its formal shape and to develop into a body and independent subject of study. Western writers such as Schacht present a different picture of the development of the Islamic law. The popular and administrative practice of the late Umayyed period, according to them, was transformed into Islamic Law. (See Majid Khadduri, *Law in the Middle East*, Washington, 1955, p. 40, article 'Pre-Islamic background and early development of jurisprudence', by Joseph Schacht). The Orientalists ignore the fact that the Muslims had the Qur'ān and the precedents left by the Prophet and the Companions. Where there was no precedent or clear instructions, they exercised their personal opinion. But this, too, was not against spirit of the teachings of the Qur'ān and the *Sunnah* of the Prophet. All this raw material, practised and produced by the early Muslims, developed into a systematic law. Certain popular customs no doubt permeated the law; but these did not deviate from the fundamental principles of Islam. The view that the law of Islam is purely based on the popular practice of the Umayyads, and does not take its thread from the Qur'ān and the *Sunnah* of the Prophet is contrary to facts and untenable.

18. Al-Shaybānī refers only to three schools, that is, Iraq, Syria and Medina. This shows that Egypt had no independent status in legal thought. See his *al-Siyar al-Kabīr* (with commentary by al-Sarkhsī), Cairo, 1957, vol. I, p. 230.

قال محمد رحمه الله : الشهيد اذا قتل فى المعركة لم يغسل و يصلى
عليه فى قول اهل العراق و أهل الشام و به ناخذ - و فى قول
أهل المدينة لا يصلى عليه و ممن قال ذلك مالك بن الس -

19. The letter of al-Layth b. Sa'd to Mālik has been reported by Ibn Qayyim (d. 751 A.H.) in *I'lām al-Muwaqqi'īn*. But since he is too late and the letter is not traceable in any early sources, we did not take it into consideration.

20. The term 'seven jurists of al-Madīnah' (*fuqahā' Sab'ah al-Madīnah*) is not traceable in the early texts of law. Ibn Sa'd (d. 230 A.H.) lists some of them together, but does not mention this appellation (Ibn Sa'd, *op. cit.*, vol. V, p. 334). Ibn al-Nadīm (d. ca. 385 A.H.) mentions a book known as '*Kitāb ra'y al-fuqahā' al-Sab'ah min Ahl al-Madīnah wa ma'khtalafū fī hi*', *Al-Fihrist*, Cairo, 1348 A.H., p. 315) by Ibn Abī'l-Zinād (d. 174 A.H.). This shows that the term was known in the middle of the second century. Prof. Schacht regards the title of this book as Ibn al-Nadīm's own formulation (*The Origins* etc., p. 350. See also pp. 243-44). Prof. Schacht may be right in his conjecture. But to begin with, it is a mere conjecture that the title is Ibn al-Nadim's own and not by Ibn Abī'l-Zinād himself. Secondly, even if the title be late, surely the important point is that about the middle of the second century a book was written containing the legal opinion of seven lawyers of Medina. This itself clearly shows that Ibn Abī'l-Zinād considered it important to record the opinion of the seven early lawyers of Medina. Given this concept, the term becomes of comparatively little importance.

21. Prof. Schacht regards the period before Ibrahīm al-Nakha'ī (d. 96 A.H.) as legendary in the history of development of law in Kufa. According to him, the reports ascribed to Ibn Mas'ūd, his companion and Shurayḥ on legal problems are spurious. He does not think al-Ḥasan of Basra a lawyer or even a traditionist. According to him, the development of legal thought in Kufa starts from Ibrahīm al-Nakha'ī. Similarly, he easily dismisses 'Umar and Ibn 'Umar as early authorities of Medina by saying: "traditionists from Companions cannot be regarded as genuine." He, therefore, starts his investigation from 'the seven lawyers of al-Madīnah' (see Schacht, Joseph, *The Origins of Muhammadan Jurisprudence*, Oxford, 1959, pp. 229-237 and 243-244).

It may be remarked that adequate information about these early authorities is not available in the early legal texts which are the sole basis of enquiry. But even these texts throw enough light on the legal background of these authorities. To prove every statement and report ascribed to them as spurious and fictitious has become customary among the Orientalists. We could judge them only from their works, which have not, unfortunately, reached us. Lack of information on the subject does not prove that the early authorities were legendary. We may partly rely on their biographies.

It is reported about al-Ḥasan of Basra that his legal opinion and decisions were collected in seven volumes. (See Ibn Ḥazm, *al-Iḥkām, ed. cit.*, vol. V. p. 97). When al-Ḥasan, according to Schacht, was not a lawyer, how could his legal decisions be collected?

The development of legal thought in Kufa is itself a wide field for research. It requires a detailed inquiry which will examine the reports stated by Prof. Schacht as fiction. This brief study does not allow us to enter into this field.

22. Al-Shāfi'ī, *Kitāb al-Umm, ed. cit.*, vol. VII, p. 246.
23. *Ibid.*, p. 257.
24. Ibn 'Abd al-Barr, *Jāmi' Bayān al-'Ilm*, Cairo, n. d., vol. I, p. 132. Cf. Ibn Qutaybah, *al-Imāmah wa'l-Siyāsah* (as attributed to him), Cairo, n.d., vol. II, p. 155. It should be noted, however, that this anecdote coming about Mālik, although famous, has been attributed sometimes to al-Manṣūr, sometimes to Harūn al-Rashīd, and sometimes even to al-Mahdī. This may put the whole story in doubt. In any case, it throws light on the local character of the schools. (See *Shorter Enc. of Islam*, Joseph Schacht, article Mālik).
25. Al-Shāfi'ī, *Kitāb al-Umm, ed. cit.*, vol. VII, p. 129; Abū Yūsuf, *Kitāb al-Āthār*, Cairo, 1355 A.H., pp. 70, 71; al-Shaybānī, *Kitāb al-Āthār*, Karachi, n.d., pp. 112, 113.
26. Abū Yūsuf, *Kitāb al-Kharāj, ed. cit.*, pp. 50-51.
27. Al-Shāfi'ī, *Kitāb al-Umm, ed. cit.*, vol. VII, p. 245; *Ikhtilāf al-Ḥadīth, ed. cit.*, p. 47.
28. By early schools of law we mean more or less definite and identifiable traditions prevalent in different regions before al-Shāfi'ī and against which al-Shāfi'ī argues. Thus, according to our terminology, Abū Ḥanifah, al-Awzā'ī and Mālik fall among the early schools. It must be constantly borne in mind, however, that the early schools already developed and experienced certain changes, among the main ones being the development and acceptance of legal *Ḥadīth* which Abū Ḥanīfah, al-Awzā'ī and Mālik use in varying extent.
29. The phrases like *al-amr al-mujtama' 'alayh 'indanā* (the agreed practice with us) which recur in *al-Muwaṭṭa'* indicate Mālik's view.
30. Abū Yūsuf, *al-Radd 'alā Siyar al-Awzā'ī*, Cairo, n.d., pp. 1, 5, 20, 24, 30, 76 *passim*.
31. Mālik, *op. cit.*, vol. II, p. 671.
32. Al-Shāfi'ī, *Kitāb al-Umm, ed. cit.*, vol. VII, p. 247 (rendering by J. Schacht, *The Origins*, p. 11).
33. *Ibid.*, pp. 102, 147, 211, 338.
34. Al-Shaybānī, *op. cit.*, pp. 68, 71, 78 *passim*.
35. Abū Yūsuf, *Kitāb al-Kharāj ed. cit.*, pp. 43, 99, 101 *passīm*.

36. Al-Shāfi'ī, *Kitāb al-Umm*, *ed. cit.*, vol. VII, p. 257.
37. *Ibid.*, p. 207.
38. *Ibid.*, pp. 240, 257 *passim.*
39. *Ibid.*, p. 230.
40. *Ibid.*, pp. 110, 170, 194, 275; and *Ikhtilāf al-Ḥadīth*, pp. 34, 35.
41. Abu Yūsuf, *Kitāb al-Khārāj*, *ed. cit.*, p. 50.
42. Al-Shāfi'ī, *Jimā' al-'Ilm*, Cairo, 1940, p. 12; *idem*, *al-Risālah*, *ed. cit.*, p. 8.
43. Al-Shāfi'ī, *Kitāb al-Umm*, *ed. cit.*, vol. VII, pp. 170, 194 and 275.

Chapter III

THE SOURCES OF ISLAMIC LAW

I

According to Islam, the ultimate source of authority is God alone. In the ideal of Islamic law, everyone except God, including the Prophet and ruling authorities, is subordinate to Divine Law, which emanates from Divine Revelation. Islamic law, irrespective of the variety of its "sources", emanates from God and aims at discovering and formulating His will. God's will is not once-and-for-all defined as a static system; rather it comprehends all spheres of man's life and is progressively unfolded. As Islam gives guidance in all walks of life, *Fiqh*, the law of Islam, as developed from the very beginning, comprehends, with special care, religio-moral, social, economic, and political aspects of human life. That is why a man acting according to the Islamic law is, in all circumstances, deemed to be fulfilling God's will. Thus, Islamic law is a manifestation of God's will.

The term "law" in this context, as hinted above, includes both the moral law as well as the legal enactments, particularly and more properly the former. It would thus be more accurate to say that while the (moral) law was revealed in the specific context of the Qur'ān and the *Sunnah* as the will of God, the Muslims' duty is to embody it in legal enactments in their own context. Indeed, a number of legal rules have been given by the Qur'ān to embody the will of God. The Qur'ānic rulings may be divided into two broad categories, namely *ḥalāl* (permissible) and *ḥarām* (forbidden). The classical legal categories owe their origin to these two terms frequently used by the Qur'ān.[1] The Qur'ān itself does not lay down the various degrees of permissibility and prohibition.

These degrees came into existence later when *Fiqh* developed as an independent science. The terminology used by the early jurists is a little different from the five categories evolved later. Today we hear the terms *wājib*, *ḥarām*, *makrūh*, *mandūb* and *mubāḥ*. This classification is based on moral assumptions and is primarily legal. Since every act of a Muslim must fall, according to the later *Fiqh* literature, under a certain legal category, this sort of classification became essential. The early works on *Fiqh* indicate that there were no such fixed categories; the terminology of the early Muslim period was general.

Al-Awzā'ī uses the terms *lā ba'sa*, *ḥālāl*, *ḥarām* and *makrūh* in his writings. The terms *lā ba'sa* and *makrūh* have been used by him in the sense of permissible and disapproved respectively. While discussing the question of selling prisoners of war he remarks that the Muslims did not consider it objectionable (*lā ba'sa*) to sell female prisoners of war. They disapproved (*yakrahūna*) of the sale of male prisoners, but approved of their exchange for Muslim prisoners of war.[2] It seems that these two terms conveyed a sense more literal than legal. The terms *ḥalāl* and *ḥarām* recur in his reasoning. He uses these two terms even for those cases which are disputed and not categorically permitted or prohibited in the Qur'ān or the *Sunnah*.[3]

The five legal categories (*al-aḥkām al-khamsah*) are not to be found in Mālik either. His terminology is similar to that of al-Awzā'ī. The terms *lā ba'sa* (no harm) and *makrūh* (disapproved) have been used by him as opposed to each other like al-Awzā'ī. The terms *ḥalāl* and *ḥarām* are not very frequent in his work. He also uses the term *wājib* in the sense of obligatory, but does not draw any distinction between *farḍ* and *wājib* as the late Ḥanafī jurists do. Of course, he distinguishes *wājib* from *Sunnah*. For instance, he says that the sacrifice of animals (on the occasion of '*Id*) is *Sunnah* (recommended) and not *wājib* (obligatory).[4] The term *makrūh* or *yukrahu* has been used by him sometimes in the sense of forbidden and sometimes in the sense of disapproved.[5] The terms *ḥasan* (good), *astaḥibbu* (I like) are also available in his writings. They convey the sense of recommendation—categories below *wājib*. All such terms as indicate recommendation fall under *mandūb* according to late classification.

The 'Irāqīs avoid the use of the terms *ḥalāl* and *ḥarām*, except for matters permitted or prohibited categorically in the Qur'ān. That is why the use of the terms *lā ba'sa* and *makrūh* is frequent in their writings. Abū Yūsuf criticizes al-Awzā'ī for his easy use of the terms *ḥalāl* and *ḥarām*, particularly his statement: "this is *ḥalāl* from God". He says that he found his teachers disliking the practice of saying in their legal decisions: 'this is *ḥalāl* (lawful) and this is *ḥarām* (unlawful)', except what was mentioned expressly in the Qur'ān as such without any qualification. He refers to Rabī' b. Khaytham, a Successor, as having remarked: "One ought not to say that God made such-and-such lawful (*ḥalāl*) or that He liked it, lest God tell him that He did not make it lawful nor did He like it. Similarly, one should not say that God made such-and-such unlawful (*ḥarām*); lest God say that he told a lie; He did not make it unlawful (*ḥarām*) nor did He forbid it." He adds that Ibrāhīm al-Nakha'ī is reported to have mentioned about his companions that whenever they gave some legal decision, they used to say: "This is disapproved (*makrūh*), and there is no harm in so-and-so (*lā ba'sa bihī*)." Concluding he remarks: "If we say 'this is lawful (*ḥalāl*) and 'this is unlawful (*ḥarām*)' what a tall talk it would be."[6] But it is interesting that Abū Yūsuf does not strictly follow this rule himself; he uses the term *ḥalāl* even in a case which is not expressly mentioned in the Qur'ān as such. He, for instance, says: "If a Muslim in the enemy territory has no animal for riding, while the Muslims there have no animal except those of *ghanīmah*, and he cannot walk on foot, in such a situation it is not lawful (*lā yaḥillu*) for the Muslims to leave him behind."[7] It should be noted that this sort of prohibition is not available in the Qur'ān, yet he uses *lā yaḥillu* which generally stands in his writings, for explicit prohibition like *ribā'* and marrying more than four women.[8] The terms *yajūzu* and *lā yajūzu* are also found in Abū Yūsuf's works.[9]

Al-Shaybānī frequently uses the terms *jā'iz* and *lā ba'sa bihī* for 'allowed' and *lā khayra* (not good) for 'forbidden'.[10] He does not make any clear distinction between prohibition proper (*ḥarām*) and disapproved (*makrūh*). The term *makrūh* or *yukrahu* recurs in his writings standing sometimes for forbidden and sometimes for disapproved.[11] The terms *ḥalāl* and *ḥarām* are no doubt visible occasionally in certain cases but not so frequently.

The term *Sunnah* in the sense of recommended, according to traditional categories, is rarely used in this period. In a case al-Shaybānī says that the recitation of *al-Fātiḥah* in the last two *rak'ahs* of prayers is *Sunnah;* but non-recitation so is equally valid.[12] The *Sunnah* prayer said before or after *farḍ* prayers is known as *taṭawwu'* and not *Sunnah* or *nafl*[13] as the name came to be established later. Al-Shaybānī sometimes interprets *wājib* (obligatory) as *afḍal* (better or recommended). Quoting a tradition from the Prophet that bathing on Friday is obligatory (*wājib*) for Muslims, al-Shaybāni remarks: "Taking a bath on Friday is better (*afḍal*) and not obligatory (*wājib*)."[14] Since the term *wājib* has occurred in this *Ḥadīth* with reference to the Friday bath it is to be inferred that al-Shaybānī treats it as a non-technical term; hence he considers it to be better. Otherwise, it would mean that al-Shaybānī does not apparently accept the tradition which characterizes Friday bath as *wājib* (obligation).

Both *farḍ* and *wājib* have been used by al-Shaybānī for 'obligatory'.[15] But *farḍ* has been generally used for those rules that are based on the Qur'ānic injunctions.[16] It appears to be more technical than *wājib*. The term *wājib* no doubt stands for obligatory, but sometimes it is used in the non-technical sense denoting 'essential' or 'necessary'. So far it had not assumed its position next to the category *farḍ* in sense and usage. There is a clear distinction between *farīḍah* and *Sunnah* in his writings. He calls 'Id prayer *Sunnah* and Friday prayer *farīḍah*. He remarks, however, that none of them should be abandoned. For this emphasis, we presume, 'Id prayer was described as *wājib* in later *Fiqh* literature.[17]

We find the term *ḥasan* being used most frequently in al-Shaybānī's writings. It seems that this was a non-technical word used in a general approbatory sense. It stands sometimes for 'approved', often for 'recommended', and occasionally for 'imperative'.[18] We think that later on this term was divided into several categories, e.g. *wājib, sunnah, mustaḥabb* etc. In most places al-Shaybānī uses this term along with the term *afḍal* (better). He says, for instance, it is better (*afḍal*) if the *mu'adhdhin* puts his fingers in his ears (while calling for prayers), but in case he does not do so, it is all right (*ḥasan*).[19] The use of *mustaḥabb* is not frequent in al-Shaybānī's works. It is mostly used in its literal sense.[20]

In the late legal categories there appeared a clear distinction between *fāsid* and *bāṭil*. *Fāsid*, according to the late terminology, stands for 'corrupt' or 'voidable' while *bāṭil* for 'null and void'. Al-Shaybānī uses these terms in several contexts, but the distinction is not very clear. Sometimes while discussing one and the same problem he uses both these terms interchangeably which implies that here he draws no such distinction between them.[21]

When we come to al-Shāfi'ī, we notice a great deal of development in categories both by way of their subdivision and by way of introduction of new categories. These subdivisions are not found in Mālik's or al-Shaybānī's works. Prohibition, for example, is of two kinds according to him.

The first is forbidden (*ḥarām*) for intrinsic reasons, and the second is forbidden for extrinsic reasons (*tanzīhan*). He demonstrates the distinction between them with complete illustrations'.[22] Similarly, he divides *wājib* into two sub-categories: *wājib* proper and *wājib* optional (*fi'l-ikhtiyār*). According to him, taking a bath on account of *janābah* (major impurity) is *wājib* proper, while a bath for the purpose of general cleanliness is *wājib* optional. He says that the term *wājib* which occurs in the *Ḥadīth* for Friday bath is capable of having both meanings. First, apparently it means that Friday bath is as obligatory as the bath for major impurity. But it might simply mean desirability for the purpose of good deportment and cleanliness. He refers to 'Uthmān b. 'Affān as having said his Friday prayer without taking a bath which corroborates the second meaning. Further, he argues on the basis of a *Ḥadīth* of the Prophet and a tradition (*athar*) of 'A'ishah which indicate that Friday bath was not meant for the validity of Friday prayer but for cleanliness. Therefore, al-Shāfi'ī does not hold taking a bath on Friday to be *wājib* proper.[23]

The term[24] *mubāḥ* which stands for actions in relation to which the *Sharī'ah* is neutral, appears for the first time in al-Shāfi'ī. He elaborates it and gives its implications. He mentions several prohibitions made by the Prophet in *mubāḥ* actions. For instance, he says that the Prophet forbade wearing *ṣammā'* (single robe) sitting in *iḥtibā'* condition (to lean against a single cloth by drawing together and covering one's back and shanks with it), and commanded to take food at one's own side from the plate and prohibited taking food from the middle, and forbade halting on the road at night. He draws a distinction between such prohibitions in *mubāḥ* acts and the prohibitions proper. He thinks that this sort of prohibition was made for etiquette. Therefore, these prohibitions, according to him, do not render these *mubāḥ* acts *ḥarām*, while the prohibition with regard to sale and marriage contracts made them *ḥarām*. Nevertheless, he regards violation in both the cases as disobedience, but disobedience in the latter is greater than in the former[25].

Al-Shāfiʿī also introduced the term *farḍ kifāyah* which is not to be found before him. He defines it as 'the *farḍ* which if performed by a sufficient number of Muslims, the remaining Muslims who did not perform it would not be sinful.' He justifies this sort of *farḍ* on the basis of the Qur'ānic verses 9 : 5, 36, 41, 111, 122 and 4 : 95 concerning *Jihād*. He regards *Jihad*,[26] saying funeral prayers for a Muslim, his burial and return of salutation (*salām*) as *Kifāyah*. He thinks that in this category of *farḍ* the intention is sufficiency, i.e. devolving upon the community as a whole and hence requiring a "sufficient number" of agents as distinguished from what devolves as a duty upon every individual. As regards *farḍ ʿayn*, he does not use this term in his writings. But it seems that the concept is there. He divides legal knowledge into *ʿāmmah* and *khaṣṣāh*. Under *ʿāmmah* he mentions five prayers, fasting during Ramaḍān, *Ḥajj* and *Zakāh*, and prohibition of murder, usury, (fornication), theft and drinking. With regard to these acts he remarks that all individuals are obligated therewith (*kullifa*). It is this concept which appeared in the form of *farḍ ʿayn* in the later *Fiqh* literature.[27]

The process of development of these categories from the early schools to al-Shāfiʿī and from him onward is not very much clear from the available early literature. It is, however, clear that these categories began to take their formal shape from al-Shāfiʿī and resulted in five fixed values (*al-aḥkām al-khamsah*) after him with the passage of time.

II

The above categories are based on four foundations (*uṣūl*). According to the classical legal theory, they are: the Qur'ān, the *Sunnah*, *Ijmāʿ* and *Qiyās*. Works on Islamic jurisprudence composed since the time of al-Shāfi'ī (d. 204 A.H.), and certain reports[28] claiming to go back earlier, convince us that the present sequence of the sources of Islamic Law was in existence in the earliest days of Islam. It is, however, difficult to accept that the present order of the legal theory dates back to the time of the Companions. There are various reasons for our doubt. Firstly, the scheme of this legal theory, i.e. the Qur'ān, the *Sunnah*, *Ijmā'* and *Qiyās*, is itself the result of historical development starting from the time of the Companions. Secondly, the technical order of the sources of law, as the reports claim to show, is actually a later product; hence such reports cannot be genuine. Thirdly, the idea of the rightly-guided leaders (*a'immat al-hudā*)' must have emerged after the first four Caliphs. Therefore, the reports showing the use of the term *Qiyās* by 'Umar, the second Caliph, in his instructions to the judges, appear to be doubtful. Fourthly, the Concept of *Ijmā'*, particularly the *Ijmā'* of the Companions, most probably appeared after the first generation (i.e. the Companions). Hence, the question of its existence in a legal theory in the days of the Companions does not arise. Fifthly, *Qiyās* developed as a technical doctrine during the second and the third generations, although the idea was present in the form of *ra'y* (considered opinion) during the first generation. From al-Shāfi'ī's discussions with his opponents it appears that the jurists of the early schools placed *Qiyās* before *Ijmā'*. The change in the order of the sources of law first appeared in al-Shāfi'ī; though the ground seems to have been prepared long before him. We analyse here a few examples in order to illustrate that before al-Shāfi'ī *Ijmā'* was placed after *Qiyās*.

While discussing the principle of *Ijmā'*, al-Shafi'i's opponent seeks to establish the authority of *Ijmā'* in opposition to the isolated traditions advocated by al-Shāfi'ī. The opponent remarks that *Ijma'* of the scholars (*'ulamā'*) on the points of detail should be followed, because they alone have the legal knowledge and are agreed upon an opinion. *Ijmā'*, according to him, stands as an authority for those who have no legal knowledge, in case the scholars are agreed. But if the scholars differ, their opinions do not have any binding authority. Further, he suggests that the unsettled points in which there is difference of opinion should be referred back to *Qiyās* on the basis of their agreed points[29]. This implies that, according to him, *Qiyās-Ijma'* process should go on continuously and that *Qiyās* precedes *Ijmā'*.

In addition to al-Shāfi'ī's controversies, we find numerous other instances that confirm our view. Ibn al-Muqaffa' (d. 140 A.H.) suggests to the Caliph al-Manṣūr that he should apply his own reason to the heritage of the past on the basis of *Sunnah* or *Qiyās*. Concluding, he remarks that the collection of these practices (*siyar*) along with the personal opinion of the Caliph himself may likely form the nearest approach (*qarīnah*) for future agreement.[30] This argument indicates that Ibn al-Muqaffa' puts *Ijmā'* at the end of the scheme and assigns the third position to *Qiyās* after the *Sunnah.*

Further, Wāṣil b. 'Aṭā' (d. 131 A.H.) is reported to have said that a right judgment can be arrived at through four sources: 'the express word of the Book, unanimously recognized traditions, logical reasoning, and consensus of the Community.[31] Here, too, we notice that *Qiyās* is given priority over *Ijmā'* and *Ijmā'* comes in the last. Ample evidence can, however, be produced to prove that a change occurred in the order of the terms of the legal theory later, and the early procedure was reversed.

From a purely theoretical point of view also the interaction of *Qiyās* and *Ijmā'* is absolutely essential. If there were no *Qiyās* (*Ijtihād*), how could an *Ijmā'* be considered? For *Ijmā'* can be arrived at only through the difference of opinion as a result of the exercise of *Qiyās* by several persons. Out of these diverse opinions, an accepted general opinion emerges through a process of gradual integration. This means that *Qiyās* (*Ijtihād*) and *Ijmā'* are two complementary factors of a continuous process. *Ijmā'*, being an agreed and accepted opinion, implies that it carries more weight and force than other non-agreed individual opinions based on *Qiyās*. This might be the reason why al-Shāfi'ī and the later jurists gave priority to *Ijmā'* over *Qiyās*. The process, however, requires that *Qiyās* must precede *Ijmā'*.

The primary source of Islamic legislation is the Qur'ān. The *Sunnah* explains and elaborates the Qur'ān. While *Sunnah* undoubtedly constitutes also an independent source, it is closely linked with and is secondary to the Qur'ān. *Qiyās* is the systematic form of *ra'y* (considered individual opinion) and is based on the Qur'ān and the *Sunnah*. Personal opinion results in *Ijmā'* when it receives the universal acceptance of the Community. In a word, the Qur'ān, the *Sunnah*, *Qiyās*, and *Ijmā'* are interlinked; the same spirit pervades these sources for which the final authority is the Qur'ān.

The basic material sources of Islamic law are the Qur'ān and the *Sunnah*. Their authority is unchanged in all times and circumstances. *Qiyās* and *Ijmā'* are, in fact, instruments or agencies for legislation on new problems for whose solution a direct guidance from the Qur'ān and the *Sunnah* is not available. It is, therefore, obvious that *Qiyās* and *Ijmā'* are considered to be an authoritative source of law being subservient to the Qur'ān and the *Sunnah*. The authenticity of these auxiliary sources shall be determined only by the degree of their consonance with the other two original and unchallenged sources of law.

III

We may now discuss briefly each of these sources of law. The Qur'ān, as we said before, is the primary source of legislation. Several Qur'ānic verses expressly indicate that it is the basis and main source of law in Islam.[32] The Prophet lived at Mecca for thirteen years and at Medina for ten years. The period after the *Hijrah,* unlike that of Mecca, was no longer a period of humiliation, and persecution of the Muslims. The type of guidance which the Muslims required at Medina was not the same as they had needed at Mecca. That is why the Medinese *sūrahs* differ in character from those revealed at Mecca. The latter are comparatively small in size, and generally deal with the basic beliefs of Islam. They provide guidance to an individual soul. The Medinese *sūrahs,* on the other hand, are rich in laws relating to civil, criminal, social, and political problems of life. They provide guidance to a nascent social and political community. We do find the term *zakāh* in several Meccan *sūrahs*;[33] but *zakāh* was not in existence at Mecca in its institutional form. At Mecca, this term has been used in the sense of monetary help on a voluntary basis or in the sense of moral purity. It was not an obligatory social duty of the opulents. Moreover, at Mecca no administrative staff was recruited for this purpose.

Apart from the controversy over the number of the legal verses in the Qur'ān, it is clear that the Qur'ān is neither a legal code in the modern sense, nor is it a compendium of ethics. The primary purpose of the Qur'ān is to lay down a way of life which regulates the relationship of man with man and his relationship with God. The Qur'ān gives directions for man's social life as well as for his communion with his Creator. The laws of inheritance, rulings for marriage and divorce, provisions for war and peace, punishments for theft, adultery and homicide, are all meant for regulating the ties of man with his fellow beings. In addition to these specific legal rules, the Qur'ān abounds in moral teachings. Therefore, it is not correct to say, as Coulson presumes, that "the primary purpose of the Qur'ān is to regulate not the relationship of man with his fellows but his relationship with his Creator."[34]

The Qur'ānic quasi-legislation is not couched in purely legal terms. There is an amalgam of law and ethics. The Qur'ān, in fact, addresses itself to the conscience of man. That is why the legal verses were revealed in the form of moral exhortation, sometimes exhorting people to the obedience of God and occasionally instilling a keen sense of fear of God in the minds of Muslims. Hence, it contains emphatic statements about certain specific attributes of God, e.g. God is all-hearing, all-seeing and the like, at the end of its verses. Further, it goes without saying that the Qur'ān does not seek to be pan-legistic, i.e. to lay down once and for all the details of life. Broadly speaking, it should be borne in mind that the legislative part of the Qur'ān is the model illustration for future legislation and does not constitute a legal code by itself. History tells us that the revelation came down when some social necessity arose, or some Companion consulted the Prophet in connection with certain significant problems. Thus, the specific rules, the legal norms, and the juridical values furnished by the Qur'ān constitute its legislative side which, however, is in no way less important than its purely ethical side.

A common reader begins to read the Qur'ān with an idea that it is a versatile code and a comprehensive book of law. He does not find in detail the laws and by-laws relating to the social life, culture, and political problems. Further, in the Qur'ān he reads numerous verses to the effect that everything has been mentioned in this Book and nothing has been left out. Besides, he notices that the Qur'ān lays great emphasis on saying prayer and giving *zakāh*, but at the same time he finds that it does not mention their specific definitions or details. Questions, therefore, arise in the mind of the layman as to the nature of the comprehensiveness of the Qur'ān.

The difficulty arises from ignoring the fact that God did not reveal the Qur'ān in a vacuum, but as a guide to a living

Prophet, who was engaged in an actual struggle. The Qur'ān, however, instead of giving the minutiae, indicates basic principles that lead a Muslim to a certain direction, where he can find the answer by his own effort. Moreover, it presents the Islamic ideology in a general form, suited to the changing circumstances in all ages and climes. The Qur'ān calls itself 'guidance' and not a code of law. It should be noted that the Qur'ān sometimes explains itself, and as a book of guidance (*hidāyah*) it did not leave untouched anything relating to the fundamentals. As regards the actual practical shape of life to be led by a Muslim and the community as a whole, it shows and demarcates the borders of the various aspects of life. It was the task of the Prophet to present the ideal practical life in the light of those limits enunciated by the Qur'ān. The Prophet was, in fact, sent primarily to exemplify the teachings of the Qur'ān. That is why the *Sunnah* by its very nature never goes against the Qur'ān, nor the Qur'ān against the *Sunnah*.[35]

In his work, '*The Origins of Muhammadan Jurisprudence*,' Prof. Joseph Schacht holds that "apart from the most elementary rules, norms derived from the Koran were introduced into Muhammadan law almost invariably at a secondary stage." He illustrates this by quoting the cases of divorce, the maxim that spoils belong to the killer, and the policy of not laying waste the enemy country, the oath of the plaintiff in confirmation of the evidence of one witness and the evidence of minors. From the difference of pinion among the early jurists in the aforesaid cases, he draws the conclusion that these people argued on the basis of their personal judgments, which they sought to justify through the Qurān.[36] This, however, appears to be incorrect, as it stands. Prof. Schacht, of course, admits that the clear rules provided for in the Qur'ān—for example, those of inheritance, evidence, punishment, etc. were from the very beginning operative, and, in fact, formed the nucleus of the *Sharī'ah*. What causes him to reach his conclusions about the secondary introduction of the Qur'ānic norms is that, in cases where the Qur'ān did not provide any explicit guidance, the Muslims formed their own opinion. However, this considered opinion was never expected to be opposed to or independent of the spirit of the Qur'ān and, if someone at a later stage, thought of a verse which could have possible relevance to this question, he quoted the verse. But this certainly does not show that the Qur'ān was introduced at a secondary stage.

It is needless to say that Islamic law underwent a long process of evolution. The interpretation of the Qur'ān in the early period was not so complex and sophisticated as it developed in the later ages. The legal rules not derived from the specific verses of the Qur'ān in the early period were sought to be so drawn later on. This was a continuous activity. The methodology of inference from the Qur'ān grew more and more intricate and philosophical in the wake of the deep and minute study of the Qur'ān by jurists in the later ages. The corpus of Islamic law is rich in examples where, with regard to a problem, some jurists argued on the basis of the Qur'ān, while the others did so on the basis of traditions or personal opinion, for these latter did not think the Qur'ānic verse relevant to the point at issue. Such differences do not imply that "in every single case the place given to the Koran", in Prof. Schacht's words, "was determined by the attitude of the group concerned to the ever-mounting tide of traditions from the Prophet;" and that "the Koran taken by itself, apart from its possible bearing on the problem raised by the traditions from the Prophet, can hardly be called the first and foremost basis of early legal theory."[37]

Prof. Schacht does admit that "a number of legal rules, particularly in family law and law of inheritance, not to mention cult and ritual, were based on the Koran from the beginning."[38] It is of supreme importance to note that the

Qur'ān's position as the first and foremost basis for legal theory does not mean that it treats of every problem meticulously. The Qur'ān, as we know, is not basically a code of law, but a document of spiritual and moral guidance. The presentation of the details of legal rules does not fall under the basic objectives of the Divine Book. The instances quoted by Prof. Schacht relate mainly to the cases, where detailed manner of application has not been prescribed by the Qur'ān. Although, generally, the legal verses of the Qur'ān are quite definite, nevertheless all such verses are open to interpretation, and different rules can be derived from the same verse on the basis of *Ijtihād*. This is the reason for the difference of opinion among the jurists in the cases mentioned by Prof. Schacht. According to one jurist, a law can be deduced from some verse but the same verse is silent on the same problem according to the other. Hence, one argues on the same point on the basis of the Qur'ān, while the other on the basis of the *Sunnah*. It is reported, for example, that during the caliphate of Abū Bakr a grandmother approached him asking her share from the heritage of her deceased grandson. Abū Bakr reportedly replied: "Neither in the Book of Allāh is there anything for you, nor do I know of anything in the *Sunnah* of the Prophet. . . ."[39] Abū Bakr's reference in the first instance to the Qur'ān clearly shows that this was the practice from the earliest days of Islam.

Let us take another example. A slave of Ibn 'Umar, who deserted him, a report says, committed theft. Ibn 'Umar asked Sa'īd b. al-'Ās, the governor of Medina, to amputate his hand. But Sa'īd refused to do so on the plea that the hand of a deserting slave is not amputated. Thereupon Ibn 'Umar reportedly asked: "In which Book of Allāh did you find it?"[40] This sort of report represents the trend of the early generations towards the Qur'ān, and shows its primary role in the process of law-making.

The doctrine of abrogation (*naskh*) of the individual verses in the Qur'ān is also significant in Islamic jurisprudence. The classical concept of this doctrine affirms that a number of verses in the Qur'ān, having been repealed, are no longer operative. These repealed verses are no doubt part of the Qur'ān, but they carry no practical value. This raises a very serious question: When the Qur'ān is eternal and its injunctions are valid for all ages, how is it possible that some of its passages lost their practical value? It seems that such a concept of abrogation was not in existence in the lifetime of the Prophet or in the early generation. It must have emerged sometime later for reasons of legal consistency not definitely known to us. We shall discuss this problem in detail in the next chapter.

IV

Another important source of Islamic law is the *Sunnah*. *Sunnah* essentially means exemplary conduct of some person. In the context of Islamic jurisprudence, it refers to the model behaviour of the Prophet. The Islamic concept of the *Sunnah*, as we shall discuss in greater detail in Chapter V, originates with the advent of the Prophet. Since the Qur'ān enjoins upon the Muslims to follow the conduct of the Prophet, which is distinguished as 'exemplary and great,'[41] it became 'ideal' for the Muslim Community.

The Qur'ān asks the Prophet to decide the problems of the Muslims according to the Revelation.[42] As such, the basic authority for legislation, as we have already pointed out, is the Qur'ān. Nevertheless, the Qur'ān declared the Prophet to be the interpreter of the Qur'ānic texts.[43] Moreover, it describes the functions of the Prophet, namely, announcing of the revelation before people, giving moral training to them, and to teach them the Divine Book and wisdom.[44] The *Sunnah* is therefore closely linked with the Qur'ān and it is, therefore, rather difficult to maintain that these are two separate sources.

It is the *Sunnah* that gives the concrete shape to the Qur'ānic teachings. The Qur'ān, for instance, mentions *ṣalāh* and *zakāh* but does not lay down their details. It is the Prophet who explained them to his followers in a practical form. Moreover, the Divine Book made obedience to the Prophet obligatory; hence, the *Sunnah*, i.e. the model behaviour of the Prophet, be it in the form of precept or example, became ultimately a source of law. The decisions taken by the Prophet were elevated by God to such a degree that their acceptance and willing submission to them was declared to be a fundamental of the faith. The Qur'ān, accordingly, says: "But nay, by thy Lord, they will not believe (in truth) until they make thee judge of what is in dispute between them and find within themselves no dislike of that which thou decidest, and submit with full submission".[45]

The source of law is the "ideal *Sunnah*" or the model behaviour of the Prophet. *Ḥadīth* is the index and vehicle of the *Sunnah*. The early schools of law, as we pointed out previously, generally accepted those traditions that were well-known and practised by the Muslims. That is why the early jurists arguing on the basis of the *Sunnah* differed from one another. Their differences were mainly due to the differences in the interpretation and application of a particular *Ḥadīth* to a particular case. One jurist might consider one particular incident in the life of the Prophet as more relevant than others to a given situation; while another jurist might single out another incident. Through this activity more or less regional interpretation of the *Sunnah* came into existence. They were all termed *Sunnah* but each one of them was associated with the *Sunnah* of the Prophet and ultimately based on it. This question will occupy us in the chapter on *Sunnah*.

According to al-Shāfi'ī, the *Sunnah* coming direct from the Prophet in the form of *Ḥadīth* through a reliable chain of narrators is a source of law, irrespective of whether it was accepted by the people or not, and even if it was an isolated tradition. He emphasized the value of the traditions from the Prophet in preference to the opinions of the Companions or their practice (*'amal*). In some cases, the early jurists followed the practice or the opinion of the Companions even in the presence of a tradition from the Prophet. But al-Shāfi'ī vehemently opposed this practice. He contended that in the presence of the Prophet's tradition, no other authority can stand. He tried to convince his opponents that they should not set aside a *Ḥadīth* from the Prophet even if it came through a single narrator, unless another *Ḥadīth* on the same subject carried over by a chain of reliable narrators is available. In case of conflict between two reports from the Prophet, the one which is more authentic must be preferred.[46]

Al-Shāfi'ī interprets the word '*ḥikmah*' occurring in the Qur'ān together with 'the Book' as the *Sunnah* of the Prophet.[47] He argues that since God made obedience of the Prophet obligatory on people, this means that what comes from the Prophet comes from God.[48] He believes that the *Sunnah* of the Prophet is revelation from God. He reports that Ṭā'ūs, a Successor, had possessed a document which contained a list of wergilds (*'uqūl*) which were divinely inspired. Again he says: "Whatever the Prophet made obligatory he did so on the basis of a divine revelation, because there is a kind of revelation which is recited (*mā yutlā*, i.e. the Qur'ān) while there is another kind which is sent to the Prophet and forms the *Sunnah*." He elaborates this point by quoting several reports to show that there used to come revelation to the Prophet in addition to the Qur'ān.[49] It appears that the concept of two kinds of revelation, namely, *jaliy* (patent) and *khafī* (assumed), begins rather earlier than al-Shāfi'ī as the reports quoted by him indicate. We do not think he was non-committal in regarding the *Sunnah* of the Prophet as revelation, as Prof. Schacht holds.[50]

The next important basis of law which is, in fact, a supplement to the *Sunnah*, is the opinions and practice (*āthār* and *'amal*) of the Companions. From the early days of Islam the Muslims have taken the legal decisions of the Companions as the source of law. The reason behind this is that the Companions were the immediate observers of the *Sunnah* of the Prophet. Having been in association with him for years together, they were expected to be acquainted not only with his sayings and behaviour but also with the spirit and character of the ideal *Sunnah* left by him for the coming generations. Their legal opinions, despite differences, carried the spirit of the Prophetic *Sunnah*, whence they cannot be divorced. That is the reason why the jurists of the early schools frequently argued on the basis of the Companions' legal decisions. The practice and opinions of the Companions were so important a source of law that Mālik sometimes sets aside a tradition from the Prophet in their favour. Al-Shāfi'ī, for instance, reports a tradition on the authority of Mālik that Sa'd b. Abī Waqqāṣ and Ḍaḥḥāk b. Qays were once discussing the question of performing *'Umrah* along with *Ḥajj*. Ḍaḥḥāk said that only a man who was ignorant of God's commands would combine the two. Further, he remarked that 'Umar, the second Caliph, had forbidden such practice. Rejecting his opinion, Sa'd replied that the Prophet had performed *'Umrah* along with *Ḥajj*, and he himself did so with him. Mālik reportedly held that the opinion of Ḍaḥḥāk was more to his liking than that of Sa'd, and that 'Umar knew the Prophet better than Sa'd.[51] Why the Medinese sometimes follow the opinion of the Companions or the local practice and set aside Prophetic traditions is a serious question which we shall discuss in detail in the chapters on *Sunnah* and *Ijmā'*.

The Companions played a vital role in establishing the *Sunnah* of the Prophet. Hence, it became more or less customary with the early schools to argue on the basis of the practice of the Companions. They must have considered that their action was based on the Prophetic *Sunnah* or they were better equipped to take decisions in the light of the *Sunnah*. But al-Shāfi'ī was strongly opposed to this view. He does not regard the sayings of the Companions or their practice as necessarily the *Sunnah* of the Prophet unless there exists an explicit tradition from the Prophet. In the absence of a tradition from the Prophet, he no doubt follows the opinions of the Companions. In case of difference of opinion among them, he prefers the opinion of the first four Caliphs to those of others, or the opinion which coincides with the Qur'ān, or the *Sunnah* or *Ijmā'* or the opinion which is correct according to *Qiyās*.[52] His utmost endeavour, however, was to adhere to the *Sunnah* of the Prophet to which he gave absolute priority and which he radically distinguished from the subsequent practice and opinions.

The Successors, too, played a major role in the development of Islamic law. Since they had association with the Companions, their opinions, too, carried weight in law. Their legal decisions constituted a source of law for the early schools. Not infrequently, we find cases where the opinion of a Successor was even preferred to that of a Companion.[53] Early works on *Fiqh* are replete with the legal opinions of the Successors. The early schools quote their opinions in support of their doctrines, and occasionally make them the sole basis of their arguments. After quoting the traditions from the Prophet and the Companions, Mālik quotes the practice and opinions of the Successors. But from this it does not follow that he always adheres to them, because on occasions he does not act upon the traditions from the Companions either. Abū Yūsuf clearly bases the principle of 'avoiding to inflict *ḥadd* punishment on the accused in case of doubt' on the opinions of the Companions and the Successors.[54] As the practice and opinions of the Companions and the Successors reflected the *Sunnah* of the Prophet, the early schools regarded them as an important source of law.

We have previously shown that al-Shāfi'ī regards the opinions of the Companions as a source of law. Sometimes he calls following their practice *taqlīd*.[55] But he does not make any mention of the Successors in his theory of law. It appears from *Kitāb al-Umm* that he follows the opinions of the Successors as a support of his thesis and not as a basis of his argument. He quotes, for instance, Shurayḥ, al-Sha'bī, Sa'īd b. al-Musayyib 'Aṭā', Ṭā'ūs and Mujāhid in the case of accepting the evidence given by a slanderer (*qādhif*).[56]

V

Another source of Islamic law is *Qiyās* (analogical deductions). It is, in fact, a systematic and developed form of *ra'y* (considered opinion). The most natural and simple mode of reasoning is *ra'y* that played a paramount role prior to the dominance of *Qiyās*. In the early days of Islam, *ra'y* was a generic term that covered a variety of modes of *Ijtihād*. We find its use in the Prophet's time as well as after him by the Companions. The Qur'ān and the *Sunnah* no doubt provide us with some legal rules with regard to the individual and social life of Muslims. But human life, being dynamic, requires laws that should change with the changing circumstances. *Ra'y* is an instrument that enables the coverage of diverse situations and enables Muslims to make new laws according to their requirements. The period of 'Umar's Caliphate abounds in such instances.

We first meet with a semi-technical use of the term *Qiyās* in the alleged letter of 'Umar, the second Caliph, to Abū Mūsā al-Ash'arī (d. 44 A.H.). 'Umar is reported to have advised him to acquaint himself with the "parallels and precedents" (of legal cases) and then to "weigh up" the cases (*qīs al-umūra*), deciding what in his judgement would be the most pleasing to God and nearest to the truth.[57] From such beginnings as this reported advice of 'Umar, *ra'y* appears to have developed later into legal and technical concept of *Qiyās*, viz. to find out an essential common factor between two similar cases and to apply the rule of one to the other. It is, however, noteworthy that the result after the application of *Qiyās* by different persons is not necessarily one and the same. The reason is that the actual location of the common factor (*'illah*) is open to difference of opinion. As such a given rule inferred by applying *Qiyās* is always subject to challenge, and can be denied by those who think differently.

Qiyās comes last in al-Shāfi'ī's scheme of the legal theory. He regards it as weaker than *Ijmā'*. He does not allow the use of *Qiyās* in the presence of a tradition (*khabar*). He takes it as something for the sake of need (*manzilatu ḍarūratin*). As *tayammum* is allowed, he argues, in the absence of water during a journey, so is the case with *Qiyās*. Further, he contends that since no *ṭahārah* is valid with *tayammum* when water becomes available, similarly use of *Qiyās* is invalid in the presence of a *khabar*.[58] He seeks to prove the validity of *Qiyās* on the basis of the Qur'ānic verse: "Whencesoever thou comest forth turn thy face toward it so that men may have no argument against you."[59] From this verse he infers that the use of *Qiyās* in reasoning is obligatory on Muslims. Explaining this verse he remarks that the man who is far away from the *Ka'bah* depends on the indications (*dalā'il*) like stars and mountains. Similarly, he says, one should depend on the indications to reach a certain conclusion.[60] These pro-*Qiyās* and pro-*Ijtihād* arguments are, in fact, aimed at the refutation of the use of unrestricted *ra'y*, which he thinks arbitrary and subjective.

VI

The last source of Islamic law, according to the scheme, is *Ijmā'*. We have already explained in this chapter its position in the order of the legal theory. *Ijmā'* is a principle for guaranteeing the veracity of the new legal content that emerges as a result of exercising *Qiyās* and *Ijtihād*. It is, in fact, a check against the fallibility of *Qiyās*. There are points which have been universally accepted and agreed upon by the entire Community. This sort of *Ijmā'* that allows no difference of opinion is generally confined to obligatory duties (*farā'iḍ*). This is known as *Ijmā'* of the Community. On the other hand, there are certain rules which we may call positive law that are agreed upon by the learned of a particular region, but they do not carry the force of the consensus of the Community. This is known as *Ijma'* of the learned (*Ijmā' al-Khāṣṣah*). The *Ijmā'* of the learned (*Ijmā' al-Khāṣṣah*), in the early schools, was a mechanism for creating a sort of integration of the divergent opinions which arose as a result of the individual legal activity of jurists. It seems that the whole system of law in the pre-Shāfi'ī period was held together and strengthened by this implicit or explicit principle. It represents the average general opinion of each region in respect of the positive law. It sets aside the stray and 'unsuccessful' opinions circulating in each locality. It is important to note that the *Ijmā'* of the learned is not the name of the decisions on legal issues taken by an assembly of Muslim jurists. It emerges, in fact, by itself through a process of integration, and creates for itself a position in the Community.

It is significant to note that al-Shāfi'ī's concept of *Ijmā'* is different from that of the early schools. He holds, as is evident from his writings, that *Ijmā'* is something static and formal having no room for disagreement. That is why he is reluctant in accepting the validity of the *Ijmā'* of the learned as a source of law due to the differences among them. Only the *Ijmā'* of the Community is valid according to him. In support of his argument he says that the Community at large cannot neglect the *Sunnah* of the Prophet, which, however, the individuals may neglect. Further, he contends that the Community—God willing—can never agree on a decision opposed to the *Sunnah* of the Prophet nor on an error.[61] As such, he restricted *Ijmā'* only to the *farā'iḍ*. *Ijmā'*, therefore, according to al-Shāfi'ī, became merely a theoretical source of law than a practical one. We shall discuss his controversies on *Ijmā'* in Chapter VIII.

However, despite his real position on *Ijmā'*, al-Shafi'ī regards it as a source of law after the Qur'ān and the *Sunnah* of the Prophet. In case these sources are silent on a point, he follows first the agreed opinion of the Companions. Then, in case of differences among them, he adopts the opinion of one Companion specially of each of the first four Caliphs. He argues finally on the basis of *Qiyās* which is strictly based on the Qur'ān and the *Sunnah* of the Prophet alone.[62] In fact, al-Shāfi'ī confines legal knowledge to the two basic sources, namely, the Qur'ān and the *Sunnah*, which he calls *aṣlān* (the two bases). He regards these two sources as independent entities (*'aynān*), while *Ijtihād*, according to him, is not an *'ayn* (entity), but something created by human intelligence.[63] He believes that the Qur'ān and the *Sunnah* provide answers to all possible problems concerning religion. Thus, the whole emphasis throughout his writings centres around these two sources.

NOTES

1. Qur'ān, 2 : 173, 275; 4 : 19; 5 : 3, 96.
2. Abū Yūsuf, *al-Radd 'alā Siyar al-Awzā'ī*, Cairo, n.d., pp, 61-62.
3. *Ibid.*, pp. 70, 96.
4. Mālik, *al-Muwaṭṭa'*, Cairo, 1951, vol. II, p. 487.
5. *Ibid.*, vol. I, p. 230, and vol. II, p. 984.
6. Abū Yūsuf, *op. cit.*, pp. 72-73.
7. *Ibid.*, p. 15. His remark كيف يحل هذا مادام فى المعمعة ويحرم بعد ذلك is significant. See also p. 66.
8. *Ibid.*, pp. 97, 105.
9. *Ibid.*, p. 70.
10. Al-Shaybānī, Muḥammad b. al-Ḥasan, *al-Aṣl*, Cairo, 1954, pp. 3, 4, 5, 6 *passim*.

11. Al-<u>Sh</u>aybānī, *al-Jāmi' al-Ṣag<u>h</u>īr*, Lucknow, 1291 A.H., pp. 8, 9, 10, 92, *passim*.
12. Al-<u>Sh</u>aybānī, *al-Muaṭṭā'*, Deoband, n.d., p. 104.
13. *Ibid.*, pp. 162, 192.
14. *Ibid.*, pp. 72-73.

قال محمد : الغسل افضل يوم الجمعه" و ليس بواجب

15. *Ibid.*, pp. 16, 76, 103.
16. Al-<u>Sh</u>aybānī, *al-Siyar al-Kabīr* (with commentary by al-Sarak<u>h</u>si), Cairo, 1957, vol. I, pp. 23, 94, 187.
17. Al-<u>Sh</u>aybānī, *al-Jāmi' al-Sag<u>h</u>īr*, p. 20.
18. *Ibid.*, pp. 10, 37; *idem, al-Muwaṭṭā'*, pp. 105, 110, 123 *passim.*
19. *Ibid.*, p. 10.
20. *Ibid.*, pp. 112, 149; *al-Siyar al-Kabīr*, vol. I, p. 226.
21. Al-<u>Sh</u>aybānī, *al-Aṣl*, pp. 3, 6, 20, 86 and 100 *passim*.
22. Al-<u>Sh</u>āfi'ī, *Kitāb al-Umm*, Cairo, 1325 A.H., vol. VII, p. 265; cf. *idem, al-Risālah*, Cairo, 1321 A.H., p. 48 f.
23. Al-<u>Sh</u>āfi'ī, *al-Risālah, ed. cit.*, p. 43.
24. The term *mubāḥ* has been used by al-<u>Sh</u>aybānī in non-technical sense. See his *al-Siyar al-Kabīr, ed. cit.*, vol. I, pp. 191, 318.
25. *Ibid.*, p. 49.
26. It appears that the term *Kifāyah*, a subdivision of obligatory, was first introduced by al-<u>Sh</u>āfi'ī, but the concept of *farḍ 'ayn* and *kifāyah* was already in existence before him. For, al-<u>Sh</u>aybānī regards *Jihād* as obligatory (*wājib*) on all the Muslims individually in case of emergency, and insists that this struggle should continue at all times. In case, he adds, the Muslims *en masse*, abandon this struggle, all will be sinful. Further, he remarks that if the purpose of *Jihād* is fulfilled by some of them, the rest will be exonerated from the performance of this duty. This view has been attributed by him to Abū Ḥanīfah. Al-<u>Sh</u>aybānī, *al-Siyar al-Kabīr, ed. cit.*, vol. I, pp. 187, 189.

    It seems that institutions like funeral prayer, *Jihād*, return of salutation in a gathering, must have been performed by some of the Muslims and not by all and sundry from the early days of Islam. This practice has been described by al-<u>Sh</u>āfi'ī as *kifāyah* in legal terminology.
27. Al-<u>Sh</u>āfi'ī, *al-Risālah, ed. cit.*, pp. 50-51.
28. Ibn Ḥazm, *al-Iḥkām fi Uṣūl al-Aḥkām*, Cairo, 1345 A.H., vol. VI, p. 29f.

عن الشعبى قال : كتب عمرالى شريح : اذا اتاك امر فى
كتاب الله فاقض به، و لا يلفتنك عنه الرجال. فان لم يكن
فى كتاب الله فبما فى سنه" رسول الله صلى الله عليه وسلم .
فان لم يكن فى كتاب الله وسنه" رسول الله صلى الله عليه وسلم

و لا فيما قضى به ائمة الهدى فانت بالخيار ، ان شئت ان
تجتهد رأيك ، و ان شئت أن توأمرنى ، و لا أرى موأمرتك
اياى الا خيرالك

Cf. Ibn 'Abd al-Barr, *Jāmi' Bayān al-'Ilm wa faḍlihī*, Cairo, n.d., vol. II, pp. 56-57.

29. Al-Shāfi'ī, *Kitāb al-Umm, ed. cit.*, vol. VII, p. 255.
30. Ibn al-Muqaffa', *Risālah fi'l-Ṣaḥābah* in *Rasā'il al-Bulaghā'*, Cairo, 1954, p. 127.
31. Abū Hilal al-'Askari, *Kitāb al-Awā'il* quoted in the article *Islām mayn 'ilm wa ḥikmat ka āghāz* (beginning of learning and philosophy in Islam), by Shabbīr Aḥmad Khān Ghawrī. *Ma'ārif*, 'Āzamgarh, April, 1962, vol. LXXXIX, No. 4, p. 278.

و هو اول من قال : الحق يعرف من وجوه اربعة : كتاب
ناطق ، و خبر مجتمع عليه ، و حجة عقل ، و الاجماع من الامة

32. Qur'ān, 5: 47, 48, 49, 50.
33. Qur'ān, 7 : 156; 23 : 4.
34. Coulson N. J., *A History of Islamic Law*, Edinburgh, 1964, p. 12.
35. Qur'ān, 6 : 38; 7; 52; 12 : 111.
36. Schacht, Jeseph, *The Origins of Muhammadan Jurisprudence*, Oxford, 1959, pp. 224, 226.
37. *Ibid.*, p. 224.
38. *Ibid.*,
39. Mālik, *op. cit.*, vol. II, p. 513.
40. *Ibid.*, p. 833.
41. Qur'ān, 33 : 21; 68 : 4.
42. Qur'ān, 5 : 48, 49.
43. Qur'ān, 16 : 44.
44. Qur'ān, 3: 164.
45. Qur'ān, 4 : 65.
46. Al-Shāfi'ī, *Kitāb al-Umm, ed. cit.*, vol. VII, pp. 177, 179, 184 *passim.*
47. Al-Shāfi'ī, *al-Risālah, ed. cit.*, p. 13.
48. *Ibid.*, p. 7.
49. Al-Shāfi'ī, *Kitāb al-Umm, ed. cit.*, vol. VII, p. 271.
50. Schacht, Joseph, *op. cit.*, p. 16.
51. Al-Shāfi'ī, *Kitāb al-Umm ed. cit.*, vol. VII, p. 199.
52. *Ibid.*, p. 246; cf. al-Shāfi'ī, *al-Risālah, ed. cit.*, p. 82.
53. Al-Shaybānī, *al-Siyar al-Kabīr*, Hyderabad Deccan, 1335 A.H., vol. II p. 260.

54. Abū Yūsuf, *Kitāb al-Kharāj*, Cairo, 1302 A.H., p. 90.
55. Al-Shāfi'ī, *Kitāb al-Umm*, *ed. cit.*, vol. VII, pp. 221, 246.
56. *Ibid.*, p. 41.
57. Al-Mubarrad, *al-Kāmil*, Cairo, 1936, vol. I, p. 14.
58. Al-Shāfi'ī, *al-Risālah*, *ed. cit.*, p. 82.
59. Qur'ān, 2: 150.
60. Al-Shāfi'ī, *al-Risālah*, *ed. cit.*, p. 66 *passim*; *idem* ,*Kitāb al-Umm*, vol. VII, p. 272f.
61. Al-Shāfi'ī, *al-Risālah*, *ed. cit.*, p. 66.
62. Al-Shāfi'ī, *Kitāb al-Umm*, *ed. cit.*, vol. VII, p. 246.
63. *Ibid.*, vol. VI, p. 203.
64. *Ibid.*, p. 271; *idem*, *al-Risālah*, *ed. cit.*, p. 4.

Chapter IV

THE THEORY OF *NASKH*

Literally *naskh* means annulment; for instance, it is an old Arab saying, نسخت الشمس الظل[1] meaning 'the sun annulled the shade.' In classical *Fiqh*, however, when used in the context of the Qur'ān it conveys three-fold meaning. First, it means that the Qur'ān abrogated the laws enunciated in the earlier Divine Scriptures like the Old and the New Testaments. Secondly, it is applied to the repeal of some Qur'ānic verses whose texts are said to have been blotted out of existence. Such textually repealed verses are further divided into two types: first, those verses whose text and law are both supposed to have been repealed; second, those whose text only is believed to have been abrogated but the law remained in force. Thirdly, it denotes the abrogation of some of the earlier commandments of the Qur'ān by the later revelations, while the texts containing those earlier commandments remain embodied in the Qur'ān. The classical theory of *naskh* in the above-mentioned three-fold meaning and the problems that arise from it are the subject of the present inquiry.

I

Historical evidence shows that the Prophet, in his grim struggle against his opponents, was sometimes attracted towards a compromise by accommodating some of their demands without, of course, conceding any point on the essentials of Islam. The Qur'ān itself bears unequivocal testimony to this and constantly warns him against any compromise whatever. A passage of the Qur'ān reads: "And they indeed strove hard to beguile thee (Muḥammad) away from that wherewith We have inspired thee, that thou shouldst invent other than it against Us; and then would they have accepted thee as a friend. And if We had not made thee wholly firm, thou mightest almost have inclined unto them a little. Then had We made thee taste a double (punishment) of living and a double (punishment) of dying, then hadst thou found no helper against Us."[2] The following Qur'ānic verse also refers to a similar situation: "Never sent We a messenger or a prophet before thee but when he desired, Satan cast in his desire. But Allāh abolishes that which Satan casts. Then Allāh establishes His revelations. Allāh is Knower, Wise."[3] The Prophet was offered similar compromise in Medina where he faced Jews and Christians as is implied from the following verse: "And the Jews will not be pleased with thee, nor will the Christians, till thou follow their creed. Say: Verily, the guidance of Allāh (Himself) is guidance. And if thou shouldst follow their desires after the knowledge which hath come unto thee, then wouldst thou have from Allāh no protecting friend nor helper."[4] This increasing anxiety of the Prophet to succeed in his mission brought it about that he sometimes nearly yielded to effect a compromsie but the compromising verses were abrogated. History mentions one such incident, that is, the so-called episode of *al-gharānīq al-'ulā*.

This story found its place in the early biographies of the Prophet. It is reported that the Prophet once desired that some revelation might come down to bring the unbelievers nearer towards Islam. Meanwhile *Sūrat al-Najm* was revealed to him. He recited it in a big assembly of the unbelievers. During the course of his recitation Satan is said to have made him pronounce the following words: "Verily they (the idols) are the exalted maidens (*gharānīq*) and their intercession is to be hoped for."[5] Towards the end of the *sūrah* the Prophet is further alleged to have prostrated and the unbelievers also followed suit. This reportedly gave great satisfaction to the Meccans. Subsequently, Gabriel came and repudiated the revelation of this passage. It is said that the above-quoted verse, "And they strove hard to beguile thee...." was revealed on this occasion. Thereupon the Prophet is reported to have been deeply grieved until the following verse came down: "Never sent We a messenger or a prophet before thee but when he desired, Satan cast in his desire."[6] This passage is said to have abrogated the verse of Satanic origin.[7]

A number of classical scholars like Mūsā b. 'Uqbah, Ibn Mardawayh, and Ibn Hajar al-'Asqalānī have accepted the report about this episode as genuine, because, according to their standards, its *isnād* (chain of the narrators) is sound enough to warrant the accepting of its authenticity. But at the same time it has been vehemently criticized and finally rejected by another group of equally eminent scholars of classical times like al-Mundhirī, al-Bayhaqī al-Qāḍī 'Iyāḍ, Fakhr al-Dīn al-Rāzī, al-Nawawī and al-'Aynī.[8] It is quite possible that this alleged account is not correct and most probably has been made up to establish this type of Qur'ānic verses.[9]

We have underlined earlier on the fact that the Prophet sometimes was swayed to effect some kind of compromise with his opponents. We have already quoted the verse clearly alluding to this persistent trait of the Prophet which was in the interest of the success of his cause. It is in such circumstances, viz. when he wanted a compromise of some sort that the Qur'ān prevented him from doing so and, in fact, imposed itself upon the wishes of the Prophet. The famous Qur'ānic verse, "Do not move your tongue so that you may hasten with it (and thus over-race the Revelation)"[10] refers undoubtedly to such situations. So does the well-known verse which is quoted by the classical authorities in favour of the *naskh* of the Qur'ānic verses, "Such of our revelations as we abrogate or cause to be forgotten, We bring (in place) one better or the like thereof. Knowest thou not that Allāh is able to do all things?"[11] It is, however, impossible to say exactly as to which were the points of which he thought of making compromise. To understand these verses, what is required is merely an inclination on the part of the Prophet to compromise and not an actual compromise. Anyhow, he could not have yielded on the essentials of his faith because otherwise his whole mission and cause would have lost their meaning. On the basis of this argument the above story seems to be historically untenable, because this would undermine the very essentials of the Prophet's faith. We have pointed out earlier in this connection, that the spirit of compromise arose from the Prophet's anxiety to make his cause succeed. It would, therefore, be absurd to assume that he wanted to commit a compromise that would absolutely destroy his essential stand on *Tawḥīd.*

The entire classical theological literature of Islam, however, suffers from the fundamental defect that it ignores the human aspect of the Prophet, including the phenomenon of the desire of compromise and artificially depicts him as a divine automaton. It lies in the very nature of such a development that real points of the intended compromise of the Prophet were concealed and certain equally artificial stories were invented to the effect that in certain of his moments the Prophet's mind was invaded by the devil and subsequently redeemed by God. This story may well have been invented and further exaggerated in this context.

II

How and when the idea of the abrogation of certain Qur'ānic verses emerged in the early history of Islam is not easy to establish. It seems, however, most probable that when the commentators and the jurists could not reconcile certain apparently contradictory verses, they propounded this theory. They found the following verses lending support to this notion:

(1) "Such of our revelations as We abrogate or cause to be forgotten, We bring (in place) one better or

the like thereof. Knowest thou not that Allāh is able to do all things?"[12]

(2) "And when We put a revelation in place of (another) revelation—and Allāh knoweth best what He revealeth—they say: Verily, thou art but inventing."[13]

(3) "Allāh effaceth what He will, and establisheth (what He will), and with Him is the source of ordinance."[14]

The classical scholars construed these verses as saying that some verses of the Qur'ān have been repealed by other verses.

The idea of abrogation of the Qur'ānic verses must have already appeared towards the end of the first century of the Hijrah, because it existed in the early schools of law. Ibrāhīm al-Nakha'ī (d. 96 A.H.) is reported to have said that verse 5:106 has been abrogated. Explaining this, al-Shaybānī says that the verse in question allows a non-Muslim to bear witness on the bequest of a Muslim during a journey, if the latter dies. But since it has been repealed, only a Muslim is now allowed to bear witness in the affairs of Muslims. He ascribes this opinion to Abū Ḥanīfah.[15] Mālik also regards the verse 2:180 as abrogated. On this basis, Mālik disallows any testator to make a will of his property in favour of a legal heir, except with the permission of all the heirs.[16] This shows that the idea of *naskh* was already in existence in the early stages of the development of Islamic jurisprudence in different centres. Later on, this theory won for itself a dominating position in Islamic legal theory to the extent that it was claimed that it carried the approval of the *Ijma'* of the Community.[17]

The Mu'tazilah justified the doctrine of the createdness of the Qur'ān on the basis of verse 2:106. They contended that because the Qur'ān was subject to abrogation, it could not be eternal.[18] But a group of them, we are told, denied the theory of abrogation. They did not take any verse of the Qur'ān to be abrogated.[19]

The significance attached to the doctrine of *naskh* in the later ages may be estimated from the fact that a large number of independent works were produced on the subject. Ibn al-Nadīm (d. ca. 385 A.H.) mentions eighteen works[20] while al-Suyūṭī (d. 911 A.H.) is of the view that the works produced on this subject are countless.[21] Besides, in the literature on the theory of *naskh*, we find a number of reports attributed to the Companions which emphasize the necessity of acquiring the knowledge of the abrogating and the abrogated verses of the Qur'ān. 'Alī, for example, is reported to have seen a man in the mosque of Kufa, who was replying to the religious questions put to him by the people around him. 'Alī asked him whether he could distinguish the abrogating verses from the abrogated to which he replied in the negative. 'Alī then pointed out to him that he was deceiving himself as well as others. Therefore, he prohibited him from speaking in the mosque again.[22] This sort of report cannot be genuine because, even according to reports, there seems to be no agreement among the Companions themselves on the number of the abrogated verses. Hence, if this story is to be believed, hardly anybody would be qualified to speak on religious subjects.

The change in the meaning of '*naskh*' in the different phases of the development of the doctrine is responsible for a good deal of confusion concerning it. Some Companions and the early authorities, we are told, had used the word in the sense of (1) exception, (2) particularizing the meaning (*takhṣīṣ*) and (3) the clarification of a previous verse.[23] So, we are told, when they stated that a certain verse was *nāsikh* for another, they intended thereby that this verse explained and removed the misconception that could arise from a certain passage by comparing it with an earlier related one; they did not mean that the latter was totally abrogated and rendered out of force by the former. These different meanings of this word were, however, confused in the later ages and no distinction was drawn between them. It is quite evident that some Qur'ānic pronouncements are general while others explain and fix their meaning. This is the meaning of the saying that the Qur'ān explains itself. These explanatory verses seem to have been called *nāsikh*, if the reports are genuine, in the early days. Abū Isḥāq al-Shāṭibī (d. 790 A.H.) has devoted a full chapter in *al-Muwāfaqāt* to this subject.[24] He has given a large number of examples to illustrate this view. We may quote here a few of them. Ibn 'Abbās has reportedly said that the passage: "Whoso desireth that (life) which is immediate, We hasten for him therein We will for whom We please"[25] abrogates the passage: "And whoso desireth the harvest of the world, We give him thereof, and he hath no share in the Hereafter."[26] In these verses, it is clear that through the phrase: 'for whom We please' the former verse restricted the latter verse which is general. Occasionally, the term *naskh* is said to have been used by the Companions in the sense of exception. Ibn 'Abbās, for example, reportedly said that the passage: "As for poets, the erring ones follow them. Hast thou not seen how they stray in every valley, and how they say that which they do not practise"[27] has been abrogated by the passage: "Save those who believe and do good deeds, and remember Allāh much, and vindicate themselves after they have been wronged."[28] The latter is, in fact, an exception from the general statement contained in the preceding passage. But Ibn 'Abbās calls it *mansūkh*. These and similar other examples quoted by al-Shāṭibī signify that some of the Companions and the Successors used *naskh* in a sense quite different from its later connotation. This confusion gave rise to the emergence of the theory of *naskh*. According to Shāh Walī Allāh, the use of the term *naskh* in its general sense by the early generations highly enhanced the number of the repealed verses which reached five hundred. He thinks, on this basis, that the number of the repealed verses in the later ages was considered to be less than it was in the earlier times.[29]

The classical theory of *naskh* cannot go back to the Prophet because we do not find any information from the Prophet as to the existence of the abrogated verses in the Qur'ān in this sense. If any passage were actually abrogated, he would have definitely pointed out to the people. As the teachings of the Qur'ān are meant for all ages and climes, it is inconceivable that the Prophet had left such an important problem, concerning the understanding of the Qur'ān, to the discretion of the people. Moreover, the Companions themselves are reported to have differed among themselves with regard to the abrogation of certain verses. Ibn 'Umar, for example, is reported to have said that the verse, "And for those who can afford it there is ransom: the feeding of a man in need,"[30] has been abrogated by the verse, "And whosoever of you is present (in the month), let him fast it."[31] But Ibn 'Abbās reportedly holds that the verse in question was not repealed. He regards it as operative in the case of aged and disabled persons. He suggests that they may feed a poor man every day in lieu of each day of fast. In this connection, it is reported that Anas b. Mālik used to feed the indigent in his old age during the month of Ramaḍān and did not keep fast.[32] This is not the only passage where the Companions differed as to its abrogation. Such examples are abundant in the commentaries of the Qur'ān and the *Ḥadīth* literature. Almost every passage which is held as abrogated by one authority is questioned by the other. The difference of the Companions in this respect imply that they had not received any instruction from the Prophet.

It has been the trend of Muslim scholars to reduce the number of the abrogated verses which had reached appalling proportions.[33] For example, the verse relating to *Jihād* (*āyat al-sayf*)[34] is said to have abrogated one hundred and thirteen verses that contained instructions for Muslims to have patience, forgiveness, and tolerance in hardships.[35] This trend shows that the abrogation of individual verses in the Qur'ān was not generally favoured. Abū Muslim al-Isfahānī (d. 322 A.H.) denied the theory of *naskh* entirely.[36] Al-Suyūṭī reduced the number of the abrogated verses from many hundreds to twenty,[37] while Shāh Walī Allāh reduced them to five only.[38] This reduction was done by means of harmonizing the passages that were deemed contradictory and hence subject to abrogation.

Al-Shahristānī discusses this problem at some length and substantiates it on rational grounds. He says: "Islam abrogates all previous codes of which it is the perfection.... If contemporary law is subject to constant alteration to meet changing conditions, why is it impossible that laws given to one people at one time should be abrogated elsewhere at another time? Law corresponds to actions, and the active changes of death and life, man's creation and annihilation, sometimes gradually, sometimes instantaneously, correspond to the legal changes of the permitted and the forbidden. God orders men's actions as He pleases and must not be asked what He is doing. If we consider the formation of man from his pre-embryonic beginning to his full stature, we see that each progressive form abrogated its predecessor. Similarly, man progressed from code to code till the perfection of all codes was reached. Nothing lies beyond it but the Resurrection."[39] In this passage, al-Shahristānī takes the doctrine of abrogation in a broader sense and emphasizes the repeal of previous codes by Islam. He thinks that abrogation is not an innovation but is a continuous process of change of law which culminated in Islam. But he is not clear as regards the question of the repeal of the particular verses of the Qur'ān. He might have taken, we presume, the abrogation of previous codes by Islam as a precedent justifying the *naskh* in the Qur'ān.

Among the modern writers on the subject, Muḥammad Abduh accepted this theory on principle, but practically he,[40] too, denied the repeal of the verses in the Qur'ān. In all such cases he tries to harmonize the so-called contradictory verses.[41] Other writers go a step further and totally reject this theory. Sir Sayyid Aḥmad Khān vehemently refuted it. According to him, the word *naskh* in the Qur'anic verse 2:106 meant the abrogation of the codes of law revealed to the earlier Prophets.[42] Muḥammad al-Khuḍarī in a more restrained and reasoned manner harmonizes all the verses which al-Suyūṭī supposed to have been abrogated.[43] Aslam Jayrājpūrī concludes his discussion of the subject by the pithy remark that 'God's words are too lofty to be abrogated by human opinion'.[44] The more recent writings on the subject also reject this theory.[45]

Among the kindred religions Judaism does not appear to accept the idea of abrogation of the Divine Revelation in any form, while Christianity holds the concept of the abrogation of the Mosaic Law.[46] In the Bible it is implied that the Christian idea of abrogation comprehends repeal of the text as well as that of the law[47]. On the basis of this resemblance, Nöldeke considered the theory of *naskh* in Islam to have originated from the Christian idea. He says, "That one revelation is abrogated by another is such an unprecedented (*unerhörter*) notion that it could not very well have been invented by Muḥammad. Somewhat similar appears to me the Christian idea of abrogation through the Gospel."[48] We agree with Nöldeke that the theory of *naskh* belongs more to the realm of fantasy than that of fact, but we cannot accept his contention that because it is such an unprecedented (or shocking: *unerhörter*) notion, it must be derived from the Christian idea. The theory might have been put forward by the Muslims themselves under necessity of legal harmony. Prof. Von Grunebaum, too, seems to differ with Nöldeke but he has different reasons for it. According to him, "the

Koranic concept seems somewhat more mechanical."[49] Guillaume accepted this theory, which, according to him, proved that "the Qur'an was subject to alteration in its initial stages." He bases his argument on the alleged anecdote of *al-gharānīq*,[50] which is, as we have shown earlier, incredible on principle.

III

Let us now discuss the three verses which are regarded as the basis for the classical theory of *naskh*. The first verse reads: "Such of Our revelations (*āyah*) as We abrogate or cause to be forgotten, We bring (in place) one better or the like thereof."[51] If we read this verse with reference to its context, there remains no doubt that the Qur'an is speaking about the annulment of the Law revealed to the Prophets of the Children of Israel. The first half of the *Sūrat al-Baqarah* in which this verse (No. 106) occurs, comprises a long disputation with the Jews which culminates in the Divine order to change the *Qiblah* from Jerusalem to the *Ka'bah* at Mecca, signifying a complete break with the abrogated laws of Judaism. In fact, Ibn Isḥāq definitely states that verses 1-141 were revealed concerning the Jewish rabbis and such of the new converts to Islam as were half-hearted and inclined to them.[52] In this context it is obvious that the reference is to the Jewish code, parts of which were lost ("forgotten") due to the political convulsions that the Jews suffered in their long chequered history. But, perhaps, the worst blow that this Jewish Revelation received was at the hands of a great Jew, St. Paul, who completed the process of its abrogation which was started by Jesus. In view of the evident context of the verse under reference and its corroboration by history it looks strange that some of the most eminent authorities of *Tafsīr* have missed the central point of this verse. It looks as though they were misled by the word *āyah*, which commonly came to signify 'a verse of the Qur'ān'. But this is an error. '*Āyah*' literally means 'a sign, token, or mark by which a person or thing is known and is synonymous with '*alāmah*'.[53] It also means by implication 'a message, or communication sent from one person or party to another' and is in this sense synonymous with *risālah*.[54] Hence, the secondary meaning, a "verse" of the Qur'ān, or more strictly, 'a portion of the Qur'ān after which a suspension of speech is approvable'.[55] The Qur'ān uses it to signify 'a sign of God',[56] 'His miracle',[57] 'His ordinance',[58] 'His message',[59] 'His revelation'.[60] To restrict its connotation to its secondary meaning, in complete disagreement with its context, appears to us an arbitrary act.

The second verse adduced in support of the theory of *naskh* reads: "And when We put a revelation in place of (another) revelation,—and Allāh knoweth best what He revealeth—they say: Verily, thou art but inventing. Most of them know not."[61] Here again the advocates of *naskh* have jumped at their interpretation without looking into the context of the verse. The internal evidence of one of the verses which follow the above-quoted verse[62] incontrovertibly puts it in the historical perspective of the early days at Medina when the Muslims faced the challenge from the Jewish tribes and from the newly converted Muslims who had still great misgivings whether the revelation of an *ummī* (unlettered) from amongst themselves could replace the time-honoured revelation of the Hebrew Prophets. The charge of invention put forward by this group makes our point still more clear, especially in view of the elaboration of it offered in the succeeding verse which reads: "And We know well that they say: Only a man teacheth him. The speech of him at whom they falsely hint is outlandish, and this is clear Arabic speech."[63] It is evident that the charge made by the *munāfiqs* (hypocrites) of "invention" did not refer to the supposed substitution of one verse of the Qur'ān for another; because they accused that the whole Qur'ān was dictated not "by the Holy Spirit" but by a Christian Slave, for, they argued, how could Muḥammad, an *ummī* Arab, be capable of receiving revelations which was the sole prerogative of the People of the Book."

The third verse (13:39) if read along with its preceding ones (13:36-38) reveals the same sad story of taking the Qur'ānic verses out of their context.

IV

It is sometimes said that there were earlier versions of some Qur'ānic verses which were later abrogated.[64] Having examined them closely we arrive at the conclusion that these alleged verses are historically quite untenable. Take for instance, the celebrated case of the *āyat al-rajm*. 'Umar, the second Caliph, is reported to have said: "But for the fear that the people would say: 'Umar had made an addition to the Book of Allāh: I would have written it (in the Qur'ān) ... because we have read it."[65] Another abrogated passage of the Qur'ān is reported by 'Ā'ishah. She says that earlier a Qur'ānic commandment was revealed that ten feedings of a suckling child were necessary to establish foster-mother. But later on, she adds, it was abrogated and only five feedings were considered enough. 'Ā'ishah further says that when the Prophet died, it was read as part of the text of the Qur'ān.[66] These two passages are the basis of certain legal rules in Islamic law. The idea that a certain passage was part of the Qur'ān arose from the clause "we read it in the Book of Allāh", or from the word 'revealed' which occurs in the reports. We presume that such words were used either by the Companions or the reporters themselves to show the significance of the injunction. In other words, they might have thought that these injunctions were not inferior to the Qur'anic commands. Hence, they used these words to signify their legal importance. This we assume provided that the reports are genuine. But are they genuine?

As to the alleged verse containing the commandment of the punishment of stoning the adulterer and the adulteress to death, its wordings appear to be manifestly of a different style from that of the Qur'ānic verses. The report has been ascribed to 'Umar. If this alleged verse had really been part of the Qur'ānic text, 'Umar would certainly have included it in the Qur'ān and would not have been afraid that he was making an addition to the Qur'ān. On this basis we can safely conclude that the reports ascribing this alleged verse in question to 'Umar are unreliable. We do not believe that the practice of stoning the adulterer and the adulteress in Islam is based on any Qur'ānic verse. It is true that this punishment was part of the Jewish law in the lifetime of the Prophet, who himself is reported to have prescribed this punishment in some cases. It is clear, therefore, that it is based on the *Sunnah* of the Prophet. It is useless to seek its justification from the Qur'ān.

The alleged verse which recommends five feedings of a child for the validity of foster-relationship has been accepted as genuine and even followed literally[67] by al-Shāfi'ī. Mālik quotes this report in *al-Muwaṭṭa'*, but does not follow it because, as he says, it is not practised in Medina.[68] The 'Irāqīs agree with Mālik and do not take this report into consideration. According to them, even one feeding of a child by a foster mother is enough to establish the relationship.[69] The rejection of this report by the early schools implies that the story is doubtful; let alone its theory being part of the Qur'ān. But it is probable that it arose from a practice among some Arabs.

Reports stating that a certain passage was originally part of the Qur'ān might also be based on some misunderstanding. Ibn Qutaybah (d. 276 A.H.) has given an example in this regard. He says that Ibn Mas'ūd did not take the last two *sūrahs* (*mu'awwadhatān*) as part of the Qur'ān. For this he gives the explanation that he (Ibn Mas'ūd) had witnessed the Prophet reciting these *sūrahs* before al-Ḥasan and al-Ḥusayn repeatedly in order to bless them. From this he discerned, according to Ibn Qutaybah, that these two verses were merely prayers (*du'ā*) like others and not part of the Qur'ān. Conversely, he adds, Ubayy b. Ka'b regarded the prayer known as *qunūt* as part of the Qur'ān because he had heard the Prophet reciting it in the prescribed prayers (*ṣalāh*). Hence, he included these two *sūrahs* in his copy of the Qur'ān.[70] This makes it highly probable that certain Companion might have heard something from the Prophet and took it as part of the Qur'ān.

V

Another problem relating to *naskh* is whether any Qur'ānic command can be annulled by the *Sunnah* and vice versa. The opinion of the jurists is divided on this point. Al-Ash'arī gives four different opinions,[71] while al-Naḥḥās gives five.[72] One of them is the well-known dictum which says: "The *Sunnah* decides upon the Qur'ān, while the Qur'ān does not decide upon the *Sunnah*".[73] Al-Āmidī has listed a number of examples where the Qur'ān had abrogated the *Sunnah*.[74]

Having studied the earlier literature on the subject one cannot help feeling that the posing of this problem itself is a result of the rigid formalization of the juristic doctrines and the absolute fixation of the relative position of the Qur'ān and the *Sunnah* therein. What seems to be the case is that where long standing customs, particularly those including fundamental policy, were sought to be changed whereby great opposition was feared, the Qur'ān had to intervene; and this may, in a loose sense, be regarded as an abrogation of the *Sunnah* by the Qur'ān. This leaves little doubt that the Qur'ān wielded higher authority than the Prophetic sayings themselves. However, there are many cases in which the precise sense and the manner of application of the Qur'ānic injunctions and statements was determined by the *Sunnah*—the question whether in some case it was done rightly and in others wrongly is irrelevant here. There are cases like the

Qur'ānic law of evidence on the point of minimum number of witnesses being two and on the question whether the evidence of two women is equal to that of one man. On these and many other points, the *Sunnah* apparently determined the application of the Qur'ān, and in some cases went against the literal meaning of the Qur'ān. This process was also inevitable. In the face of this situation and, when we take into account both sides of the picture, the whole complexion of the problem changes.

Al-Shāfi'ī has dealt with the problem of abrogation at a greater length in his work *al-Risālah.* He maintains that the Qur'ānic commands can be abrogated only by the Qur'ān, and those of the *Sunnah* only by the *Sunnah.* He is opposed to the view that the *Sunnah* can abrogate the Qur'ān and vice versa. In support of his view, he adduces the Qur'ānic verse 2:106 which explicitly speaks, according to him, of the abrogation of the Qur'ān by the Qur'ān. He argues that the Prophet was ordered by God to follow the revelation and not to change the Qur'ān himself. He quotes several Qur'ānic verses which indicate that God alone can change revelation.[75]

Let us now see why the Qur'ān cannot abrogate the *Sunnah* according to al-Shāfi'ī. He contends that if the Qur'ān abrogates any *Sunnah* of the Prophet, while the Prophet himself does not point to its abrogation, this means that all the commands from him not conforming to the Qur'ān would be taken as abrogated by the Qur'ān. For the abrogation of a *Sunnah* he thinks it necessary that the Prophet should have informed the people specifically, even if it is abrogated by the Qur'ān. Thus, he takes this information by the Prophet as abrogation of the *Sunnah* by the *Sunnah.* He gives several illustrations of how a host of rules framed by the Prophet would be abrogated if the Qur'ān is accepted to abrogate the *Sunnah.* He says that various types of sale which the Prophet had made unlawful would be considered to be abrogated by the Qur'ānic verse: "Whereas Allāh permitteth trading and forbiddeth usury."[76] Again, the *Sunnah* with regard to stoning the adulterer and the adulteress would be regarded as repealed by the verse: "The adulterer and the adulteress, scourge ye each one of them (with) a hundred stripes."[77] Similarly, he contends that one-fourth of *dinār* as minimum value for amputating the hand of a thief would be taken for abrogated by the Qur'ānic injunction: "As for the thief, both male and female, cut off their hands."[78] For this he gives the reason that the Qur'ān does not lay down any minimum value of theft. But al-Shāfi'ī also believes that no *Sunnah* of the Prophet contradicts the Qur'ān; on the contrary it elaborates it.[79] Therefore, the Qur'ān does not abrogate any *Sunnah*.

Likewise, no *Sunnah* of the Prophet, according to al-Shāfi'ī, abrogates the Qur'ānic injunctions. He contends that the function of the *Sunnah* is to point out which of the Qur'anic passages are abrogating and which abrogated. Again, he argues that the *Sunnah* follows the spirit of the Qur'ān. In cases of the clear-cut injunctions it follows the Qur'ān *in toto*; while in case of general or ambiguous commands, it explains and elaborates them.[80] As such there is no question of the abrogation of the Qur'ān by the *Sunnah*. Further, he gives several examples of how the *Sunnah* points to the abrogation of the individual verses. He says that the Qur'an, in verse 2:180, commands to leave a will in favour of the parents and other near relatives at the time of death. Similarly, in passage 2 : 240 it commands the husbands to bequeath in favour of their wives before their death. Simultaneously, the Qur'ān prescribes respective shares in the inheritance of the deceased for his parents, widows, and the near relatives. Now, al-Shāfi'i says that there may be a two-fold meaning of these passages. Firstly, the parents and the wives may receive the bequest together with their shares from the inheritance fixed by the Qur'ān. Secondly, the Qur'ānic verses that name the share of the wives and parents in the inheritance may be treated as abrogating (*nāsikh*) the injunction about making a will contained in the passages 2: 180, 240. But of these two alternatives, he chooses the latter in the light of the *Sunnah*. He quotes a *Ḥadīth* which states that no will is valid in favour of a legal heir. This *Ḥadīth* shows, according to him, that the injunction with regard to leaving a will at the time of death had been abrogated by the fixation of the shares in the inheritance.[81] It should be noted that al-Shāfiʻī does not regard the *Ḥadīth* quoted above as repealing the Qur'ānic injunction about leaving a will at the time of death, as held by the classical jurists. According to him, the Qur'ānic rulings, as we explained earlier, can be abrogated only by the Qur'ān and not by the *Sunnah* (*Ḥadīth*).

This whole edifice, however, has been erected on the concept that the Qur'ān contains some abrogated verses. In this respect al-Shāfiʻī was no exception. But one may differ from him on the verses held by him as abrogated. They can be shown to be operative if interpreted in a different manner. Suppose the parents of a deceased are non-Muslim, he can leave a will in their favour at the time of his death. Mālik holds that a person can bequeath in favour of his legal heirs with the permission of other heirs.[82] Similarly, there is no harm if the husband leaves a will for the maintenance of his wife for one year, as the Qur'ān is clear on this point. The matter, however, depends on adequate interpretation of the Qur'ānic passages.

VI

In the preceding paragraphs we have analysed the classical theory of abrogation. This theory, as we have previously pointed out, contradicts the eternal validity of the Qur'ān. From this it follows that the abrogated Qur'ānic injunctions were eternally operative prior to their abrogation, but lost their eternity as a result of abrogation. Now despite their existence in the Qur'ān, they are defunct and inoperative.

Their mere existence in the Qur'ān, it may be remarked, is not the sign of eternity unless they carry a practical value. The concept of the eternity of the Qur'ān presupposes that all its laws should remain effective in the Muslim *Ummah* for ever. Hence, in the face of this belief, there can be no reasonable ground for the thesis that some of the Qur'ānic verses are abrogated.

The Qur'ān was revealed piecemeal in twenty three years. Each revelation generally came down in the context of specific social conditions. As the nascent Muslim society was developing, the Qur'ānic revelations also kept pace with the changing conditions and environment. The revelations that came earlier and in certain circumstances were modified or enlarged or amended later cannot be said to have been strictly abrogated. Thus, to implement the Qur'ānic rulings in different times and places, one must study the historical context of each revelation and then the Qur'ān in its totality must be implemented. We can, therefore, generalize that the Qur'ānic injunctions were revealed in a given situation. Instead of abrogating the previous rulings by the subsequent ones, it seems proper to implement them in the conditions similar to those in which they were revealed.

Let us give an example. There are many passages in the Meccan *sūrahs* that ask the Muslims to be patient and to tolerate the aggression of the infidels.[83] On the contrary, the Medinese *sūrhas* consist of a few verses that call upon the Muslims to launch an attack on the infidels and kill them wherever they are found.[84] There is apparently a contradiction between these two sets of verses. It seems that the commentators could not reconcile them and, therefore, held that the former had been abrogated by the latter. But the question arises: Are the Meccan verses in question actually abrogated? In other words, should the Muslims never tolerate the aggression of the non-Muslims in all conditions; or, should they always fight and kill them whatever the circumstances may be? We do not think this is the purpose of the Qur'ān. It is a known fact that the Meccan verses containing the order of tolerance were revealed in a situation when the Muslims were weak and could not retaliate the aggression of the infidels, while the verses containing the command of *Jihad* belong to a period when the strength of the Muslims had grown considerably. Thus, these different types of rulings belong to different situations. Hence, there is no contradiction between them. From this it may be inferred that, in the first place, if the Muslims anywhere are weak, they may tolerate the aggression of the non-Muslims temporarily. But simultaneously they are duty-bound to make preparations and make themselves powerful. Secondly, when they grow powerful they are required to live in a state of preparedness and to shatter the power of the enemies of Islam. It is, therefore, clear that the rulings of the Qur'ān revealed in different situations may be implemented in view of their perspective and situational context.

NOTES

1. Ibn Manẓūr, *Lisān al-'Arab* (s.v.). See also commentaries under the verse 2: 106. There are some other similar expressions, e.g. نسخت الريح اثر المشى and نسخ الشيب الشباب Cf. al-Āmidī, Sayf al-Dīn Abu'l-Ḥasan 'Alī, *al-Iḥkām fī Uṣūl al-Aḥkām*, Cairo, 1914, vol. III, p. 146.
2. Qur'ān, 17 : 73-75.
3. Qur'ān, 22: 52.
4. Qur'ān, 2: 120.
5. Tr. by Alfred Guillaume, *Islam*, Edinburgh, 1962, p. 189.
6. Qur'ān, 22: 52.
7. Ibn Isḥāq, *Maghāzī*, MS. fo. 56 b. quoted by Alfred Guillaume, *New Light on the Life of Muhammad*, Cambridge, n.d., p. 38; Ibn Sa'd, *al-Ṭabaqāt al-Kubrā*, Beirut, 1957, vol. I, p. 205; Al-Ṭabarī, *Jāmi' al-Bayān fī Tafsīr al-Qur'ān*, Cairo, 1328 A.H. vol. XVI, p. 131 ff.
8. Al-Zurqānī, Muḥammad b. 'Abd al-Bāqī, *Sharḥ al-Zurqānī 'ala'l-Mawāhib al-laduniyah*, Cairo, 1291 A.H., vol. I, pp. 326-27 f.

9. It is important to note that the verse cast by the Satan was not new for the Meccans. It is reported that the Quraysh, while circumambulating the *Ka'bah*, used to recite the words

تلك الغرانيق العلى و ان شفاعتهن لترتجى

See Yāqūt, *Mu'jam al-Buldān*, under the word. العزى. Thus it may be that some infidel had recited these words, as Shiblī Nu'mānī holds, while the Prophet was reciting the *sūrat al-Najm*. The story then assumed a different form through changing reports with the passage of time. Cf. Shiblī Nu'mānī, *Sīrat al-Nabī*, A'zamgarh, n.d., 6th edition, vol. I, p. 242.

10. Qur'ān, 75 : 16.
11. Qur'ān, 2 : 106.
12. Qur'ān, 2 : 106.
13. Qur'ān, 16 : 101.
14. Qur'ān, 13 : 39.
15. Al-Shaybanī, Muḥammad b. al-Ḥasan, *Kitāb al-Āthīr*, Karachi, n.d., p. 282.
16. Mālik, *al-Muwaṭṭa'*, Cairo, 1951, vol. II, p. 765.
17. Al-Āmidī, *op. cit.*, vol. III, pp. 167, 201.
18. Al-Rāzī, Fakhr al-Dīn, *al-Tafsīr al-Kabīr*, Cairo, 1307 A.H., vol. I, p. 446.
19. Al-Tabarī, 'Abd al-Muta'āl Muḥammad, *al-Naskh fi'l-Sharī'at al-Islāmiyah*. Cairo, 1961, p. 61.
The Shī'ah have the doctrine of *badā'* as a counterpart of *naskh*, although there is a big difference between both the conceptions—the former being more sharp and extreme than the latter. For the difference between the two see al-Āmidī, *op. cit.*, vol. III, p. 157. Cf. *Enc. of Islam*, article '*Badā*'.
20. Ibn al-Nadīm, *al-Fihrist*, Cairo, 1348 A.H., p. 56.
21. Al-Suyūṭī, Jalāl al-Din, *al-Itqān fī 'Ulūm al-Qur'ān*, Cairo, 1317 A.H., vol. II, p. 20.
22. Al-Naḥḥās, *Kitāb al-Nāsikh wa'l-Mansūkh fi'l-Qur'ān al-Karīm*, Cairo, 1323 A.H., pp. 4, 5.
23. Ibn Qayyim, *I'lām al-Muwaqq'īn*, Delhi, 1313 A.H., vol. p. I, p. 12.
24. Al-Shāṭibī, *al-Muwafaqāt*, Tunis, 1302 A.H., vol. III, p. 58 ff.
25. Qur'ān, 17 : 18.
26. Qur'ān, 42: 20.
27. Qur'ān, 26 : 224.
28. Qur'ān, 26 : 224.
29. Shāh Walī Allāh, *al-Fawz al-Kabīr* (Urdu translation), Karachi, 1960, p. 78.

30. Qur'ān, 2 : 184.
31. Qur'ān, 2 : 185.
32. Al-Bukhārī, *al-Jāmi' al-Ṣaḥīḥ*, Leiden, n.d., vol. III, p. 202. Similar other examples may be seen in the same *sūrah*. The verse 2 : 240 is reported to have been abrogated, according to Ibn al-Zubayr, while Mujāhid holds it as operative (*Ibid.*, p. 207). Similarly, some regard the verse 2 : 180 as repealed, while others deny this. Al-Ṭabarī, *al-Tafsīr*, Cairo, n.d., ed. *Shākir*, vol. III, p. 285 f. About the verse 4 : 7 Ibn 'Abbās is reported to have said:

إن ناسا يزعمون أن هذه الآية نسخت ، ولا و الله ، ولكنها مما تهاون الناس

Al-Bukhārī, *op. cit.*, vol. II, p. 191, (*Kitāb al-Waṣāyā*).
33. The alleged abrogated verses are enumerated below:

(i)	Individual abrogated verses	201
(ii)	Verses abrogated from *sūrah al-Aḥzāb*.	213
(iii)	A complete abrogated *sūrah* corresponding to *sūrah* IX.	130
(iv)	Two combined abrogated *sūrahs* known as *al-Khala' wa'l-Ḥafd*.	18
(v)	Two verses relating to feeding a child and stoning an adulterer	2
	Total	564

Al-Jabarī, 'Abd al-Muta'āl, *op. cit.*, p. 71.
34. Qur'ān, 9 : 5.
35. Qur'ān, verses like 15 : 85. Ibn Khuzaymah has listed such verses together. See his *al-Mūjaz fi'l-Nāsikh wa'l-Mansūkh*, Cairo, 1323 A.H., p. 265.
36. Al-Rāzī, Fakhr al-Dīn, *op. cit.*, vol. I, p. 444; al-Āmidī, *op. cit.*, vol. III, p. 165.
37. Al-Suyūṭī, *op. cit.*, vol. II, p. 23.
38. Shāh Walī Allāh, *op. cit.*, p. 96. Also see pp. 78-96.
39. Al-Shahristānī, *Kitāb Nihāyat al-Iqdām fi 'Ilm al-Kalām*, ed. and trans. by Alfred Guillaume, Oxford, 1934, pp. 158-59, quoted by Donaldson, Dwight M., *Studies in Muslim Ethics*, London, 1953, p. 52.
40. Muḥammad 'Abduh, *Tafsīr al-Manār*, Cairo, 1954, vol. II, p. 138 ff.
41. *Ibid.*, p. 141.
Muḥammad 'Abduh seems to be moderate towards this theory. He, however, warns against easily accepting Qur'ānic verses as abrogated.
42. Sayyid Aḥmad Khān, *Tafsīr al-Qur'ān*, Lahore, n.d., pp. 137-140 f.

43. Muḥammad al-Khuḍarī, *Uṣūl al-fiqh*, Cairo, 1938, pp. 246-51, ft. n.
44. Quoted by Baljon, J.M.S., *Modern Muslim Koran Interpretation*, Leiden, 1961, p. 49.
45. The work entitled *al-Naskh fi'l-Sharī'at al-Islāmiyah* by 'Abd al-Muta'āl, is an attempt at refuting the theory of abrogation. Even Shāh Walī Allāh, although he accepted five verses as abrogated, does not seem to be much pleased to recognize this theory, as he asks to be careful in accepting the opinions of the jurists in this respect. Shāh Walī Allāh, *al-Tafhīmāt al-Ilāhiyah*, Bijnor, 1936, vol. II, p. 173. Mawlānā 'Ubayd Allāh Sindhī may also be referred to in this connection.
46. Al-Āmidī, *op. cit.*, vol. III, p. 165.
47. New Testament, Epistles of Paul, Epherians 2: 15, Colossians 2 : 14.
48. Nöldeke, Theodor, *Geschichte des Qorāns*, Hildesheim, 1961, p. 52.
49. Von Grunebaum, G. E., *Islam*, London, 1961, p. 85.
50. Guillaume, Alfred, *Islam, ed. cit.* p. 189; cf. his '*New Light on the Life of the Prophet*', *ed. cit.* p. 38.
51. Qur'ān, 2 : 106.
52. Ibn Hishām, Abū Muḥammad 'Abd al-Malik, *Sīrat al-Nabī*, (ed. Muḥammad Muḥī al-Dīn 'Abd al-Ḥamīd), Cairo, n.d., vol. II, pp. 152-176.
53. Lane, Edward William, *Arabic-English Lexicon*, London, 1863, Book I, Part I, p. 135.
54. *Ibid.*, p. 135.
55. *Ibid.*, p. 135.
56. Qur'ān, 17 : 12; 19 : 21.
57. Qur'ān, 6 : 35; 7 : 106.
58. Qur'ān, 6 : 125.
59. Qur'ān, 20 : 47; 36 : 46.
60. Qur'ān, 6 : 4.
61. Qur'ān, 16 : 101.
62. Qur'ān, 16: 102. It reads: "Say: The Holy Spirit hath revealed it from thy Lord with truth, that it may confirm (the faith of) those who believe, and as guidance and good tidings for those who have surrendered (to Allah)."
63. Qur'ān, 13 : 103.
64. Such verses have been listed together by 'Alī Ḥasan 'Abd al-Qādir, in his '*Naẓrah 'ammah fī Ta'rīkh al-Fiqh al-Islāmī*, Cairo, 1956, pp. 46-49.
65. The full statement of 'Umar goes:

قال عمر: اياكم أن تهلكوا عن آية الرجم أن يقول قائل:
لانجد حدين فى كتاب الله فقد رجم رسول الله صلى الله عليه وسلم

و رجمنا ، و الذى نفسى بيده لولا أن يقول الناس : زاد عمر بن الخطاب فى كتاب الله تعالى لكتبتها : الشيخ و الشيخة اذا زنيا فارجموهما البتة ، فانا قد قرأناها -

Mālik, *op. cit.*, vol. II, p. 824. In other classical collections of *Ḥadīth* this verse reads:

الشيخ و الشيخة اذا زنيا فارجموهما البتة ، [نكالا من الله ، و الله عزيز حكيم

Al-Bayhaqī, *al-Sunan al-Kubrā*, Hyderabad, Deccan, 1354 A.H., vol. VIII, p. 211.

Another statement has been ascribed to ʻUmar which is, as it were, explanation of the former statement. It goes:

الرجم فى كتاب الله حق على من زنى من الرجال و النساء ، اذا قامت البينة اوكان الحبل او الاعتراف

Mālik, *op. cit.*, vol. II, p. 823.

The term *Kitāb Allāh* has been interpreted by some scholars as Torah or code of law (*sharīʻah*) in a broader sense and not as the Qur'ān itself. See *Maʻārif* (Urdu), Azamgarh, vol. LXXXII, No. 5, November, 1958, p. 386, Muḥammad Ismāʻil, article *Chand Nāskh wa Mansūkhāyāt*

The notebook (*saḥīfah*) in which the verse about stoning was recorded is reported to have been eaten by a goat. Ibn Qutaybah, *Ta'wīl Mukhtalif al-Ḥadīth*, Cairo, 1326 A.H., pp. 397-98. The spuriousness of this verse is clear from such reports.

66. Mālik, *op. cit.*, vol. II, p. 608.

The statement of ʻA'ishah goes:

كان فيما انزل من القرآن عشر رضعات معلومات يحرمن ثم نسخن بخمس معلومات ، فتوفى رسول الله صلى الله عليه وسلم و هو فيما يقرأمن القرآن -

67. Al-Shāfiʻī, *Kitāb al-Umm*, Cairo, 1324 A.H., vol. VII, p. 208.
68. Mālik, *op. cit.*, vol. II, p. 608.
69. Al-Shaybānī, Muḥammad b. al-Ḥasan, *al-Muwaṭṭa'*, Deoband, n.d., p. 278.
70. Ibn Qutaybah, *op. cit.*, p. 32.
71. Al-Ashʻarī, *Maqālāt al-Isl–miyyīn wa Ikhtilāf al-Muṣallīn*, Cairo, 1950. vol. II, p. 251.
72. Al-Naḥḥās, *op. cit.*, p. 5.
73. Al-Dārimī, *Sunan*, Cairo, 1349 A.H. Vol. I, p. 145.

السنة قاضية على القرآن ، و ليس القرآن بقاض على السنة

74. Al-Āmidī, *op. cit.*, vol. III, p. 213.
75. Al-Shāfi'ī, *al-Risālah*, Cairo, 1321 A.H., p. 17.
76. Qur'ān, 2 : 275.
77. Qur'ān, 24 : 2.
78. Qur'ān, 5 : 38.
79. Al-Shāfi'ī, *al-Risālah*, pp. 17-18.
80. *Ibid.*, p. 17.
81. *Ibid.*, pp. 21-22.
82. Mālik, *op. cit.*, vol. II, p. 765.
83. Qur'ān, 16 : 126, 127.
84. Qur'ān, 9 : 5.

Chapter V

THE *SUNNAH*—ITS EARLY CONCEPT AND DEVELOPMENT

In Chapter III, we briefly discussed 'the *Sunnah*' as a source of law and its relation to the Qur'ān. In the present chapter we shall examine its early concept, its distinction from *Ḥadīth* and phases of its development.

Loosely speaking, the terms *Sunnah* and *Ḥadīth* convey the same meaning, namely, the Traditions of the Prophet. But a critical study of these terms will show that in the early phase their meaning was not identical. *Sunnah* primarily means 'pathway', 'behaviour', 'practice', 'manner of acting' or 'conduct of life'.[1] The term implies the normative practice or the model behaviour, whether actually good or bad, of a particular individual, sect or community. The manner in which God dealt with the former generations is termed God's *Sunnah*[2] in the Qur'ān; while the *Sunnah* of the past generations[3] refers to their practices and mores. A number of Qur'ānic verses clearly indicate that the term *Sunnah* denotes practice or behaviour.[4]

'*Sunnah*' was not new for the Muslims. It was already in vogue in the pre-Islamic Arabia. The Arabs had used it for the past customs and exemplary conduct left by their ancestors, i.e. for their customary or common law. They strictly followed these customs because they regarded them as norms for themselves. Labīd b. Rabī'ah, in his famous *mu'allaqah*, says:

من معشر سنت لهم آباؤهم
و لكل قوم سنة و امامها

(He comes) from a tribe for whom their ancestors have left a normative behaviour; every people has a *Sunnah* and its originator.[5]

The break with the old customs and discontinuity of the established practices was decried by them. This discontinuity from the *Sunnah* was known as *bid'ah* (innovation). Thus, *bid'ah* was the antithesis of *Sunnah*. The earliest Islamic Arabic literature leaves clear testimony to this.[6]

Sunnah, be it used in the sense of a people's practice or an individual's behaviour, carries a normative element. It is this normativeness that distinguishes it from other synonyms. Let us establish this proposition by some illustrations. Abū Yūsuf admonishes the Caliph to revive the *Sunnahs* originated by righteous men, because revival of the *Sunnahs*, according to him, is a virtue which survives and never perishes.[7] While discussing the problem of the conquered lands of Basra and Khurasan, to give another example, he remarks that these lands are on a par with other lands of Iraq and hence should be governed by the principles adopted in the case of Sawād. But, he adds, since a particular *Sunnah* (practice) was prevailing in these lands (i.e. Basra and Khurasan) and the succeeding caliphs have also enforced the same *Sunnah* (practice), these lands should be left as they had been, and the practice be followed.[8] In both these examples the word *Sunnah* has been used in the sense of normative practice.

So far we have discussed the etymology of the term *Sunnah*. When this term is used in Islamic law and doctrine, it refers to the normative practice set up by the Prophet as a model, which, so long as he was alive, was his unique privilege. In the succeeding generations it stood for the usage of the early Muslims as representing the *Sunnah* of the Prophet. It should be pointed out that, according to the terminology of the doctors of *Ḥadīth* in the post-Shāfi'ī period, *Ḥadīth* and *Sunnah* are identified. But this is not correct. *Ḥadīth* and *Sunnah* are two different things carrying different meanings. *Ḥadīth* is the narration of the behaviour of the Prophet while *Sunnah* is the law deduced from this narration. In other words, *Ḥadīth* is the "carrier" and "vehicle" of the *Sunnah*.

Sunnah is contained in *Ḥadīth*. Therefore it has been well said that a certain *Ḥadīth* contains five *Sunnahs*,[9] or there are three *Sunnahs* in the incidence of Barīrah, a slave girl.[10] Further, it is not necessary that *Sunnah* be always deduced and known from *Ḥadīth*, i.e. a report. Early texts on law show that the term *Sunnah* was used in the sense of the established practice of the Muslims claiming to have come down from the time of the Prophet. That is why *Sunnah* sometimes contradicts *Ḥadīth* and sometimes it is documented by *Ḥadīth*. The following dictum throws light on distinction between these two terms. 'Abd al-Raḥmān b. Mahdī (d. 198 A.H.) is reported to have said: "Sufyān al-Thawrī is *Imām* in *Ḥadīth* and not *Imām* in *Sunnah*, while al-Awazā'ī is *Imām* in *Sunnah* and not in *Ḥadīth*, but Mālik is *Imām* in both." Abū Yūsuf, too, has been called by his biographers "master of *Ḥadīth* and master of *Sunnah* (*Ṣāḥibu Ḥadīth wa Ṣāḥibu Sunnah*)".[11] Abū Yūsuf insists on following the *Ḥadīth* which is in conformity with the Qur'ān and the *Sunnah*.[12] All these examples clearly indicate the difference between the meanings of *Ḥadīth* and *Sunnah*. In short, the difference between the early meanings of *Sunnah* and *Ḥadīth* is that the former carried in its gamut the well-known traditions, the established practice and the agreed usages of the Muslims, while the latter was the narration of the fixed and definite laws enunciated by the Prophet. But al-Shāfi'ī put up a strong opposition to the current meaning of *Sunnah* and insisted on taking the *Sunnah* from the genuine traditions of the Prophet. He preferred a genuine *Ḥadīth* from the Prophet to the agreed and established practice of the Muslims. Henceforth *Sunnah* was identified with *Ḥadīth*.[13]

The early *Fiqh* literature also shows that the word *Ḥadīth* was not used exclusively for the sayings and the actions of the Prophet. We find that in pre-Shāfi'ī period it was applied also to the statements of the Companions and the Successors. On the question of allotting share out of booty to the rider and the horse, the decision taken by the governor of Syria and later approved by 'Umar, the second Caliph, is called *Ḥadīth* by Abū Yūsuf and it is followed by Abū Ḥanīfah in preference to established traditions from the Prophet.[14] It appears that this term came to be restricted to the sayings and actions of the Prophet only when the distinction between the *Sunnah* and *Ḥadīth* was set aside.

Let us now discuss the concept of the Prophetic *Sunnah*. The Western writers have painted a picture that the Prophetic *Sunnah* in Islam is no more than another name for the *Sunnah* of the pre-Islamic Arabia, as it stood modified by the Qur'ān. Moreover, according to some of them, the concept '*Sunnah* of the Prophet' is a late concept, because for the early Muslims *Sunnah* meant merely the practice of the Muslims themselves. Here it may be remarked that the concept '*Sunnah* of the Prophet' in Islam, as we pointed out earlier in Chapter III, owes its origin to the advent of the Prophet. The Qur'ān time and again makes obedience to the Prophet obligatory on the Muslims and speaks of his behaviour as 'Ideal'. The Muslims, therefore, from the very beginning accepted his conduct as 'model' for them on the basis of the teachings of the Qur'ān. They did not take it as an institution prevalent among the Arab tribes in the pre-Islamic days. The Qur'ān has used the word '*uswah*'[15] for the 'exemplary conduct' of the Prophet. As a concept, therefore, it has no relation to the *Sunnah* of the Arab tribes. No doubt, most of the customs in pre-Islamic Arabia remained in the post-Islamic era after the Prophet had reformed some and introduced other afresh. But by this very reason even the pre-Islamic customs retained in Islam bear the hall-mark of the Prophetic sanction. Thus, they ceased to be mere customs of pre-Islamic days.

Besides, although the actions of the Community were governed by the Qur'ān, it was the Prophet who gave its injunctions a practical shape and concrete form. Thus, the way in which the Prophet acted upon the Qur'ān became the law of the Community. How, then, is it reasonable to suppose that the Companions around the Prophet neglected the activity of the Prophet through whom the Qur'ān was taught to them? We have previously pointed out that the Qur'ān and the *Sunnah* of the Prophet are so related to each other—rather interwoven in such a way—that they cannot be separated from each other. We may call them an 'integral whole'. Moreover, the Prophet was not a record merely to transmit the divine message. Perforce, therefore, the concept of the 'Prophetic *Sunnah*' must have existed since the very dawn of Islam.

So much for the concept of the *Sunnah* of the Prophet. One reason for the rejection of its concept by the orientalists is the rare use of the phrase '*Sunnah* of the Prophet' in early literature. Prof. Schacht could not find this term in the biography of the Prophet by Ibn Hishām (d. 218 A.H.) except in one place. Of this he says that the term has been used in a different context.[16] But it is strange that he does not refer to the speech of the Prophet made by him on the occasion of the Farewell *Ḥajj*. In this speech Ibn Hishām records clearly the words, 'the Book of Allāh and the *Sunnah* of His Prophet.'[17] Moreover, we are told that 'Umar, the second Caliph, sent emissaries to different towns in order to teach them the religion (*dīn*) and the *Sunnah* of the Prophet.[18] The epistle, written by al-Ḥasan of Basra (d. 110 A.H.) to 'Abd al-Malik b. Marwān (d. 86 A.H.), contains the phrase '*Sunnah* of the Prophet'.[19] The term is also available in the early legal literature before al-Shāfi'ī.[20] Further, the existence of this term is not the necessary index for the existence of its concept. What constitutes our argument is that the Muslims considered the Prophet's behaviour an ideal pattern and example for them since the inception of the Revelation. This is an adequate proof for the existence of its concept from the early days of the Prophet.

Prof. Schacht has also tried to prove that "*Sunnah* in its

Islamic context originally had a political rather than a legal connotation; it referred to the policy and administration of the caliphs." He links it with the *Sunnah* of Abū Bakr and 'Umar. He thinks that the concept of the *Sunnah* of the Prophet appeared in connection with the assassination of 'Uthman, the third Caliph, who was killed on the charge that he had diverged from the policy of his predecessors. According to him, the term '*Sunnah* of the Prophet' was first used by the Khārijī leader, 'Abd Allāh b. Ibāḍ, in his letter addressed to 'Abd al-Malik. The same term, he presumes, appeared in a theological connotation in the letter of al-Ḥasan of Basra addressed to the same Caliph. Further, he observes that this term was introduced into Islamic law towards the end of the first century of the Hijrah by the 'Irāqīs.[21] Prof. Schacht, in fact, bases his thesis on mere conjectures, and perhaps purposely ignores the testimony of the Qur'ān to the necessity of this concept. Also, positive evidence is required to show that the term had only a political connotation and that its concept appeared in connection with the assassination of 'Uthmān. The Qur'ān commands Muslims in general terms to follow the pattern of the Prophet's behaviour in all fields of life. According to a report in *al-Muwaṭṭa'*, Abū Bakr is said to have referred to this term in legal context.[22] There seems to be no reason to doubt this report. Besides, it is unthinkable that the Muslims had ignored the precedents of the Prophet in their legal affairs for one full century.

As to the early development of the *Sunnah*, it should be remarked that this institution has undergone a process of evolution since its very beginning. The early available works show that for the early schools of law *Sunnah* was the practice of the Community as supported by the well-known traditions from the Prophet, or the conduct of the Companions or the Successors. Al-Shāfi'ī, on the other hand, regarded every well-founded authentic *Ḥadīth* even though it may be an isolated one and whether accompanied by practice or not as *Sunnah* of the Prophet. The conflict between the early schools and al-Shāfi'ī was, therefore, centred around the status of the solitary *Ḥadīth* which was not recognized in the general practice. This has led Prof. Schacht to conclude that (1) the *Sunnah* was originally the practice of the Community and not the *Sunnah* of the Prophet which is a late development and (2) that, as this concept came to be accepted, *Ḥadīth* came to be forged on a large scale so much so that there is probably hardly any *Ḥadīth* which may be genuinely from the Prophet himself.[23] This thesis culminates in the rejection of the whole corpus of *Ḥadīth* which may be genuine from the Prophet himself. In view of the present writer the practice and the transmission of *Ḥadīth* after the lifetime of the Prophet went hand-in-hand. Earlier, practice was stressed because being in conformity with the ideal conduct of the Prophet it did not require documentation by any statute or law. It was a proof by itself.[24] But when in the first place this practice lost its resemblance with the ideal *Sunnah* because of the gap in time, the need of *Ḥadīth* became more and more acute. Hence, the early schools emphasized the practice (*'amal*) of the Community, more than al-Shāfi'ī. Even among the pre-Shāfi'ī *fuqahā'* those who were nearer to the time of the Prophet laid more stress on practice than those who were farther from his time. The latter, despite their occasional reference to the practice, frequently quote *Ḥadīth* for its proof. That is why in Abū Yūsuf and al-Shaybānī the emphasis on *Ḥadīth* is greater than in al-Awzā'ī and Mālik. Even those who rely on practice are not unmindful of *Ḥadīth*. Therefore, we can safely conclude that *Ḥadīth* and *Sunnah* (practice) were running parallel. In the following pages we shall try to show various phases of the development of the *Sunnah*.

During the lifetime of the Prophet *Sunnah* implied the conformity of the acts of the Companions to the acts of the Prophet. They regulated their lives according to the Qur'ān as exemplified in and illustrated by the behaviour of the

Prophet No separate law was needed to support the veracity of their actions except the sayings and model conduct of the Prophet. After his lifetime, the Companions had with them the Qur'ān, the conduct of the Prophet and their own practice prevalent while he was alive. The Companions settled in different towns outside Arabia. They were not only the transmitters of the *Sunnah* of the Prophet but also its interpreters and elaborators. This widened the scope of the *Sunnah* to receive within its orbit new contents. Being representatives of the life and conduct of the Prophet the conduct and opinions of the Companions began to be regarded as exemplary by the succeeding generation. 'Umar, the second Caliph, we are told, once awarded a punishment of one hundred lashes to one of his governors. 'Amr b. al-'Āṣ came up to him and said: "If you introduce such types of punishment for your governors, this will prove too much for them and it will become a *Sunnah* later...."[25] This report shows that the conduct of the Companions was being assimilated to the *Sunnah*.

The practice that originated from the lifetime of the Prophet continued in its pure form more or less until the time of the first four Caliphs. They managed to protect this continuous tradition and tried to close the avenues for the penetration of incongruent accretions. People around the Companions must have asked them about the conduct of the Prophet on different problems. This narration of the behaviour of the Prophet by the individual Companions was known as *Ḥadīth*. *Ḥadīth* must naturally conform to the established practice continued since the time of the Prophet. Now there were two channels before the people for knowing the real *Sunnah* of the Prophet, namely, (1) practice so far it was pure and continuous and (2) *Ḥadīth*. But there were apprehensions that solitary *Ḥadīths* might come to the surface which may not conform to the established practice. Hence, precautionary measures were adopted by the first four Caliphs to keep the practice intact at least in the legal sphere. Any report given by a Companion was put to severe tests, in case it disagreed with the practice. Such examples are abundant as indicate that these early caliphs were conscientious in regard to recognizing any individual and isolated *Ḥadīth*. Abū Bakr is reported to have got a solitary *Ḥadīth* confirmed by another Companion.[26] 'Umar, the second Caliph, seems to be even more cautious than his predecessor. We are told that he used to accept a tradition from the Prophet on the evidence of two witnesses. Similarly, 'Alī, the fourth Caliph, is said to have recognized an individual *Ḥadīth* when confirmed by an oath.[27] On a number of occasions 'Umar is reported to have consulted the Companions as on the occasion of a *Ḥajj* or in a similar public gathering.[28] When on a certain point lonely reports reached him, he is reported to have made official announcement to let the public know the real *Sunnah* of the Prophet against these reports.[29] This procedure safeguarded the *Sunnah* against intrusive extraneous ingredients. That is why we do not find, during the time of the first four Caliphs, the chaotic state of affairs in law that developed with the free transmission of *Ḥadīth* later on. No doubt, differences did exist there because the individual opinions could not be eliminated. Indeed, it was in order to removes differences among individual opinions in law that the main emphasis began to be laid on *Ḥadīth* from the Prophet. But this did not check the differences, because *Ḥadīth* itself began to reflect the differences. In the early phase, however, the Community was integrated by the Qur'ān, and by the established practice as coming down from the time of the Prophet. This phase of *Sunnah* is characterized by its continuity and relative purity. Hence, *Ḥadīth* was not much needed for its documentation.

After the time of the first four Caliphs, the life of the state diverged from this pure and continuous tradition. In the Community itself, theological heresies emerged among

Muslims. Each sect endeavoured to prove its doctrines as a part of the Islamic teaching and sought to endorse them by a certain authority. The restrictions imposed on the free transmission of *Ḥadīth* were now dissipated. Consequently, people began to narrate *Ḥadīth* frequently and, in the long run, it increased tremendously. The *bid'ah* (innovation) and *fitnah* (general corruption) raised their heads in Islam.[30] The Umayyad Caliphs in general were not interested in protecting the purity and continuity of the ideal practice. The whole legal system became a private matter and jurisconsults (*muftīs*), in their private capacity, continued law-building activity. The judges and judicial authorities appointed by the Umayyad rulers were more or less working under their control. Therefore, it was not guaranteed that the decisions taken by them would be objective. Hence, the established ideal practice could not survive in its practical form after the end of the orthodox caliphate. This gave stimulus to rely on *Ḥadīth* and to prove *Sunnah* by *Ḥadīth*. The confidence vested in practice was gradually weakened and ultimately *Ḥadīth* was regarded as the only channel for the ideal *Sunnah*. In these circumstances, 'Umar b. 'Abd al-'Azīz reportedly ordered Abū Bakr b. 'Amr b. Ḥazm to collect *Ḥadīth* or *Sunnah* of the Prophet, and the *Ḥadīth* of 'Umar, the second Caliph.[31] With the passage of time, the practice of the Muslims was no longer *ipso facto* regarded as *Sunnah* of the Prophet unless it was supported by a genuine *Ḥadīth*. With this background in view, it is easy to understand that *isnād* (chain of transmitters) in *Ḥadīth* gained significance at the stage when the confidence in practice was lost and the Community morally deteriorated. Although free narration of *Ḥadīth* resulted in a good deal of fabrication, it would not be reasonable to hold that the legal sphere was altogether swamped by forgers. The reason is that a large part of the legal decisions being practised by the Muslims was living and known to all. Where differences arose, it was the result of conflicting *Ḥadīth* circulated in different places. These differences were not so basic and crucial that they affected fundamentals. The immunity of the legal sphere may be judged from the fact that the Shī'ah, although they had their own *Ḥadīth* in law, differ but on a few points from the *Ahl al-Sunnah.*[32] This is due to the reason that law was based more on actual and continuous practice than on legal doctrines which came to be formulated later.

The Companions went about their business in a normal and natural manner participating in all social, religious and political affairs. The only distinguishing feature of their life was naturally that their conduct was followed by other people as being an approximation to the ideal life of the Prophet. The practical aspect of their life had, therefore, a far-reaching effect on the conduct of the next generation of the Successors. That is why when they exercised their own *Ijtihād* in certain matters, people accepted it as authoritative and it ultimately tended to become the *Ijmā'* of the Community. This was, in fact, the *Sunnah* of the Companions (*Sunnat al-Ṣaḥābah*). The reason why the *Ummah* accepted their *Ijtihād* as part of the *Sunnah* is obvious enough. People knew well that the Companions of the Prophet, especially the first four Caliphs, being the true devotees of Islam, could never deviate from the spirit of the *Sunnah* of the Prophet. There is a long list of cases wherein the Companions, especially 'Umar, the second Caliph, exercised their own opinion (*ra'y*) which was natural with the progress of human life. Thus, with the *Ijtihād* of the Companions the element of personal opinion entered into the *Sunnah.* But it may be remarked that anything that appeared novel as compared with the established practice coming down since the time of the Prophet, was recognized as *bid'ah* (innovation) by the Companions. 'Umar's famous remark in respect of *tarāwīḥ* prayer[33] is very conclusive. It shows how the Companions were careful to draw a sharp distinction between the real *Sunnah* of the Prophet and the

Sunnah that evolved out of it. The so-called *bid'ah* of *tarāwīḥ* prayer being said in public during Ramaḍān has been ultimately recognized as *Sunnah* and is practised throughout the Muslim world until today. There is no doubt that the *Sunnah* of *Ṣaḥābah* in many cases was based on their personal opinions, but it, too, was assimilated to the term *Sunnah* in the early days. This gave rise to a controversy among the jurists of the second century of the Hijrah as to whether an isolated *Ḥadīth* should be taken as *Sunnah* or conduct of the Companions. That is why the early schools, in respect of certain problems, as we shall see later, preferred the behaviour of the Companions to a lonely *Ḥadīth*. This was, indeed, a comparison between the two channels of the *Sunnah* of the Prophet, namely, practice and transmission.

The establishment of the Umayyad rule ushered in a new era for the development of the *Sunnah*. In this period, the scope of the *Sunnah* widened further. Now it came to include the rulings of the administrative authorities and the consensus of the jursits of each region. We find vestiges of this new content of the *Sunnah* in a number of statements of early authorities. Al-Shaybānī attributes to Mu'āwiyah or 'Abd al-Malik the practice of taking decision on the basis of one witness together with an oath by the plaintiff,[34] while this practice is called *Sunnah* by Mālik.[35] Ibn al-Muqaffa' (d. ca. 140 A.H.) states that blood had been shed on the authority of *Sunnah*; but when this *Sunnah* was closely inquired into, the answer forthcoming was that 'Abd al-Malik or some other ruler (*amīr*) behaved in this or that manner.[36] Abū Yūsuf blames al-Awzā'ī and the jurists of Hejaz for their frequent use of the phrase *maḍat al-Sunnah* (so has been the *Sunnah* in the past). According to him, the *Sunnah* to which they had referred might have been the decision of a market inspector or of some district governor.[37] Al-Shāfi'ī became aware of the distinction between the *Sunnah* of the Prophet and its later evolution after he went to Iraq from Medina.

He, therefore, began attacking *'amal* (practice) ruthlessly and did not regard it as authoritative *Sunnah*. During this period, we think, terms like *a'immat al-huda*[38] came into existence in order to draw a distinction between the rightly-guided and worldly caliphs.

With the acceleration of individual independent thinking in law the personal opinions of the jurisconsults, too, came to be part of the *Sunnah* in different regions. That is why Abū Yūsuf regards those who have understanding in law (*fuqahā'*) as an authoritative source of legal knowledge.[39] We hear the early authorities repeatedly say: "It has been the practice" (*maḍat al-Sunnah*), or "we found our scholars say so-and-so", etc.[40] These phrases, in fact, refer to the consensus of the local scholars that was also recognized as a source of law. Thus, *Sunnah* and local *Ijmā'* had come so close to each other that it is hard to draw a distinction between them. It is almost agreed that *Sunnah* in Mālik refers to the consensus of the people of Medina. We shall come to this issue in due course.

Let us now take up the *Sunnah* according to the early authorities, namely, al-Awzā'ī, Mālik, Abū Yūsuf and al-Shaybānī, and examine briefly their points of view.

Being the oldest of these authorities, al-Awzā'ī (d. 157 A.H.) of Syria refers frequently to the practice of the Muslims as came down to him from the time of the Prophet. During the course of his controversies with Abū Ḥanīfah, he depends in most cases on the conduct of the Prophet in the first instance. Then to reinforce his argument he refers to the practice of the Companions and the early Muslims. Occasionally, he mentions the conduct of the political leaders (*a'immah* or *wulāt al-Muslimīn*) and even to the usage of Banū Umayyah until the murder of Walīd b. Yazīd (126 A.H.)[41] as corroborating evidence. We have previously pointed out how Abū Yūsuf criticizes him for his use of the phrase '*maḍat al-Sunnah*'. He objects to his frequent reference to the practice of the

Muslims and political leaders saying that this practice might be the opinion of the scholars of Syria who are not good in the knowledge of rituals and jurisprudence.[42]

From Abū Yūsuf's controversies with al-Awazā'ī it is evident that in any given situation the *Sunnah* may differ, because one legist singles out a certain incident from the life of the Prophet as relevant to that situation while the other argues differently. Let us give an example. According to Abū Ḥanīfah, if a non-Muslim embraces Islam, leaves his home and property, his property will be included in the booty in case the non-Muslim territory falls to the Muslims. Al-Awzā'ī rejects this view and adduces the precedent of the fall of Mecca when the Prophet did not take into possession the properties of the Muslims there, nor did he make them captives. Further, he remarks: "The person most worthy to be followed and whose *Sunnah* is to be adhered to is the Prophet." He also quotes Shurayḥ as having said: "The *Sunnah* outstripped this analogy of yours. Therefore, follow and do not make innovations. You will not be misguided so long as you follow tradition". Defending the view of his teacher, Abū Yūsuf points out that the fall of Mecca was an exception. He argues that people are not like the Prophet; nor is the case of the non-Arabs and the *Ahl al-Kitāb* similar to that of the Arabs. Poll-tax (*jizyah*) is not levied, he adds, on the Arab unbelievers who are not *Ahl al-Kitāb*; they will be killed. Poll-tax, according to him, is levied only on the non-Arab unbelievers. It has been the *Sunnah* in Islam, he contends, to distribute booty among the warriors and the *Imām* had no authority to withhold it from them. But the Prophet, he says, had not done so at the fall of Mecca. Again, he continues, if this practice of the Prophet (i.e. fall of Mecca) is taken as established practice (*al-amr*), no one should be allowed to capture any person and to take booty in the war. To strengthen his argument Abū Yūsuf points out another similar exception, namely, the battle of Hawāzin. In this battle, he says, the Prophet returned the captives to Banū Hawāzın. It is remarkable that he characterizes as *Sunnah* even what he regards as having been an exception. Further, he asserts that the Prophet's behaviour was right for him but others are not to take it as a precedent.[43]

From the above example we may draw certain conclusions. Firstly, others, too, can establish the *Sunnah* according to al-Awzā'ī on which the *Sunnah* of the Prophet over-arches. Secondly, in the problems where clear instructions were not available *Sunnah* can be determined by *ra'y*, applying a relevant incident of the Prophet's life to the situation. Thirdly, there may be differences in determining the *Sunnah* on the basis of argument. Fourthly, even an exception from a general rule can be called *Sunnah* and can be basis of argument. Although Abū Yūsuf describes the exception as *Sunnah*, he does not recognize it as an *established Sunnah* to be followed.

The views of Abū Yūsuf and al-Awzā'ī on *Sunnah* do not differ much in their consequences. None the less, we find certain points in their approach that distinguish the one from the other. Al-Awzā'ī does not quote generally any tradition from the Prophet in the formal way with the chain of narrators. In the first instance, he refers to a particular incident from the life of the Prophet without any formality of narration. Abū Yūsuf, on the contrary, quotes traditions from the Prophet in a formal manner, although not with perfect *isnād* like al-Shāfi'ī. Moreover, he insists on transmitting *Ḥadīth* from reliable persons (*thiqāt*). But we find no such indication in al-Awzā'ī. The emphasis on *Ḥadīth* in Abū Yūsuf is greater than in al-Awzā'ī. In some cases, he bases himself only on practice without reference to the Prophet, but this is rare in Abū Yūsuf. Al-Awzā'ī sometimes argues on the basis of exceptional precedents left by the Prophet, while Abū Yūsuf always bases himself on the general practice of the Prophet. Al-Awzā'ī's reasoning, however, is important because it gives us a rule that every *Sunnah* of the Prophet, whether general or exceptional, should be followed (unless the Qur'ān or the Prophet himself points out that such-and-such *Sunnah* was reserved for the Prophet—an argument adduced by al-Shāfi'ī in support of al-Awzā'ī).[44]

Mālik's method in *al-Muwaṭṭa'* is that on each legal topic he first relates the relevant *Ḥadīth* from the Prophet, if available, then from some Companion, and lastly the practice and opinions of the lawyers of Medina, generally the opinion of one of the seven lawyers. He occasionally quotes the precedents left by the Umayyad authorities like Marwān b. al-Ḥakam, 'Abd al-Malik, and 'Umar b. 'Abd al-'Azīz. Afterwards he states the views of his own school, the people of Medina through certain particular phrases. These are: *maḍat al-Sunnah* (it has been the practice), *al-Sunnah 'indanā* (the practice with us), *al-Sunnah allatī lā ikhtilāfa fīhā 'indanā* (the practice in which there is no difference among us), *al-amr 'indanā* (our practice), *al amr al-mujtama' 'alayhi 'indanā* (our generally agreed practice), and *al-amr alladhī lā ikhtilāfa fīhi 'indanā* (our practice in which there is no difference among us). These phrases recur in *al-Muwaṭṭa'* interchangeably to show the established practice of the people of Medina. Mālik in some cases rejects, as we have pointed out before,[45] a tradition coming from the Prophet in favour of the opinion of a Companion or a Successor. This is due to the fact that the agreed and established practice of Medina was the ideal practice according to him. This led the 'Irāqī jurists[46] and al-Shāfi'ī to accuse him of negligence of *Ḥadīth*. The reason for the emphasis on *Ḥadīth* by the 'Irāqīs and al-Shāfi'ī as compared to the Medinese is that Medina had an established practice coming down from the Prophet, while Kufa or Basra had none. The 'Irāqīs, in fact, were creating their own tradition by combining *Ḥadīth* with *ra'y*. Al-Shāfi'ī wanted to establish a universal standard of prophetic tradition against regional traditions.[47] From this phenomenon, Dr. Schacht concludes that "it was the Iraqians and not the Medinese to whom the concept of the *Sunnan* of the Prophet was familiar before the time of Shāfi'ī".[48] We, have, however, shown previously that the concept '*Sunnah* of the Prophet' was not new either in Iraq or in Medina but had existed from the very beginning in Islam.[49]

Sunnah in Mālik does not purely consist of tradition from the Prophet. Nor is it always the traditions from the Companions or the Successors, because he occasionally rejects their reported conduct as the established *Sunnah*. *Sunnah*, according to him, is sometimes based on the traditions from the Prophet, sometimes on the behaviour of the Companions and the Successors, and occasionally on the practice prevalent among the people of Medina.[50] The established practice of the Muslims in Medina seems to be the channel to judge the real *Sunnah*. That Mālik uses the term *Sunnah* in the sense of the established practice in Medina can be proved by his own statements. Firstly, he uses the word *Sunnah* and terms like '*al-amr al-mujtama' 'alayhi 'indanā*' interchangeably. Secondly, he himself refers to the practice ('*amal*) in several cases.[51] Thirdly, at times he refers to the consensus of the scholars of Medina.[52] Fourthly, some chapters in *al-Muwaṭṭa'* have been entitled as '*Sunnah* in such-and-such problem,' while others are captioned as '*amal* in so-and-so.'[53] This implies that *Sunnah* and '*amal* were identical for him. Addressing a Medinese opponent al-Shāfi'ī says: "You establish the *Sunnah* on a two-fold basis: first, what conforms to the opinion of the Companions, and secondly, which involves no difference of opinion of the people."[54] This shows that al-Shāfi'ī was referring to the *Ijmā'* (agreed practice) of the people of Medina which the Medinese called *Sunnah*.

The reason why Mālik and the Medinese followed the established practice is that the Companions had seen the Prophet behave in all sorts of conditions, and thus they themselves were taken by the next generation to be acting according to his model conduct. Thus, by the time of the third generation, the *Sunnah* of the Prophet was taken to have been established in the Community. On this hypothesis, as time went on, the Prophetic *Sunnah* became more and more visible and exposed to the common man. If any Companion had not known it on certain points previously, he came to know it later. There were about thirty thousand Companions living at Medina. Their recognized, known, and established practice was more reliable than an isolated tradition. Moreover, a tradition was based on the transmission of one, two or at the most six persons, whereas practice was known to thousands of people. Hence, the channel of practice was more reliable for them than a chain of transmission to know the real *Sunnah*. This is résumé of an argument advanced by a Medinese opponent to al-Shāfiʿī's objections.[55] This sort of argument was also challenged and rejected by al-Shāfiʿī.

Let us now discuss how Mālik is clear about the concept "*Sunnah* of the Prophet" in his argumentation. The problem before us is whether *Sunnah* for Mālik was the established practice, of Medina without reference to the Prophet. He captions a chapter as '*Sunnat al-Iʿtikāf*'. Under this topic he states that he heard no scholar speaking of any condition in *Iʿtikāf*. Further, he argues that *Iʿtikāf* is a religious action like other actions, say, prayer, fasting, and *Ḥajj*. Any person who performs them should follow what has been the practice in the past (*mā maḍā min al-Sunnah*). He should not institute something new and contrary to the practice of the Muslims in the past. He should neither impose any condition nor innovate an institution. Concluding, he remarks: "The Prophet had performed *Iʿtikāf* and the Muslims implemented the *Sunnah* of *Iʿtikāf*."[56] In this example, Mālik explicitly refers to the Prophet's *Sunnah*. Sometimes, however, he refers generally to "the practice since the time of the Prophet". This is more obvious from his sporadic remarks on certain problems that "so has been the practice since the time of the

Prophet."[57] Moreover, in most cases he bases himself expressly on the conduct of the Prophet as narrated to him in the form of *Ḥadīth*. For instance, he holds the view that no compensation is necessary for the injuries in the head below the injury known as *al-mūḍiḥah*. For this he gives the reason that the Prophet, in his letter to 'Amr b. Ḥazm, ended the compensations on the injury *al-mūḍiḥah* for which he prescribed five camels.[58]

The remarks of Ibn Qāsim (d. 191 A.H.), a disciple of Mālik, throw further light on Mālik's position with regard to the acceptance of *Ḥadīth*. Mālik stipulates the permission of *walī* (guardian) for the validity of the marriage of a woman. In this case he argues on the basis of a tradition (*athar*) from 'Umar b. al-Khaṭṭāb and the practice of the two legists of Medina, namely, al-Qāsim b. Muḥammad, and Sālim b. 'Abd Allāh. Now, Mālik does not follow the *Ḥadīth* from the Prophet which requires no permission of *walī* for the validity of the marriage of a woman. Supporting his teacher, Ibn Qāsim says that if the opponents' *Ḥadīth* had been accompanied by practice he would have accepted it, but the fact is not so. Several traditions, he adds, have been reported from the Prophet and his Companions, but these traditions were not corroborated by practice. The Companions and the people in general followed the traditions accompanied by practice. Therefore, such traditions as were not accompanied by practice survived, neither belied nor yet acted upon. The Successors received these traditions from the Companions and so did the following generations without discrediting and rejecting what reached them. Therefore, what is eliminated from practice, he concludes, is neglected but not theoretically discredited, and what is accompanied by practice is followed and ratified.[59] From this it may be concluded that both practice and traditions from the Prophet, as we explained before, came down simultaneously. Mālik followed the traditions that were practised generally, although he did not discredit others too.

In a certain case he is reported to have said: "The *Ḥadīth* is there, but we do not know what it really means."[60] Therefore it would be incorrect to draw the general conclusion about Mālik and the Medinese that they give preference to traditions from the Companions over traditions from the Prophet.[61] There was no problem of preference before them, but of the proper channel to approach the ideal *Sunnah*.

From Abū Yūsuf begins the period when *Ḥadīth* came to be referred frequently to support the *Sunnah*, although both still remained separate. In fact, the ground was prepared for appearance of al-Shāfi'ī on the scene.

Abū Yūsuf regards the *Sunnah* as the conduct and behaviour of the Prophet as practised by the Muslims after him. The terms *Sunnah* and *Ḥadīth* run parallel in his arguments. He is radically opposed to accepting the lonely traditions which run counter to the well-known *Sunnah* and the traditions known to the legists. He does not recognize the vague term *maḍat al-Sunnah* used by al-Awzā'ī unless its source is known. The *Sunnah*, according to him, must be known to the men of understanding in law and of learning (*Ahl al-fiqh and Ahl al-'ilm*). In the following paragraphs we shall illustrate these points with examples.

The Caliph Hārūn al-Rashīd inquired of Abū Yūsuf whether an invitation should be extended to the infidels before waging war with them or not. In addition, he asked him to inform him of the *Sunnah* in respect of extending invitation and giving battle to them and of capturing their children. In response to his queries Abū Yūsuf recounted a host of instructions which the Prophet used to give to the Companions at the time of sending them to fight the infidels. Besides, he enlightened him on the practice of the Companions especially of Abū Bakr and 'Umar.[62] This shows that the *Sunnah* for him was not the practice of the Community alone. He takes the *Sunnah* primarily from the behaviour of the Prophet which became well known for being acted upon and practised by the early Muslims.

The terms *Sunnah* and *Ḥadīth* occur generally simultaneously in his writings. This he does, we presume, to document the *Sunnah* by *Ḥadīth* because the time was approaching when practice was no longer regarded as its own proof. He disagrees with al-Awzā'ī's view that some fixed share should be given to the women and the *dhimmīs* who take part in the battle alongside of the Muslims. Defending Abū Ḥanīfah, he quotes certain traditions from the Prophet. Concluding, he remarks: "On this point *Ḥadīth* is abundant and the *Sunnah* is well known." It may be remarked that al-Awzā'ī himself argues on the basis of the behaviour of the Prophet and the practice of the Muslims and their political leaders. But Abū Yūsuf rejects his view because it is not known to "the men having understanding in law (*Ahl al-fiqh*)", and because it runs counter to a number of traditions known to him.[63] This example shows that Abū Yūsuf depends mostly on the generally known traditions and a mere reference to the Prophet or the practice was not enough for him.

On the question of allotting shares from the booty to each of two horses possessed by a single warrior in a battle, Abū Yūsuf differs from al-Awzā'ī purely on the basis of *Ḥadīth*. He describes the *Ḥadīth* adduced by al-Awzā'ī lonely (*shādhdh*) which is, therefore, not recognized by him.[64] It may be remarked that in this case he does not refer to any practice. A lonely *Ḥadīth*, according to him, we suppose, is one which is foreign to the established practice and the abundant and well-known traditions on the subject. This instance also demonstrates how Abū Yūsuf is receding from practice towards *Ḥadīth*.

Abū Yūsuf no doubt quotes *Ḥadīth* frequently, but he seems to be very strict in the question of its acceptance. He had certain criteria to judge its authenticity. He does not recognize any *Ḥadīth* which goes against the Qur'ān and the well-known *Sunnah*. He insists on making the Qur'ān and the well-known *Sunnah* (*al-Sunnat al-ma'rūfah*) the standard and guide and requires that the new situation be "measured" on these standards alone.[65] He was aware that transmission of Ḥadīth was on the increase, and lonely traditions were coming to the surface. He, therefore, warns against solitary traditions and requires adherence to the Ḥadīth followed by the Community (*jamā'ah*) and that which is well known to the lawyers and the one which is in consonance with the Qur'ān and the *Sunnah*.[66] In this connection he also quotes a Ḥadīth from the Prophet which is challenged by al-Shāfi'ī.[67]

Abū Yūsuf is angry with al-Awzā'ī and the lawyers of Hejaz for their frequent use of the phrase *maḍat al-Sunnah* vaguely. But it should be noted that he accepts it from al-Zuhrī because, we think, it expressly refers to the Prophet and the Companions. Al-Zuhrī remarks: "It has been the *Sunnah* from the Prophet and the first two Caliphs after him that the evidence of a woman is not valid in cases of punishment."[68] He himself uses similar phrases occasionally in the course of his reasoning.[69] The source of the *Sunnah*, according to him, is of vital importance. The following remarks speak of his point of view in this respect. He says: "Judgements should not be taken in the matters of lawful and unlawful merely on the basis of the statements, like: the people have always been doing such-and-such, for people have been practising much what is unlawful and what should not be practised. A decision should be based on the *Sunnah* of the Prophet and practice of the early generations (*salaf*), i.e. his Companions and those who have understanding in law."[70] But it is curious that Abū Yūsuf does not take into consideration the scholars of Syria to whom al-Awzā'ī refers in the course of his arguments. He asks al-Awzā'ī as to who are those scholars and political leaders whose practice he was referring to so that he could judge them whether they were reliable and competent.[71] From this we conclude that the early schools had more reliance on their local authorities than others. This gave birth to the emergence of the local *Ijmā'* of the scholars and differences in the *Sunnah*.

Al-Shaybānī does not differ much from Abū Yūsuf in respect of *Sunnah*. His wont in the arguments is that he first points out the *Sunnah* on a particular problem, then he supports it by quoting traditions from the Prophet and the practice of the Companions. In the last, he states the opinion of Abū Ḥanīfah and the scholars of Iraq in general. For instance, he says that it is the *Sunnah* to levy *jizyah* on the magians, not to marry their women and not to eat their slaughtered animals. Then he remarks: "So has been reported to us from the Prophet."[72]

Like Abū Yūsuf, he also bases himself on the well-known *Ḥadīth* and on occasions uses the phrase '*al-Sunnat al-ma'rūfah*.'[73] But his repeated remarks 'this is the opinion of Abu Ḥanīfah and our jurists in general' reflect the regional colour in his conclusions.

He vehemently criticizes Mālik and the Medinese for neglecting traditions of the Prophet which are reported by themselves. In this respect he seems to be already half-way towards al-Shāfi'ī. Mālik, for example, maintains that there is no harm to pass across the man at prayer. Al-Shaybānī ruthlessly attacks the Medinese remarking that they transmit the traditions which they do not themselves follow. If he intends, he says, to argue against them on the basis of their own reports, he can do so. Concluding, he remarks that on this point they set aside the traditions and follow what they like which is not supported by any *athar* or *Sunnah*.[74]

On many problems he differs from Abū Ḥanīfah and agrees with the Medinese on the basis of *Ḥadīth*. We give an example. The point at issue is whether a man can lead the prayer in sitting condition while the people behind him are standing. Al-Shaybānī follows the view held by the Medinese that the *Imām* should lead the prayer standing. But

Abū Ḥanīfah holds the opposite view. Quoting a *Ḥadīth* from the Prophet al-Shaybānī says: "Nothing has reached us to the effect that any of the rightly-guided leaders (*a'immat al-huda*), Abū Bakr, 'Umar, 'Uthmān, 'Alī and others, had ever led prayers in sitting condition. Therefore, we follow this because this is more authentic."[75] In this case, although he does not mention the word '*Sunnah*', he bases himself on *Ḥadīth* and the practice of the early Muslims. Therefore, this practice as supported by *Ḥadīth* seems to stand as *Sunnah* for him.

To give the definition of *ṭalāq al-Sunnah,* as he calls it, he quotes a *Ḥadīth* from the Prophet. The method which the Prophet taught to Ibn 'Umar for giving divorce is known, according to him, as *ṭalāq al-Sunnah.*[76] From this and similar other examples we can conclude that in this phase the *Sunnah* and *Ḥadīth* had come so close to each other that there remained little distinction between them. Al-Shāfi'ī removed even this little distinction.

From the views of the early authorities on the *Sunnah,* as analysed above, it is evident that the *Sunnah* carried in its content personal opinion of the jurists and the local colour of each region. Since every region had a different milieu and materials of law-making, the differences in the *Sunnah* were natural. The acuteness of differences in the *Sunnah* may be estimated from the following example. Mālik holds that walking behind the dead body in a funeral procession is against the *Sunnah* (*min khaṭā' al-Sunnah*),[77] while al-Shaybānī thinks it better (*afḍal*) to follow the dead body.[78] These differences in the *Sunnah* were not confined to such minor cases as we have so far quoted. They extended even to acts clearly prohibited in the Qur'ān like *ribā* (usury). Abū Yūsuf agrees with al-Awzā'ī on the point that *ribā* (usury) is forbidden in enemy territory (*arḍ al-ḥarb*), while Abū Hanīfah allows it on the basis of a tradition from the Prophet reported by Makḥūl. It is surprising that al-Awzā'ī, living in

Syria, is not aware of the *Ḥadīth* narrated by Makḥūl (or he does not at least regard it as genuine). On the contrary, he adduces several arguments to the effect that *ribā* (usury) was forbidden in the transactions between the Muslims and the infidels in the Prophet's time.[79] It appears that the tradition reported by Makḥūl was not widely known in Syria. But this lonely report became well known in Iraq, and this view was held by Ibrāhīm al-Nakha'ī, Sufyān al-Thawrī[80] and al-Shaybānī.[81] This shows how *Sunnah* in its early stages was characterized by provincialism even in respect of such crucial problems. Keeping this background in view we can well understand the meaning of the well-known dictum that "the *Sunnah* decides upon the Qur'ān and not the Qur'ān upon the *Sunnah*."

From the emphasis of the early jurists on the practice of the Muslims it would not be correct to infer that *Ḥadīth* is a late product. We have earlier analysed the reasons for the emphasis on practice by the early jurists. *Ḥadīth* was in existence since the time of the Prophet. Quite apart from the conventional reports about the collection of *Ḥadīth*, its existence in the lifetime of the Prophet and after him cannot reasonably be doubted. The reason is that people around the Prophet must have talked about his deeds, sayings and conduct, especially since his obedience was made obligatory on them by God. Now after his death this sort of talk must have assumed more importance than before, because the Prophet was no longer among them. How could the Arabs who were noted for their marvellous memory fail to narrate and transmit the deeds and sayings of their Prophet whose conduct was 'exemplary' for them according to the Qur'ān? "Rejection of this natural phenomenon, to quote Prof. Fazlur Rahman, is tantamount to a grave irrationality, a sin against history."[82]

NOTES

1. Vide all the major dictionaries.
2. Qur'ān, 17 : 77, 33 : 62.
3. Qur'ān, 8 : 38, 15 : 8.
4. Qur'ān, 35 : 43, 48 : 23.
5. *Al-Mu'llaqāt al-Sab'ah* (with commentary by al-Zawzanī), Cairo, 1315 A.H., p. 102.
6. Ḥassān b. Thābit says:

إن الذوائب من فهر و اخوتهم   قد بينوا سنة للناس تتبع

سجية تلك منهم غير محدثة   إن الخلائق فاعلم شرها البدع

See *Dīwān Ḥassān b. Thābit* (ed. 'Abd al-Raḥmān al-Barqūqī), Cairo, 1926, p. 248.

7. Abū Yūsuf, *Kitāb al-Kharāj*, Cairo, 1302 A.H., p. 3.
8. *Ibid.*, p. 33.
9. Abū Dā'ūd, *Sunan*, Cawnpore, 1928, vol. II, p. 105.
10. A statement of 'Ā'ishah goes:

كان فى بريرة ثلاث سنن

Mālik, *al-Muwaṭṭa'*, Cairo, 1951, vol. II, p. 562.

11. Abū Nu'aym al-Isfahānī, *Ḥilyat al-Awliyā'*, Cairo, 1936, vol. VI, p. 332.
12. Abū Yūsuf, *al-Radd 'alā Siyar al-Awzā'ī*, Cairo, n.d., p. 31. Al-Sha'bī and al-Zuhrī are reported to have been 'most aware of the past *Sunnah*', Ibn Sa'd, *al-Ṭabāqāt al-Kubrā*, Beirut, 1376 A.H., vol. II, p. 389; vol. VI, p. 254.
13. It appears that al-Shāfi'ī was not the first jurist who identified *Sunnah* with *Ḥadīth*, but there had been in the past some people, e.g. Ṣāliḥ b. Kaysān (d. 140 A.H.) who held this view. Ibn Sa'd, *al-Ṭabāqāt al-Kubrā*, *ed. cit.*, vol. II, p. 388f.
14. Abū Yūsuf, *Kitāb al-Kharāj*, p. 11; about an *athar* of 'Umar b. al-Khattāb Mālik says:

ليس هذا الحديث بالمجتمع عليه و ليس عليه العمل

See Mālik, *op. cit.*, vol. II, p. 449. 'Umar *b.* 'Abd al-'Azīz calls the judgements of 'Umar the *Ḥadīth* of 'Umar. See al-Shaybanī, *al-Muwaṭṭa*, Deoband, n.d., p. 391. Al-Shaybānī calls the saying of Makḥūl, the Successor, *Ḥadīth*. Al-Shaybānī, *al-Siyar al-Kabīr* (with commentary by al-Sarakhsī), Hyderabad, Deccan, 1335 A.H., vol. II, p. 259.

15. Qur'ān, 33 : 21.
16. Schacht, Joseph, *The Origins of Muhammadan Jurisprudence*, Oxford, 1959, p. 349 (Addenda); cf. Ibn Hishām, *Sirat al-Nabī*, Cairo, n.d. (ed. Muḥammad Muḥī al-dīn 'Abd al-Ḥamīd), vol. IV, p. 337.
17. Ibn Hishām, *op. cit.*, vol. IV, p. 276.
18. Abū Yūsuf, *Kitāb al-Kharāj, ed. cit.*, pp. 8, 66.
19. Ibn al-Murtaḍā, Aḥmad b. Yaḥyā: *Kitāb Ṭabāqāt al-Mu'tazilah*, Beirut, 1961, p. 19.

و قدا در كنا السف الذين قاموا الامر الله و استنوا بسنة رسول الله صلى الله عليه وسلم

Cf. *Der Islam*, Band 21, p. 68.
20. Mālik, *op. cit.*, vol. II, pp. 833, 899, 983; Abū Yūsuf, *al-Radd 'alā Siyar al-Awzā'ī, ed. cit.*, pp. 57, 67, 131; Abū Yūsuf, *Kitāb al-Kharāj, ed. cit.*, pp. 8, 43, 66; Al-Shaybānī, *al-Muwaṭṭa', ed. cit.*, pp. 317, 391.
21. Schacht, Joseph, *An Introduction to Islamic Law*, Oxford, 1964, pp. 17-18.
22. Mālik, *op. cit.*, vol. II, p. 513.
23. Schacht, J., *The Origins of Muhammadan Jurisprudence, ed. cit.*, pp. 4, 5, 20, 30, 40, 61, 63, 76, 80. See also his article entitled 'pre-Islamic background and early development of jurisprudence, in *Law in the Middle East* (ed. Majid Khadduri), Washington, 1955, vol. I.
24. Cf. Yusuf, S. M., 'The *Sunnah*—its Transmission, Development and Revision' *Islamic Culture*, vol. XXXVII, No. 4, October, 1963, pp. 276, 279.
25. Abū Yūsuf, *Kitāb al-Kharāj, ed. cit.*, p. 66. 'Umar's following remarks in this respect are also significant:

انكم ايها الرهط ائمة يقتدى بكم الناس and والله لوفعلتها لكانت سنة

See Mālik, *op. cit.*, vol. I, pp. 50, 326.
26. Mālik, *op. cit.*, vol. II, p. 513.
27. Abū Yūsuf, *al-Radd 'alā Siyar al-Awzā'ī, ed. cit.*, pp. 30-31, 'Umar is reported to have imposed a ban on the narration of *Ḥadīth* (*Ibid.*, p. 30), and to have taken three Companions under arrest for violation of this order. (Haykal, Muḥammad Ḥusayn, *al-Fārūq 'Umar*, Cairo, 1346 A.H., vol. II, p. 288).
28. Abū Yūsuf, *Kitāb al-Kharāj, ed. cit.*, p. 106.
29. Al-Shaybānī, *Kitāb al-Ḥujaj*, MS, p. 40. Cf. Abū Yūsuf, *Kitāb al-Āthār*, Cairo, 1355, A.H., No. 872.

See Al-Shāfi'ī, *Ikhtilāf al-Ḥadīth*, Cairo, 1325, A.H., p. 17 (on the margin of *Kitāb al-Umm*, vol. VII).

30. A poet in the elegy of 'Umar b. 'Abd al-'Azīz says:

و أحييت فى الاسلام علما و سنة ولم تبتدع حكما من الحكم اضجعا [اصحما]

ففى كل يوم كنت تهدم بدعة و تبنى لنا من سنة ماتهدما

Cf. al-Shāṭibī, *al-I'tiṣām*, Cairo, n.d., vol. I, p. 102. Al-Ḥasan of Basra is reported to have remarked:

ظهر الجفاء و قلت العلماء و عفت السنة ، وشاعت البدعة

Al-Jāḥiẓ, *al-Bayān wa'l-Tabyyīn*, Cairo, 1949, vol. III, p. 133. Cf. Yusuf, S.M., 'The *Sunnah*—its Transmission, Development and Revision', *Islamic Culture*, vol. XXXVIII, No. 1, January, 1964, p. 19, footnotes. Al-Awzā'ī's remarks حتى هاجت الفتنة are also significant. Abū Yūsuf, *al-Radd 'alā Siyar al-Awzā'ī, ed. cit.*, p. 20.

31. Al-Shaybānī, *al-Muwaṭṭa'*, *ed. cit.*, p. 391.

32. 'Alī Ḥasan 'Abd al-Qādir, *Naẓrah 'āmmah fi Ta'rīkh al-Fiqh al-Islāmī*, Cairo, 1956, p. 189. Goldziher mentions seventeen points of difference between *Shī'ī* and *Sunnī* law. See his *Le Dogme et la Loi de l' Islam*, Paris, 1958, p. 191.

33. Mālik, *op. cit.*, vol. I, p. 114.

نعمت البدعة هذه

34. Al-Shaybānī, *al-Muwaṭṭa'*, *ed. cit.*, p. 363.

35. Mālik, *op. cit.*, vol. II, pp. 722, 725.

36. Ibn al-Muqaffa', *Risālah fi'l-Ṣaḥābah*, in *Rasā'il al-Bulaghā*, Cairo, 1954, p. 126.

37. Abū Yūsuf, *al-Radd 'alā Siyar al-Awzā'ī, ed. cit.*, p. 11.

38. *Ibid.*, p. 238, cf. Abū Yūsuf *Kitāb al-Kharāj, ed. cit.*, p. 32. The term *al-Khulafā' al-Rāshidūn*' is not traceable upto alShāfi'ī (d. 204 A.H.). Cf. Coulson, N.J., *A History of Islamic Law*. Edinburgh, 1964, p. 36.

39. Abū Yūsuf, *al-Radd 'alā Siyaral-Awzā'ī, ed. cit.*, p. 76.

40. *Ibid.*, pp. 41, 46 *passim*, Mālik, *op. cit.*, vol. I, pp. 268, 280, *passim;* Abū Yūsuf, *Kitāb al-Kharāj, ed. cit.*, pp. 33, 99, 105.

41. Abū Yūsuf, *al-Radd 'alā Siyar al-Awzā'ī, ed. cit.*, p. 20.

42. *Ibid.*, p. 21.

43. *Ibid.*, pp. 131-135. For more examples of exception see pp. 24, 108-9. See also pp. 126-130.

44. Al-Shāfi'ī, *Kitāb al-Umm*, Cairo, 1325 A.H., vol. VII, p. 329.

45. See the treatise entitled '*Ikhtilāf Mālik wa'l-Shafi'ī*, in *Kitāb al-Umm*, vol. VII, The problem of *Khiyār al-majlis* may be referred to in *al-Muwaṭṭa'*.

46. See al-Shaybānī's criticism on the Medinese in his *Kitāb al-Ḥujaj*.

47. Coulson, N. J., *op. cit.*, pp. 50, 57, 98-99.

48. Schacht, J. *The Origins of Muhammadan Jurisprudence*, *ed. cit.*, p. 76.

49. Mālik, *op. cit.* vol. II, pp. 748, 851.

50. *Ibid.*, vol. I, pp. 61, 71, 177, 222-23, 225-26; vol. II, pp. 708-9, 788, 854, passim.

51. *Ibid.*, vol. I, pp. 18, 206 *passim*.

52. *Ibid.*, vol. I, 268, 276 *passim*.

53. *Ibid.*, vol. I, pp. 18, 40, 100; vol. II, pp. 921, 926.

54. Al-Shāfi'ī, *Kitāb al-Umm*, vol. VII, p. 240.

و زعمت انك تثبت السنة من وجهين: أحدهما أن تجد الائمة
من اصحاب النبى صلى الله عليه وسلم قالوا بما يوافقها ، و الاخر
أن لا تجد الناس اختلفوا فيها

55. *Ibid.*, p. 242.

56. Mālik, *op. cit.*, vol. I, p. 314.

57. *Ibid.*, vol. I, p. 177; vol. II, pp. 514, 854.

58. *Ibid.*, vol. II, p. 859. See also cases where the behaviour of the Prophet constitutes the main argument of Mālik. *Ibid.*, vol. I, pp. 341-42; vol. II, pp. 456, 475, 476, 650, 677.

59. Saḥnūn, *al-Mudawwanat al-Kubrā*, Cairo, 1323 A.H., vol. IV, p. 28. It is remarkable that Ibn Qāsim does not rely purely on practice as stated by Dr. Schacht (*The Origins*, p. 63, notes below), but on the tradition from the Prophet which is accompanied by practice.

60. *Ibid.*, vol. I, p. 5.

61. Schacht, J., *The Origins of Muhammadan Jurisprudence*, *ed. cit.*, p. 24.

62. Abū Yūsuf, *Kitāb al-Kharāj*, p. 118 f.

63. Abū Yūsuf, *al-Radd 'alā Siyar al-Awzā'ī*, *ed. cit.*, pp. 37-40

64. *Ibid.*, p. 41.

65. *Ibid.*, p. 32.

66. *Ibid.*, p. 31.

67. *Ibid.*, pp. 24-25; cf. al-Shāfi'ī, *Kitāb al-Umm, ed.cit.*, vol. VII, pp. 309-10.

68. Abū Yūsuf, *Kitāb al-Kharāj, ed. cit.*, p. 99.

69. Abū Yūsuf, *al-Radd 'alā Siyar al-Awzā'ī, ed. cit.*, pp. 57, 77.

70. *Ibid.*, p. 76.

71. *Ibid.*, pp. 41-42.

72. Al-Shaybānī, *al-Muwaṭṭa', ed. cit.*, p. 176.

73. Al-Shaybānī, *Kitāb al-Ḥujaj*, MS, pp. 88, 188, *passim*.

74. *Ibid.*, p. 60.

75. *Ibid.*, p. 32. Al-Shaybānī's disagreement with the Medinese on the question of the blood-money of a *dhimmī* is a stock example of his strict adherence to *Ḥadīth*. He accuses the Medinese of rejecting the traditions of the Prophet and the practice of Abū Bakr, 'Umar, 'Uthmān and of preferring to the practice of Mu'āwiyah. Cf. al-Shāfi'ī, *Kitāb al-Umm, ed. cit.*, vol. VII, pp. 290-91.

76. Al-Shaybānī, *al-Muwaṭṭa', ed. cit.*, p. 254.

77. Mālik, *op. cit.*, vol. I, pp. 225-26.

78. Al-Shaybānī, *al-Muwaṭṭa', ed. cit.*, p. 168.

79. Abū Yūsuf, *al-Radd 'alā Siyar al-Awzā'ī, ed. cit.*, pp. 96-98.

80. Al-Ṭaḥāwi, Aḥmad b. Muḥammad, *Mushkil al-Āthār*, Hyderabad, Deccan, 1333 A.H., vol. IV, p. 245.

81. Al-Shaybānī, *al-Siyar al-Kabīr*, Hyderabad, Deccan, n.d. vol. III, p. 228.

82. Fazlur Rahman, *Islamic Methodology in History*, Lahore, 1965, p. 32.

CHAPTER VI

EARLY MODES OF *IJTIHĀD*

Ra'y, *Qiyās* and *Istiḥsān*

The most fundamental source of law in the early phase was the Qur'ān—as elaborated, exemplified and interpreted by the *Sunnah*. Thus, the Qur'ān-*Sunnah* constituted one source of law. The society in which the Qur'ān was revealed was naturally to develop further by the outward expansion of Islam. Most of the problems that confronted the Muslims living in the time of Revelation were bound to differ from those of the coming generations in the wake of the interplay of Islam and other neighbouring cultures with which they came in contact. As such, the law furnished by the Qur'ān-*Sunnah* source in the time of the Prophet had to be supplemented and sometimes reinterpreted and elaborated to cover new problems in order to find answers for them. Islamic law, therefore, developed with the emergence of new problems from time to time since the days of the Prophet, and was created and recreated, interpreted and reinterpreted, in accordance with the varying circumstances. The process of rethinking and reinterpreting the law independently is known as *Ijtihād*. In the early period *ra'y* (considered personal opinion) was the basic instrument of *Ijtihād*. It was a generic term which preceded the growth of law under more systematic principles of *Qiyās* and *Istiḥsān*, but this term continued to be applied even to *Qiyās* by the rightmost wing.

The term *Ijtihād* in the early period was used in a narrower and more specialized sense than it came to be used in al-Shāfi'ī and later on. It conveyed the meaning of fair discretionary judgement or expert's opinion. There is a report about 'Umar, the second Caliph, that one day, during the month of

Ramaḍān, he announced the end of fast, when the sun apparently set. After a while he was informed that the sun was again seen in the sky (as it had not actually set). Upon this he reportedly remarked: "The matter is easy; we exercised *Ijtihād* (*qad ijtahadnā*).[1] This is an early example of the use of this term by the Companions standing for discretionary judgement.

Among the early authorities, we find its frequent use in Mālik. He uses this term generally for the cases where he finds no definite answer from the Prophet or in the agreed practice and, therefore, leaves the matter to the discretion of the *Imām* to decide.[2] For instance, in the case of injury to a blind eye and amputation of a paralysed hand Mālik holds no fixed compensation but leaves the matter to *Ijtijād* (fair estimate).[3] He was asked about the giving of reward (*nafal*) from the *ghanīmah* to a soldier prior to its distribution. He replied that there was no known practice except that it depended on the discretion (*ijtihād*) of the *Imām* to give *nafal* (reward) after the distribution of *ghanīmah* or before it.[4] In cases where Mālik used the term *Ijtihād*, the 'Irāqīs use the term *ḥukūmah 'adl* (fair arbitration).[5] The term *Ijtihād* is not in frequent use in the 'Irāqīs' writings. Ibn al-Nadīm, however, mentions a book entitled '*Kitāb Ijtihād al-ra'y*' by al-Shaybānī.[6]

I

Literally speaking, *ra'y* means opinion and judgement. But the Arabs had used it for the well-considered opinion and skill in affairs. A person having mental perception and sound judgement was known as *dhu'l-ra'y*. The antonym of *dhu'l-ra'y* was *mufannad*, a man weak in judgement and unsound in mind. The epithet (*mufannad*) is reported to have applied to men alone and not to women, because, according to the Arabs, she had not possessed *ra'y* even in her youth, let alone in her old age.[7] The term was also applied to the views of the Khawārij and they were known as *Ahl al-ra'y*.[8] The reason for this appears to be that their views departed from those of *Ahl al-Sunnah*. From this it follows that *ra'y* had the element of exclusive and independent idiosyncratic thinking, which might not be accepted by others. The Qur'ān indicates that the people of Noah had rejected his message because he was followed by the weak and lowly persons immature in judgement (*bādī al-ra'y*).[9]

This implies that intellectual perfection and maturity in judgement had been since long a criterion of greatness. The Qur'ān itself time and again exhorts to deep thinking and meditation over its verses.[10] It invites to the exercise of reason and personal opinion in legal matters. The Prophet himself set examples by accepting the opinion of the Companions in matters where he was not directed by Revelation. On the occasion of Badr, to give an instance, the Prophet chose a particular place for the encampment of the Muslim forces. A Companion, Ḥubāb b. al-Mundhir, asked him whether he had chosen that place on his own judgement (*ra'y*) or on revelation from God. The Prophet replied that he had done so on his own judgement. When the Companion suggested a fitter place, the Prophet told him: "You have made a sound suggestion (*laqad asharta bi'l-ra'y*)"[11] Examples are abundant where the Prophet consulted the Companions and accepted their opinions. The Qur'ān's insistence on consulting the Companions in different matters presupposes its approval of exercise of personal opinion in deciding problems.

Matters were not much complicated during the lifetime of the Prophet because his decision was the last word. But after his death problems grew more and more intricate. The reason is that the Companions had two bases for deciding fresh cases, namely, the Qur'ān and the precedents left by the Prophet. As regards the Qur'ān, it may be stated that *ra'y* was the best method to judge which of the Qur'ānic verses was applicable to a given situation and which was not. The problem of *Ḥadīth* was more delicate than that of the Qur'ān. Firstly, because it required confirmation whether a certain *Ḥadīth* actually came from the Prophet; secondly, whether the Companion rightly understood the meaning of the *Ḥadīth*. In this connection we may refer to the internal criticism of Ibn 'Abbās and 'Ā'ishāh on a number of traditions known to the students of *Ḥadīth*. Consequently, even in the presence of the Qur'ānic verses and traditions on a certain problem the employment of *ra'y* could not be avoided. The reason for this is obvious. The Qur'ānic verses and traditions are to be interpreted by the Muslims in order to be definite whether a certain verse or tradition is applicable to a certain situation. Interpretation and application, therefore, presuppose exercise of personal judgement. Hence, since the early days of Islam, there has been perpetual conflict between the letter and the spirit of the law. Thus, it is not correct to say that *ra'y* was exercised only in the absence of the Qur'ānic verses or traditions on a problem. Al-Shāfi'ī's opponent argues that difference exists over the problems where no Qur'ānic injunction or *Sunnah* is available. Al-Shāfi'ī replies that difference of opinion exists even on points on which there are explicit rules in the Qur'ān or the *Sunnah*. Thereafter al-Shāfi'ī recounts a number of the Qur'ānic verses and traditions on which the Companions and the early jurists differed because of their interpretation.[12]

On going through the cases of *Ijtihād* of several Companions, especially of 'Umar, the second Caliph, we find that *ra'y* was exercised even in the presence of the injunction in the Qur'ān or the *Sunnah*. The fact is that one Companion singled out one verse or tradition for a situation while another pointed to quite a different verse. We give below a few cases where 'Umar exercised his personal opinion, although instructions on these very points can be taken to have already existed in the texts of the Qur'ān or the *Sunnah*.

It is a well-known fact that 'Umar abolished a share of *zakāh* being given to certain Muslims or non-Muslims for "conciliation of their heart" as required by the Qur'ān.[13] The Prophet used to give this share to chiefs of certain Arab tribes in order to attract them to embrace Islam or to prevent them from doing harm to the Muslims. This share was given also to the neo-Muslims so that they might remain steadfast in Islam. But 'Umar discarded the order which Abū Bakr had written in his caliphate for donation of certain lands to some persons on this basis. He argued that the Prophet had given this share to strengthen Islam; but as the conditions had changed, this share ceased to be valid.[14] 'Umar's action seems apparently contrary to the Qur'ān. But, in fact, he considered the obtaining situation and followed the spirit of the Qur'ānic injunction. His personal judgement led him to decide that if the Prophet had lived in similar conditions, he would have done the same. 'Umar b. 'Abd al-'Azīz, during his caliphate, had given this share to a certain person for the same purpose for which the Prophet used to give in his lifetime.[15] Both these examples show how *ra'y* decided where to apply a Qur'ānic injunction and where not.

Another important illustration for the point in question is 'Umar's decision not to distribute the lands of Iraq and Syria among the Companions. The Muslims insisted on distributing the land among them according to the Prophet's practice. To all their contentions 'Umar replied that if he kept on distributing the lands, from where he would maintain the army to protect the borders and the newly conquered towns. The Companions, therefore, finally agreed with him and remarked: "Your's is the correct opinion (*al-ra'y ra'yuka*)." 'Umar later on found the justification of this decision in the Qur'ānic verses 59:6-10 which entitled the *Muhājirūn*, the *Anṣār*, and the coming generations to receive the share from *ghanīmah*.[16] 'Umar apparently departed from those Qur'ānic verses which contain the injunction of distributing booty among the Muslims. According to the rule and practice, the lands, too, should have been distributed like other articles of *ghanīmah.* But 'Umar preferred the general benefit of the Muslims to that of the individuals. Social justice demanded that these conquered lands should not be distributed among the army. This illustration provides an important example of early *Istiḥsān*, i.e. departure from the established rule in the interest of equity and public welfare.

According to a report, some slaves had stolen a she-camel, slaughtered and eaten it. When the matter was referred to 'Umar, he in the first instance ordered the cutting of the hands of the thieves, but after a moment's reflection he said, addressing the slaves' master: "I think you must have starved these slaves out". He, therefore, ordered the master of the slaves to pay double the price of the she-camel and withdrew his order for the cutting of the thieves' hands.[17] Another story runs that a man stole something from *Bayt al-Māl* but 'Umar did not amputate his hand.[18] That 'Umar desisted from cutting the hands of thieves during the days of famine is a well-known fact of history. In these cases 'Umar apparently contravened the Qur'ānic verses which contain the injunction of cutting the hands of a thief. But it should be noted that the Qur'ān is silent on the details of the punishment of the amputation of hands. It is for the *Sunnah* or *ra'y* to decide where to cut the hand and where not.

It is reported that 'Umar imposed a ban on the sale of the mother-of-the-child (*umm al-walad*), or giving her away as a gift or in inheritance. After the death of her master, he declared her to be free.[19] On this problem he discontinued the practice rampant during the time of the Prophet and the predecessor, Abū Bakr. Of course, it may be objected that he changed the *Sunnah* of the Prophet and established a new *Sunnah* through his personal opinion. Here it may be remarked that 'Umar was faced with a social situation which was radically different from that of his predecessors. People used to keep slave-girls—who abounded in 'Umar's time because of conquests—with them for some time. Then these slave-girls fell into the hands of another master with the result that none took the responsibility to look after these women's children. Moreover, this practice was giving an impetus to the growth of the institution of slavery. The following remarks of 'Umar show how grave the situation had become, and how seriously he was taking this problem. According to *al-Muwaṭṭa'*, he remarked: "Why is it that people have intercourse with their slave-girls, and why then abandon them to go out freely? If any slave-girl comes to me and her master confesses cohabitation with her, I shall assign her child to him. Henceforth, either set them free or keep hold of them.[20] From this it is clear that this problem had become acute for him and he was forced to take this stern measure due to the changed social conditions. Similar considerations explain 'Umar's exercising *Ijtihād* in the other cases mentioned above.

These are a few examples where 'Umar apparently departed from the clear injunctions or the previous practice. But it should be noted that this was not really a departure but true adherence to the spirit and intention of the command based on his personal judgement.

Let us discuss the question of the relationship of *ra'y* and *naṣṣ* which seem to be opposed to each other. Literally, *naṣṣ* means "something clear." Technically, it signifies a clear injunction which is textually evidenced with regard to a certain point in the Qur'ān or *Ḥadīth*. The problem is whether *ra'y* can be employed in taking some decision in the presence of a *naṣṣ* on some point. According to the classical legal theory, there is no room for *ra'y* in the presence of a *naṣṣ*. We have previously pointed out that every command, whether in the Qur'ān or *Ḥadīth*, requires interpretation and application to a given situation. That is why, as we saw in

Chapter III, the Companions differed in the interpretation of the Qur'ānic verses. Therefore, we think, there is no escape from the use of *ra'y* even in the presence of *naṣṣ*. But it is worthy of note that where there is no allowance of any interpretation except in one aspect, the decision will naturally be taken on the basis of *naṣṣ*.

Naṣṣ has been defined in the classical literature on jurisprudence as 'the text which conveys only one meaning', or 'whose interpretation is the text itself.'[21] We think that *naṣṣ* by this sort of definition can apply only to a few texts; texts where different interpretations are not possible are rarely found. It seems that the definition of *naṣṣ*, as stated above, is a development from its original meaning. We give below an illustration from al-Shaybānī's *al-Siyar al-Kabīr* which shows that in his time *naṣṣ* could be interpreted differently. Discussing the problem of giving protection to enemy he remarks that the protection given by a free Muslim man, whether he be an upright person (*'adl*) or a profligate (*fāsiq*), will be binding on all Muslims. He justifies this view by quoting a *Ḥadīth* from the Prophet which says: "Muslims are equal in respect of blood and they are like one hand over against all those who are outside the Community. The lowest of them is entitled to give protection on behalf of them." Commenting on the word '*adnā*' (translated here as "lowest") he says that, if it means 'minor' as in the Qur'ānic verse 58 : 7, it is a textual evidence (*tanṣīṣ*) that protection given by one man is valid. But, if it is a derivatine of *dunuw* which means 'nearness' as in the Qur'ānic verse 53 : 9, then it would be taken as (textual) evidence for giving protection by a Muslim who resides in the border area (on the enemy's territory) being close to the enemy. Further, he observes that if it is derived from *danā'ah* which means lowliness, it would be textual evidence (*tanṣīṣ*) for the validity of giving protection even by a profligate (*fāsiq*) Muslim.[22]

Al-Shaybānī is the first scholar to use the term *naṣṣ*. Authorities earlier than him have not used this term. Even al-Shaybānī uses this term in *al-Siyar al-Kabīr*,[23] which was his last work. The early jurists had generally used the terms *Kitāb* and *Sunnah* instead of *naṣṣ*. Indeed, al-Shāfiʻī uses the term *naṣṣ* in opposition to *ra'y*, which we believe must have developed somewhat prior to al-Shāfiʻī among the circle of the traditionists but which al-Shāfiʻī adopted as a principle of law. The concept of *naṣṣ* seems to be a reaction against *ra'y* in al-Shāfiʻī. The more *ra'y* was discarded and the scope of *Ijtihād* narrowed, the more the concept of *naṣṣ* dominated and was extended in its application.

The cases to which al-Shāfiʻī applies the principle of *naṣṣ* or which are regarded by him as being clear injunctions are not open to reasoning, whether they be in the Qur'ān or in *Ḥadīth*. He himself explains the idea of *naṣṣ* to his opponent. This, too, implies that his opponent, who represents the early schools, is not perfectly aware of the concept of *naṣṣ* now developing by degrees. Al-Shāfiʻī says that on the emergence of fresh problems (*nāzilah*), the Qur'ān directs explicitly (*naṣṣan*) or implicitly (*jumlatan*). Further, he remarks that *naṣṣ* means whatever had been ordered or forbidden by God in plain words (*naṣṣan*). He then cites cases which fall under *naṣṣ* and *jumlah* respectively. Under *naṣṣ* he mentions the relatives with whom marriage is forbidden, prohibited edibles like blood and pork, and the ritual purity. *Jumlah*, according to him, stands for the duties made obligatory by God like *ṣalāh*, *zakāh*, and *ḥajj*. These duties, he says, were explained and elaborated by the Prophet. Of the cases which he mentions under *naṣṣ* he remarks that the Qur'ān is enough for them and no further argumentation is needed.[24] This means that al-Shāfiʻī validates the employment of *ra'y* in cases which fall under *jumlah*.

In his *al-Risālah*, al-Shāfiʻī uses the term *naṣṣ* in different forms like *naṣṣ Kitāb*, *naṣṣ ḥukm* and sometimes *naṣṣ al-Kitāb w'al-Sunnah*. In these different places in the *Risālah* he seems to mean by *naṣṣ* the direct textual evidence whether in the

Qur'ān or in the *Sunnah*.[25]

Occasionally, he distinguishes *naṣṣ al-Kitāb* from the *Sunnah* in places where he particularly lays stress on the text of the Qur'ān.[26] He has written a chapter captioned 'the duties laid down plainly in the text of the Qur'ān (*al-frā'iḍ al-manṣūṣah*), for which the Prophetic *Sunnah* provided details. In this chapter he mentions some verses from the Qur'ān regarding ritual purity and quotes several traditions how the Prophet elaborated them. This chapter is followed by another one entitled 'the duty laid down in the text of the Qur'ān (*al-farḍ al manṣūṣ*) limited and particularized by the *Sunnah*. Al-Shāfi'ī discusses, in this chapter, several problems, namely, heritage, homicide, and usury. From the wordings of the Qur'anic verses dealt with in this chapter it appears that the injunctions contained in them were of general nature. But he, by quoting the traditions from the Prophet, explained that they had specific and definite meaning.[27] This implies that *naṣṣ* requires details, elaboration and amplification. Hence, there can be allowance for the difference of opinion. That is why we find that usury, homicide and heritage are cases subject to legal differences, although al-Shāfi'ī describes them as *manṣūṣ*. Moreover, from the detailed discussion of *naṣṣ* by al-Shāfi'ī we conclude that this problem was more or less new for the early schools and he wanted to acquaint them with it in full detail. The theory of *naṣṣ* later on became a dogmatic instrument for justifying one's own views on some legal problems and for rejecting those of others. Moreover, emphasis on *naṣṣ* closed the door to the use of *ra'y* in law.

Another problem that confronts us while discussing *ra'y* is the conflict between the two alleged groups known as *Ahl al-Ḥadīth* and *Ahl al-Ra'y*. Al-Shāfi'ī mentions the terms *Ahl al-Kalām*, *Ahl al-Ḥadīth*, *Ahl al-Qiyās* in different places in his writings. By *Ahl al-Ḥadīth* he seems to mean the experts on *Ḥadīth*, as we pointed out in Chapter II, and not the lawyers of Hejaz or those who argued exclusively on the basis of *Ḥadīth* and discarded *ra'y ab initio*. At least until al-Shāfi'ī *ra'y* and *Ḥadīth* were intermingled and the law was receiving sustenance from both of them in different centres of legal activity. The group who rejected *ra'y* and advocated *Ḥadīth* alone was not born as yet. Al-Shāfi'ī was, of course, a great champion of *Ḥadīth* and opponent of arbitrary *ra'y*; nevertheless, he could not escape from the use of *ra'y* and reason in his argumentation. During this period we hear the names of persons like al-Zuhrī (d. 124 A.H.), Shu'bah (d. 160 A.H.), Sufyān al-Thawrī (a. 161 A.H.), Sufyān b. 'Uyaynah (d. 198 A.H.), Wākī' b. al-Jarrāḥ (d. 197 A.H.) and others who devoted themselves to *Ḥadīth*. But it would be too much to contend that they wanted to banish *ra'y* and reason from law. The difference between the views of al-Shāfi'ī and those of his opponents with regard to the qualifications of *faqīh* is that the former prefers one who adheres most strictly to *Ḥadīth*, while the latter favours the person whose understanding in law is recognized even by the traditionists.[28] This shows that *Ahl al-Ḥadīth* and *fuqahā'* during this period had recourse to both *ra'y* and *Ḥadīth* in their legal reasoning—one giving greater importance to *Ḥadīth* and the other to *ra'y*.

It seems that *Ahl al-Kalām*, according to al-Shāfi'ī, were the Mu'tazilah (and probably also included the Khawārij)[29] who doubted the authenticity of *Ḥadīth*. It appears from his writings that they had different views in this respect. A group of them took only the Qur'ān as a source of law and rejected *Ḥadīth in toto*. Others accepted those traditions which conformed to the Qur'ān and rejected those which contradicted it. A third group accepted the well-known traditions and denied those narrated by a single narrator (*khabar al-wāhid*). Al-Shāfi'ī has given a brief account of their arguments and their refutation.[30] He occasionally calls them *Ahl al-'uqūl* for their emphasis on reason in law. He thinks that they (*Ahl al-'uqūl*) are more entitled to base themselves on *Ijtihād* than those who, despite possessing knowledge of '*uṣūl* like the Qur'ān and the *Sunnah*, still exercise arbitrary *ra'y* and *Istiḥsān* on the basis of reason.[31]

That in the early period there existed two separate groups one advocating *Ḥadīth* exclusively and the other *ra'y* alone does not appear to be true. The reason is that the scholars of *Ḥadīth* in this period were not free from exercising *ra'y* in their reasoning and vice versa. Mālik, although a great authority of *Ḥadīth*, frequently uses *ra'y* in *al-Muwaṭṭa'*. Similarly, the 'Irāqīs who are called *Ahl al-Qiyās* by al-Shāfi'ī are not lacking in *Ḥadīth*, as is obvious from their works. *Ra'y*, as we learn from al-Shāfi'ī's controversies with his opponents, was equally employed by the lawyers of Hejaz and Iraq. He, therefore, constantly accuses both these schools of negligence of *Ḥadīth* as compared to *ra'y*.[32] We find another clue which strengthens our stand. Al-Zuhrī is generally known as a great traditionist (*muḥaddith*) but not noted as a great lawyer (*faqīh*). Still it should be noted that al-Shaybānī calls him the greatest lawyer and the scholar of traditions (*riwāyah*) in Medina.[33] This shows that the sharp distinction between *Ahl al-Ḥadīth* and *Ahl al-ra'y* did not exist in the early period. Al-Shāfi'ī occasionally uses the term *Ahl al-'ilm bi'l-Ḥadīth wa'l-ra'y*[34] which indicates confluence of *Ḥadīth* and *ra'y*. The extreme opposition between *Ḥadīth* and *ra'y* appears to have developed in the post-Shāfi'ī period when the school-bias took root in the followers of each school. But it is obvious that the process of separation began at least with al-Shāfi'ī. Medina was already known as '*home of the Sunnah*,' as we hear from al-Shāfi'ī.[35] The appellation of *Ahl al-Ḥadīth* was, therefore, applied to the lawyers of Medina and *Ahl al-ra'y* to the lawyers of Iraq.

With the process of the compilation of *Ḥadīth* a number of doctors of *Ḥadīth* came into the field. They narrated *Ḥadīth* in support of every problem, as is evident from classical collections. Al-Shāfi'ī had already condemned unrestricted *ra'y* in his time, although he could not part with it practically. In the post-Shāfi'ī period *ra'y* began to be condemned on the basis of *Ḥadīth*. We find a chapter on 'condemnation of *ra'y* and *Qiyās*' in several collections of *Ḥadīth*. During this period, we believe, *ra'y* came to be opposed to *Ḥadīth*. This literalist (*ẓāhir*) attitude of mind towards *Ḥadīth* gave birth to a legal school known as *Ahl al-Ẓāhir*. Henceforth, the conflict between *Ḥadīth* and *ra'y* was aggravated. As a result of the acrimony of this conflict the authorities of the early age were painted as having been divided into *Ahl al-Ḥadīth* and *Ahl al-ra'y*. Among the 'Irāqīs, al-Sha'bī (d. ca. 103 A.H.) has been represented as an opponent of *ra'y*. A host of reports was attributed to him in condemnation of *ra'y*.[36] But it may be remarked that the early trend of reasoning in law belies the proposition that there had existed scholars who based themselves purely on *Ḥadīth* to the exclusion of *ra'y*. Moreover, it is curious to note that al-Sha'bī occurs in the *isnād* of a number of reports which contain the decisions taken on the basis of *ra'y*.[37] Besides, it is reported that he was appointed to the post of judge during the caliphate of 'Umar b. 'Abd al-'Azīz.[38] How can a judge avoid the use of *ra'y*? Therefore, the picture that emerges from the later reports ascribed to him does not appear to be historically true. For similar reasons the name of Rabī'at al-ra'y given to Rabī'ah b. Abī 'Abd al-Raḥmān (d. 136 A.H.) of Medina is doubtful. Mālik narrates a number of reports from him in *al-Muwaṭṭa'* but this appellation does not appear there. This, however, requires further investigation.[39]

Ra'y was the basic and natural instrument to solve the legal problems in the early schools. The differences in law between various centres of legal activity and between the lawyers of each school were generally based on *ra'y*. Ibn al-Muqaffa' portrays a hideous picture of the dissensions among the jurists. The divergence of opinion in law, he tells us, had assumed such a chaotic state of affairs that what was held lawful at Ḥīrah was made unlawful at Kufa. Such differences were evident even in the single town of Kufa. A certain thing was permitted in one quarter of Kufa, while the same was forbidden in another. The schools of Iraq and Hejaz insisted on following what was in the hands of each of them and tried to disparage one another. Even the *Sunnah*, as they call it, is nothing but the personal opinion (*ra'y*) of some individual, not supported by the Qur'ān and the *Sunnah*.[40] A similar picture emerges in the mind of the reader of the controversies of al-Shāfi'ī with his opponents. Below, we discuss a few problems, and show how *ra'y* was at work in the making of law in different legal centres.

Sa'īd b. al-Musayyib reports that 'Umar, the second Caliph, had decided one camel as compensation for injury to a molar tooth, while Mu'āwiyah decided five camels. Commenting on this he says that in 'Umar's decision the compensation decreases but, according to Mu'āwiyah, it increases. If he (Sa'īd b. al-Musayyib) were to take a decision on this point, he adds, he would fix two camels for the injury to a molar tooth, so that the compensation may become equal. Concluding, he remarks that every *mujtahid* is rewarded. It is worthy of note that the opinion of Sa'īd b. al-Musayyib is against the majority standard of the Medinese on this point. They follow the decision of Mu'āwiyah who fixed five camels for a molar tooth. Mālik argues that the Prophet fixed five camels for injury to a tooth; and since the molar is also a tooth, its compensation must also be five camels.[41] In this example we note the independence with which Sa'īd b. al-Musayyib abandons the decisions taken by 'Umar and Mu'āwiyah and gives his own opinion. Of course, Mālik refers to the tradition of the Prophet who fixed five camels for a tooth and not for a molar tooth. Hence, he exercises his *ra'y* and follows the same compensation as for a tooth.

In the case of injury to the collar bone or a rib 'Umar, the second Caliph, is said to have fixed one camel as compensation. But the Medinese do not follow this decision and maintain that there is no known compensation for the collar bone or a rib. They hold that any fair compensation (*hukūmah fi ijtihād*) can be fixed for these wounds.[42] Al-Shāfi'ī bitterly objects to this sort of arbitrary reasoning of the Medinese. He contends that compensations (*diyāt*) were fixed by the Prophet through revelation, and since 'Umar, being a Caliph, takes the place of the Prophet, his decision should not be ignored.[43] In these two cases we observe that they accepted neither Ibn al-Musayyib's opinion nor 'Umar's decision but established their own doctrine. This led al-Shāfi'ī to accuse them of sometimes accepting 'Umar's decision and ignoring *Ḥadīth* from the Prophet, while at other times doing the opposite. He, therefore, states categorically that the Medinese take their knowledge arbitrarily.[44]

According to the Medinese, the compensation for the injuries caused to a woman is half of that for the injuries caused to a man, if it amounts to one-third of the full *diyah* (i.e. 100 camels) or more, but the same is equal to that for injuries caused to man in case it amounts to less than one-third of *diyah*.[45] On the basis of this principle Sa'īd b. al-Musayyib held that the compensation for three fingers is only twenty camels. He was questioned how it was that the compensation decreased as the number of wounds increased. He replied that this was the *Sunnah* (i.e. the practice at Medina).[46] Here we note that Sa'īd b. al-Musayyib does not exercise his *ra'y* in this problem because it is based on the majority opinion and agreed practice (*Sunnah*). This doctrine is attributed to Zayd b. Thābit. On this point the 'Irāqīs do not agree with the Medinese. According to them, the compensation for the injuries caused to a woman is half of the compensation for the injuries caused to a man irrespective of the extent of *diyah*. Their principle is attributed to 'Umar and 'Alī.[47] Al-Shāfi'ī compares both these doctrines and remarks that one opinion may be more correct than the other.

It is interesting to see that he terms the principle ascribed to 'Umar, 'Alī and Zayd b. Thābit as *ra'y*. As regards the *Sunnah* referred to by Ibn al-Musayyib, he is doubtful whether this is the *Sunnah* of the Prophet or of the Companions or it is based on *ra'y*.[48] This example clearly shows how legal doctrines were formulated on the basis of *ra'y* and how the decisions of the Companions were followed in the light of reason. *Ra'y* was the major factor for the differences in legal doctrines of various schools of law before al-Shāfi'ī.

The Medinese employ their *ra'y* and reasoning in accepting the traditions of the Prophet. Their treatment of *Ḥadīth* is most objectionable in the eyes of their opponents. They narrate a *Ḥadīth* from the Prophet but do not follow it. We adduce a few examples to show how *ra'y* was working even in accepting *Ḥadīth* in Medina. Mālik narrates a *Ḥadīth* that the Prophet had said his *Ẓuhr* and *'Aṣr* prayers together and similarly he had combined *Maghrib* and *'Ishā'* prayers in the absence of any fear of rainfall. Concluding, he remarks: "I think (*ara*) it happened on a rainy day."[49] Although the *Ḥadīth* clearly mentions that the Prophet combined these prayers without any excuse, Mālik would not allow this except on an excuse such as a rainy day.

The Medinese narrate a *Ḥadīth* from the Prophet and the practice of the four Caliphs that they used to recite long *sūrahs* from the Qur'ān in *Fajr* prayer. But they do not follow these traditions because recitation of the long *sūrahs* would cause hardship.[50]

Al-Shāfi'ī criticizes the Medinese opponent for his negligence of a *Ḥadīth* in favour of raising the hands while performing *rukū'* in prayer. Thereupon the opponent retorts: "What is the purpose (*ma'na*) of raising the hands at the time of performing *rukū'*"?[51]

By quoting these examples we intend to show that Medina, the home of *Sunnah*, was not free from *ra'y*. Later, we shall show that even the 'Irāqīs criticize this attitude of the

Medinese towards *Ḥadīth*. In Chapter II we pointed out that *ra'y* in Medina was the essence and sum-total of the opinions of the jurisconsults before Mālik which crystallized in the form of the agreed practice of Medina. Hence, one cannot call it arbitrary, as al-Shāfi'ī does. The fact that Mālik narrates a *Ḥadīth* even when he does not follow it, is the greatest proof for the *Ḥadīth-ra'y* complex in the scholarly circles of that period. As an expert in *Ḥadīth* he narrates a tradition, but as a jurist he either follows or neglects it.

The 'Irāqīs are at least on a par with the Medinese in respect of exercising *ra'y* in legal problems. Al-Shāfi'ī calls them *Ahl al-Qiyās* for their frequent exercise of *ra'y* and *Qiyās* in reasoning. At times they examined a *Ḥadīth* on the basis of reason. The interpretation of the *Ḥadīth* of *muṣarrāt* is a stock example of their rationality in law. The Prophet is reported to have said: "Do not retain milk in the udders of a camel or a goat to deceptively show the yield greater. If anyone buys a *muṣarrāt* animal (the animal whose milk was kept held in its udders for some time to show its yield greater) he has the choice, after having milked it, either to keep it with him if he likes it, or to return it if he does not like it, together with one *ṣā'* of dates." Abū Ḥanīfah opines that he should return the animal together with the cost of the milk and not one *ṣā'* of dates. Ibn Abī Laylā holds that he should give one *ṣā'* of dates plus the cost of the milk. The reason for this interpretation of Abū Ḥanīfah is that the milk kept held in the udders of the animal may vary in quality and quantity according to the different types of animal. One *ṣā'* of dates prescribed in the *Ḥadīth* as a compensation for any quality and quantity of milk cannot reasonably be cost of the milk. Hence, the 'Irāqīs opine that cost of the milk should be paid instead of one *ṣā'* of dates. Al-Shāfi'ī follows the *Ḥadīth* literally and emphasizes unquestioning adherence to the *Ḥadīth* of the Prophet.[52]

The problem of giving double share from the *ghanīmah* (booty) to the horse is also disputed among the 'Irāqīs. Abū

Ḥanīfah holds that a single share should be given to a soldier and his horse respectively. He argues that 'Umar's governor in Syria did so and it was approved of by 'Umar himself. He does not recognize as authentic the traditions from the Prophet for giving a double share. He contends that it is unreasonable that the share of an animal be greater than that of a Muslim. But Abū Yūsuf and al-Shaybānī are opposed to their master on this problem. Abū Yūsuf argues that the *āthār* and traditions from the Prophet which recommend the double share of the horse are greater in number and more authentic. Besides, he says, the matter has nothing to do with discretionary preference; otherwise, on Abū Ḥanīfah's view, a man would be equal to a horse. Further, he contends that double share is given to the horse so that one may be able to carry more equipment. This would encourage people to keep horses for the sake of *Jihād*. Again, the share of the horse is returned to his master; hence the rider's share is not less than that of the animal.[53]

Refuting the view of his master, al-Shaybānī contends that there is no question of superiority of the animal over a human because the double share is given to the rider and not to the animal. The preference here is, in fact, of the rider over a foot-soldier. Then he substantiates the three shares to the rider. One, he says, is meant for the maintenance of the horse, another for his fighting on the horse, and the third for his fighting with his own body.[54] This example shows that the same *Ḥadīth* is neglected by Abū Ḥanīfah and recognized by his disciples on the basis of *ra'y* and reason.

Ḥadīth in Iraq no doubt was generally judged on rational grounds. But we find certain exceptions to this general attitude towards *Ḥadīth* According to the 'Irāqīs, fast during the month of Ramaḍān is not broken by eating and drinking in forgetfulness. Although reason demands that fast should break and be atoned for by another fast, the 'Irāqīs do not hold its atonement on the basis of a *Ḥadīth*. On this question

Abū Ḥanīfah is reported to have said: "Were there no traditions available in this matter, I would have decided in favour of atonement by another fast." But it is worthy of note that the Medinese do not accept these traditions. They maintain that the fast should be atoned for by keeping another fast in lieu. Commenting on the Medinese view al-Shaybānī remarks that this sort of decision cannot be taken on the basis of *ra'y* but must be based on traditions which cannot be rejected. He also refers to the consensus of opinion held on this point by the 'Irāqīs.[55] It may be pointed out that the rules formulated on the basis of *Ḥadīth* or *ra'y* were also supported by local *Ijmā'*. This local agreement of scholars was a decisive factor in each locality and distinguished one region from another. Hence, the scholars of every region polemize against those of others.

The 'Irāqīs no doubt are ever apt to argue on the basis of the opinions of the Companions (*āthār*). We notice the same critical and rational attitude towards the opinions of the Companions and the Successors as we have witnessed with regard to the *Ḥadīth* of the Prophet. Al-Shaybānī, for instance, does not hesitate to criticize the opinion of Abu'l-Dardā' on the following problem. Abu'l-Dardā' is reported to have held that the Muslim army is allowed to take food found by them from the enemy territory to their homes. Further, according to him, they can eat it and give presents out of it so long as they do not sell it. Al-Shaybānī comments on this opinion by saying that Abu'l-Dardā' treated giving presents like eating, as a necessity. He, therefore, does not accept the Companion's view on the basis that eating is a basic necessity while making presents is not. He regards giving presents as misappropriation. He holds this view on the basis of several traditions of the Prophet.[56]

In another case, al-Shaybānī rejects the opinions of Sa'īd b. al-Musayyib, al-Ḥasan al-Baṣrī, and Ibrāhīm al-Nakha'ī which al-Shāfi'ī adduces in support of his view. To this al-Shaybānī remarks: "The opinion of anyone of them is binding neither on me nor on you". Thereafter, al-Shāfi'ī charges him with following at times the opinion of these authorities and falling into error. But al-Shaybānī retorts by saying that their ('Irāqīs') view is based on analogical deduction (*Qiyās*) from the *Sunnah* and reason (*ma'qūl*).[57] These examples show that the opinions of the early authorities were not accepted blindly by the 'Irāqī lawyers. Reason and personal considered opinion were the instruments for deciding cases. That is why the 'Irāqīs use frequently the phrases "*ara* (I think)" and "*ara'yta* (what do you think?)" in their reasoning. From the above analysis we conclude that the jurists of Iraq and Medina had a similar attitude, with a difference in emphasis upon *ra'y* in solving legal problems.

The frequent exercise of *ra'y* in law by the early authorities created a state of chaos in different regions. Had it continued, Islamic law would have never reached any state of unity. This diversity argued for some mainstay to eliminate these dissensions and to forge a basic unity in law. This was done through *Ijmā'* about which we shall speak in the next chapter. Ibn al-Muqaffa', having been fed up with the differences in law, suggests another method to bring about unity. He assigns the right of exercising *ra'y* only to the *Imām*, i.e. the political authority. He maintains that people can make suggestions to the Caliph but have no right to stick to and implement their personal opinion. This was indeed a reaction against the free interpretation of law by individual lawyers. He rejects the idea of a "total law" which, he thinks, would make religion too rigid for the people. Therefore, he appreciates the exercise of reason and personal opinion in religion. On account of the differences caused by *ra'y* he occasionally attacks it, but does not want to eliminate its employment. He perhaps intends to restrict it in order to avoid chaos in law.[58]

II

The generic term *ra'y*, the most widespread and natural mode of reasoning in the early period, was, in the course of time, subjected to a number of conditions and limits with a view to arresting its arbitrariness, and to systematizing the process of reasoning. This systematic form of individual reasoning in law came to be known as *Qiyās*.

Prof. Schacht believes that *Qiyās* has been derived from the Jewish exegetical term *hiqqīsh*, inf. *heqqesh*, from the Aramic root *nqsh*, meaning, 'to beat together.' Further, he remarks that 'this is used: (*a*) of the juxtaposition of two subjects in the Bible, showing that they are to be treated in the same manner; (*b*) of the activity of the interpreter who makes the comparison by the text; (*c*) of a conclusion by analogy, based on the occurrence of an essential common feature in the original and in the parallel case.' The third meaning, he adds, in which Ḥellel uses the term (Palestinian Talmud 6, fol.33 a 14), is identical with that of *Qiyās*.[59] This view is not acceptable to us for the following reasons. Firstly, the method of philology has its own limitations and shortcomings in discovering the origins and sources of the institutions of *Fiqh*. If one makes a deep and extensive study to explore in different languages and cultures the terms and institutions current in one language and culture, we believe that one can find a large number of such counterparts. But from this it never follows that institutions in one culture have been taken from another culture. But in this case even this philological evidence is completely unprobative, since 'to beat together' carries us nowhere. Granted that in its technical use in Hebrew *hiqqīsh* had a meaning of *Qiyās* in Islamic law, as Prof. Schacht says, still there is no evidence to show that it was actually borrowed by the Muslims from there. It requires adequate proof to establish the foreign provenance of the term. Since Arabic and Hebrew belong to the same family, this root was apparently common having closely resembling meaning. Secondly, viewed from the sociological standpoint every community discovers its own principles and institutions according to its needs as it evolves them. It would be erroneous to assume that these institutions are always necessarily borrowed from foreign civilizations. Therefore, the correct approach is to maintain that the principles are, in fact, socially conditioned. The doctrine of *Qiyās* must have come into existence as a result of social necessity, although it acquired a theoretical basis later on. Hence, there is no question of borrowing it from anywhere. It is, in fact, a developed form of *ra'y* that already existed from the very beginning.

Although *Qiyās* is a systematic form of *ra'y*, there is a big difference between the two. *Ra'y* has a flexible and dynamic nature. It decides the cases in the light of the spirit, wisdom and justice of Islam. It is a well-considered and balanced opinion of a person who aspires to reach a correct decision. *Ra'y*, in the words of Ibn Qayyim, is a decision which the mind arrives at after thinking, contemplation and genuine search for truth in a case where indications are conflicting.[60] In other words, *ra'y* stands for the decision that would have been taken, either by Revelation if it were to come down on that occasion, or by the Prophet if he had been there. *Qiyās* is a comparison between two parallels because of their resemblance. This resemblance which is technically known as *'illah* (*sharī'ah-value*) is not always defined. One may differ in its determination. *Qiyās* indeed is an extension of a precedent. Its scope, therefore, is more limited than that of *ra'y*. In *ra'y* we find the emphasis on the actual situation, while in *Qiyās* the emphasis is on abstract analogy, whatever the situation may be. We find in Ibn al-Muqaffa' an example of this limited nature of *Qiyās*. He illustrates it by the following example. Suppose a man consults you on whether he should speak the truth or tell a lie. You would certainly suggest to him that he should speak the truth.

Again he asks you whether on every occasion, say, when a person wants to kill another, he should speak the truth and give the pursuer the trail of the fugitive. Here *Qiyās* demands that he must speak the truth but *ra'y* advises breaking of the law, i.e. not to speak the truth but to do what is generally beneficial.[61] This example shows that *Qiyās* fails on many occasions because of its restricted scope. In the early schools, especially in Iraq, *Qiyās* was exercised in a little wider sense keeping itself close to *ra'y*. But al-Shāfi'ī restricted its scope to its lowest degree. He laid down a number of rules for circumscribing *Qiyās* which brought it nearer to *naṣṣ*.[62] From al-Shāfi'ī onward, *ra'y* gave place to *Qiyās* so defined with the result that *ra'y* began to be condemned radically and *Qiyās* began to figure prominently in reasoning.

Qiyās in its early stages was simple and unsophisticated. The idea of logical major and minor premises with the common essential factor had not yet come into existence. It consisted in quoting a similar precedent or an analogous case. It was not rigid and formal as it appeared in al-Shāfi'ī. In the following paragraphs we shall give some examples to show the character and application of *Qiyās* in the early schools and its development.

In the Qur'ān or *Sunnah* there was no fixed compensation for the injury caused to a molar tooth. According to a report, Ibn 'Abbās was asked about this question. He replied that a molar tooth is as good as other teeth like fingers whose compensation, notwithstanding their differences of size, is equal.[63] On this point, Ibn 'Abbās no doubt exercised *Qiyās* but it is so direct, simple and natural that we may call it *ra'y*. An appraisal of the cases in which the Companions exercised *Ijtihād* leads us to believe that their reasoning was characterized by *ra'y* more than formal *Qiyās*.

The Syrian al-Awzā'i generally bases himself on the precedents left by the Prophet or the practice of the Muslims. No doubt the word *ra'y* has not been expressly mentioned in his arguments, nevertheless it is not difficult to see that his choice of the precedents or the Qur'ānic verses in support of his view reflects his exercise of personal opinion. He exercises *Qiyās* in a very simple form. The following example will show its character. Abū Ḥanīfah maintains that if a mother of the child (*umm al-walad*) embraces Islam in enemy territory and migrates to the Muslim territory, then in case she is not pregnant she can marry if she desires, and no *'iddah* is binding on her. Abū Ḥanīfah, according to Abū Yūsuf, argues on the basis of a *Ḥadīth* from the Prophet. But al-Awzā'ī differs from him on this point and remarks that if a woman leaves her country for the sake of God to protect her religion, her case is parallel to that of the women who migrated from Mecca to Medina in the Prophet's time. She cannot marry, he adds, until the expiry of her *'iddah*. He elaborates his argument that the female emigrants had gone to the Prophet at Medina while their husbands, who were infidels, lived on at Mecca. The Prophet returned the wives of those persons who became Muslims and found them passing *'iddah*.[64] This and similar other examples show that *Qiyās* in the early schools was a presentation of the parallel without any specific restrictions as imposed later. These parallels and border-line incidents constituted a major portion of reasoning of the early authorities. The controversies of Abū Ḥanīfah and al-Awzā'ī along with the comments of Abū Yūsuf provide a vivid picture of this sort of *Qiyās*.

The Medinese, too, exercise *Qiyās* in deciding legal cases, but it again is not very formal and rigid. Words like *mathal*, *ka* (like) and *bimanzilah* are generally used to denote the similarity between the two parallels. Even a minor resemblance is enough for them to apply *Qiyās* and to derive a rule from it. This is why they are occasionally accused of immaturity and inconsistency in *Qiyās* by al-Shāfi'ī. It should be noted that the word *Qiyās* itself rarely occurs in Medinese circles unlike the 'Irāqīs in their reasoning. We discuss below a few problems to show the attitude of the Medinese towards *Qiyās*.

Discussing the problem of cutting the hand of a thief, Mālik says that if a labourer or an employee working along with some persons steals the latter's property, his hand will not be amputated. This case is not, he adds, parallel to that of a thief but to an embezzler; and the hand of an embezzler is not amputated. He gives two further similar illustrations. If a man borrows something and refuses to return it, his hand will not be cut. His case corresponds, he says, to that of a debtor who refuses to pay the debt due on him. The hand of a debtor who refuses to pay the debt is not amputated. In the third example he observes that if a thief collects the property in the house in one place but he does not go out of it, his hand will not be amputated according to the agreed practice of Medina. His case is similar to that of a man who keeps wine before him to drink but actually does not drink. No *ḥadd* punishment will be inflicted on such a criminal. Similarly, if a man sits before a woman with the intention of committing adultery, no *ḥadd* punishment will be given to him.[65]

From the three examples given above we can easily understand the attitude of the Medinese towards *Qiyās*. It is important to note that cutting of a hand is a punishment prescribed by the Qur'ān for a thief. But Mālik mitigates this punishment in a number of cases on the basis of *Qiyās*. Moreover, the *Qiyās* that Mālik employs in the above examples is not so perfect and mature as can withstand serious objections. The parallels which he presents in support of his view are open to challenge. In several other cases al-Shāfi'ī criticizes the Medinese *Qiyās*. This will occupy us in Chapter VIII.

According to the Medinese, the minimum cost of the stolen goods for applying *ḥadd* (punishment) is one-fourth of a *dinār*. This provides the basis of the minimum amount of a dower of a woman. Mālik says: "I do not think (*lā ara*) that a woman should be married for a dower less than one-fourth of a *dinār*; and this is the minimum cost for which the hand is cut.[66] This shows that the minimum amount of dower according to the Medinese is based on *Qiyās*. Although this is a problem of *Qiyās*, yet Malik uses the term *ra'y* instead of *Qiyās*. This indicates that *Qiyās* was fundamentally *ra'y* in the Medinese reasoning. The early Medinese, it should be pointed out, held no fixed amount of dower. Al-Shāfi'ī, therefore, accuses Mālik of having been influenced by Abū Ḥanīfah on this and of inconsistency in *Qiyās*.[67]

Qiyās with 'Irāqīs also seems to be a more systematic kind of *ra'y*. It was no doubt systematic but not so formal and rigid as with al-Shāfi'ī. The difference between the Medinese and the 'Irāqīs' *Qiyās* is that, while with the former it emphasized more the generally accepted practice, with the latter it demanded more logical consistency. The 'Irāqīs, in order to avoid inconsistency in *Qiyās*, limited as its scope was, devised another method akin to *ra'y* known as *Istiḥsān*. Of this we shall speak later.

The 'Irāqīs no doubt sought the decision of a large number of cases on the basis of *Qiyās*. It is worthy of note that the term itself which occurs in their reasoning frequently conveys a sense more general than technical. It means rational ground, and legal rule. Al-Shaybānī in his writings often says: "We part with *Qiyās* and follow *Istiḥsān*", or "*Qiyās* would be . . . but we do not follow it."[68] Let us quote an example to clarify the point. The problem under discussion is whether an article or a slave, found defective after sale and use by the purchaser, can be returned to the seller or compensated for its defect by him. Al-Shaybānī holds that if the article is mortgaged or given to some one as a donation by the purchaser, or in case it is a slave-girl, if the purchaser had sexual intercourse with her or kissed her, all such acts, according to *Qiyās*, are indications of the purchaser's assent. Hence, the goods or the slave purchased cannot be returned on the plea of defect to the seller.[69] In this example it is evident that *Qiyās* simply means a general rational ground rather than technical *Qiyās* which explicitly involves a *maqīs 'alayh* (original basis).

Let us give some more examples of 'Irāqī *Qiyās*. In a *salam* (prepaid sale) contract, al-Shaybānī says, if the buyer and the seller differ in respect of naming the time-limit—one claims that the time-limit was named, while the other denies it—the statement of the party who asserts the naming would be accepted (on the basis of *Istiḥsān*), because the party who denies naming designs to invalidate the contract. But, according to *Qiyās* (rule), the statement of the party who denies should be accepted, and the contract be treated as invalid (as no *salam* contract is valid without naming time-limit).[70]

If a person takes possession of two pieces of cloth with the express right of option that he would buy anyone of them for ten *dirhams*, he should have one of them for ten *dirhams*. If anyone of them is lost or becomes defective, either through the buyer himself or by someone else, the buyer should take the one already lost or become defective, and return the other piece. In case both are lost, he should pay half the price of each of the two. This sort of transaction, al-Shaybānī remarks, is invalid according to *Qiyās*, because he purchased a thing not known and not named (i.e., identified). But al-Shaybānī validates it on the basis of *Istiḥsān* only in the transaction of two or three pieces of cloth, provided that the buyer takes the possession and chooses one of them.[71]

Al-Shaybānī validates the sale of wine and swine by the protected non-Muslims (*ahl al-dhimmah*) because they are valuable goods according to them. In this case again he exercised *Istiḥsān*, he remarks, and abandoned *Qiyās* because of a tradition of 'Umar reported to him on this point.[72] In all these examples word *Qiyās* has been used in the sense of general rule or rational ground.

We may now discuss a few problems to show the nature of *Qiyās* according to the 'Irāqīs. The problem of *muzāra'ah* (lease of agricutlural land) is disputed among them. Those who allow *musāqāh* (lease of a plantation of fruit trees) allow *muzāra'ah*, while those who disallow *musāqāh* disallow *muzara'ah* as well. Ibn Abī Laylā permits *musāqāh* and for this he bases himself on the contract of *musāqāh* concluded by the Prophet with the Jews of Khyber. He extends this analogy to the contract of *muzāra'ah*. Abū Ḥanīfah, on the other hand, allows neither *musāqāh* nor *muzāra'ah*. He argues on the basis of the traditions of the Prophet narrated by Rāfi' b. Khadīj and Jābir b. 'Abd Allāh which interdict such contracts. Abū Yūsuf validates *muzāra'ah* on the basis of *Qiyās*. *Muzāra'ah*, according to him, is parallel to *maḍārabah* (sleeping partnership). As the fact of profit and its amount are both undetermined in *muḍārabah*, he argues, the same is true of *muzāra'ah*. He follows the tradition of the Prophet relating to the contract of *musāqāh* with the Jews. He believes that the traditions on *musāqāh* are more authentic, greater in number and more familiar than the opposite traditions. It may be remarked that *muzāra'ah*, according to Abū Yūsuf, is based on *muḍārbah* by analogical extension and *muḍārabah* itself is an analogical deduction from the contract of *musāqāh* of the Prophet. Thus *muzāra'ah* involves double *Qiyās*, or *Qiyās* on the result of another *Qiyās*.[73] This sort of example of *Qiyās* in the 'Irāqī school reflects a phenomenon of free use of *ra'y* in a liberal but systematic manner. Besides, it shows that for *Qiyās* an original basis of precedent was not necessary but it could consist of general rational argumentation.

We find cases in 'Irāqīs where their *Qiyās* is too weak and illogical to stand the criticism of al-Shāfi'ī. Abū Ḥanīfah, according to a report, holds that a female apostate should not be executed. He argues that the Prophet prohibited the killing of women in enemy territory. Al-Shāfi'ī criticizes this analogy by saying that the killing of a woman in enemy territory is not parallel to the killing of a female apostate. Further he adds that the Prophet also interdicted the killing of the aged and servants (*ajīr*) in enemy territory. Similarly, Abū Bakr prohibited the killing of monks during a war. If these people, he asks, turn apostates, would they not be killed? Again he contends that as a woman is killed in cases of adultery and homicide, likewise she would be killed in case of apostasy.[74] In this problem the *Qiyās* of Abū Ḥanīfah is unreasonable and the objections of al-Shāfi'ī against him are sound.

Despite the critical attitude of the 'Irāqīs towards *Ḥadīth*, they occasionally accept traditions which are against reason and general principles. An 'Irāqī opponent of al-Shāfi'ī says that no *Qiyās* is valid against a binding tradition (*khabar lāzim*).[75] A burst of laughter (*qahqahah*) in prayer makes void both the ablution and the prayer according to the 'Irāqīs. The Medinese hold that only the prayer becomes void and not the ablution. Al-Shaybānī in this connection remarks that if there were no traditions (*āthār*) on the point in question, *Qiyās* required what the Medinese held. But, he adds, there is no extension of analogy in the presence of a tradition (*athar*) and adherence must be shown to the traditions.[76] In this example the Medinese exhibit themselves more rational and critical than the 'Irāqīs who are on a par with al-Shāfi'ī when he emphasizes adherence to the traditions. What we wish to point out in this connection, however, is al-Shaybānī's use of *Qiyās*; *Qiyās* is not used in a technical sense but must mean reason in general.

The 'Irāqīs, like the Medinese, produce in their arguments parallels and border-line incidents to support their view. The frequent use of the phrases *'alā tara* and *ara'yta*[77] in their writings refers to such cases. This is also use of *Qiyās* in its wider sense. This shows that *Qiyās* was more or less *ra'y* in a systematic form.

The 'Irāqī law in general seems to be more humane than the Medinese. This is best illustrated in cutting of the hands and feet of a thief. Let us give the details of this punishment. If the left hand of a thief is paralysed, his right hand, according to the 'Irāqīs, will not be amputated lest he should be left without a single hand. If his right leg is paralysed, his right hand will not be cut off lest he should be deprived of both hand and foot at one side. If his right leg has no defect and left leg is paralysed, his right hand will be cut off. If he repeats theft, his left paralysed leg will be amputated. If he does so again, he shall be put in prison until he repents. If a man commits theft four times, his both hands and both feet will not be amputated for this according to the 'Irāqīs: only the right hand shall be cut for the first time and left leg for the second time. For the third time he will be put in prison. Abū Yūsuf gives as reason that one hand and one foot should be allowed to remain to enable him to fulfil human needs.[78] But, there is no such human consideration with the Medinese. If a person commits theft four times repeatedly, his both hands and feet shall be amputated by cutting one each time. If he repeats this for the fifth time, he will be put in prison. If a man has no right hand, his left hand, according to them, will be cut off.[79]

From this account of the doctrine of *Qiyās* in the early schools, we conclude that *Qiyās* in this phase was under development. It was used in the sense of parallel, precedent and reason in general, and the concept of *'illah* was much broader than for the later jurists. That is why, it appears to us, that the term *'illah* is not met in their writings. Words like *bimanzilah* (equivalent) and *mithāl* or *mathal* (likeness) were used to indicate this simple nature and wide scope of *Qiyās*. This simple type of *Qiyās* gradually gave way to the strictly logical *Qiyās* in al-Shāfi'ī's period. An opponent of al-Shāfi'ī says: "One thing should not be extended to another analogically unless the latter's origin, source, and application, from the beginning to the end, be identical (with the original), so that it becomes completely convertible into the terms of the original."[80]

III

Ra'y, in the early period, appeared in another form known as *Istiḥsān*. It was a unique method of exercising personal opinion by setting aside the apparent and strict analogy in the interest of public benefit, equity or justice. *Istiḥsān* is an 'unreasoned preference' to an established law in a certain situation or a decision based on absolute reasoning rather than on analogical reasoning. A lawyer is sometimes forced to depart from a binding rule for a certain serious consideration. It depends, indeed, on one's legal acumen to distinguish where a rule is applicable and where it should be abandoned. *Istiḥsān* is not a whim and arbitrary opinion, but a way to take a correct decision according to the situation. This term is frequently used by the 'Irāqī jurists in their reasoning. Departure from *Qiyās* and acting in accordance with a given situation was a method not peculiar to the 'Irāqī jurists. 'Umar's acts of *Ijtihād*, e.g. stopping the amputation of the hands of thieves during the days of famine, declaring three *ṭalāq* pronouncements as triple divorce, banning the sale of slave-mothers, prohibiting marriage with the women of *Ahl al-Kitāb* in certain cases, and so on, in fact fall under *Istiḥsān*. This term was not used before the 'Irāqīs but the principle and concept was in existence there. The circumstances in which 'Umar had taken these decisions required deviation from an established rule on the grounds of public interest or equity or for similar other reason.

Who first introduced this term is disputed. Goldziher opined that Abū Ḥanīfah was the first jurist to have used it. A concept and method similar to *Istiḥsān* was, however, available, even before Abū Ḥanīfah according to Prof. Schacht, who has produced circumstantial evidence to show this. But the term itself, he maintains, was first introduced by Abū Yūsuf.[81] As the works of Abū Ḥanīfah himself on *Fiqh* are not available, it is difficult to comment on the point. Al-Shaybānī, however, attributes *Istiḥsān* in a number of cases to Abū Ḥanīfah.[82] It seems, therefore, credible that Abū Ḥanīfah had used this term for the first time. Abū Yūsuf, we presume, therefore, had borrowed the term from Abū Ḥanīfah and was not its originator, as Prof. Schacht thinks.

The 'Irāqīs do not generally give the reasons for applying the principle of *Istiḥsān*. One, therefore, cannot know for certain the reasons and the nature of expediency involved in their departure from the established rule. An appraisal of their source-material on *Istiḥsān* shows that, besides public interest, they departed from *Qiyās* even in favour of a certain tradition or a custom prevalent in their region. This does not mean that they are giving preference to the tradition as a tradition, or to the custom as a custom, to *Qiyās*, but because they think that a certain tradition or a certain custom is more in public interest than *Qiyās*. We illustrate this with instances of 'Irāqī *Istiḥsān* that will throw light on its nature and working in law.

If an *Imām* (political authority) or a ruler witnesses a man committing theft, or adultery, or drinking wine, he cannot punish the man on the basis of his personal knowledge until legally valid evidence is established. This is on the basis of *Istiḥsān*—a tradition (*athar*) reported from Abū Bakr and 'Umar. But *Qiyās* requires that the man should be penalized on the personal knowledge of the *Imām*.[83] It is remarkable that, apart from the tradition, the decision taken in the matter is itself reasonable. In the absence of the legal evidence, an *Imām* can execute any person, say his enemy, on the basis of his personal knowledge by charging him with a suitable crime.

Abū Ḥanīfah disapproved of the custom of *Ish'ār* (making incision in the flesh of sacrificial animals) on the occasion of

Ḥajj because, according to him, it is cruel disfiguration of the animal.[84] Al-Sara<u>kh</u>sī explains Abū Ḥanīfah's view saying that he was, in fact, not opposed to *I<u>sh</u>'ār* which is based on *Ḥadī<u>th</u>*, but since people in Iraq exceeded in making incisions so acute that the animal sometimes died in the scorching heat of Hejaz, and that attracted flies and caused intense trouble to the animal, he disapproved of the custom.[85] This is, in fact, an example of *Istiḥsān* to which Abū Ḥanīfah had recourse in consideration of the local custom of causing intense trouble to the animal.

If an infidel enters Muslim territory under their protection and a Muslim steals his property or cuts his hand, the hand of the Muslim, according to Abū Yūsuf, will not be amputated. He says that, according to *Qiyās*, his hand should be cut, but in this case he employs *Istiḥsān* to bring himself in agreement with those who hold this view.[86] This is a strange example of *Istiḥsān* which does not seem to be justified. The reason given by Abu Yūsuf for his departure from the rule is not intelligible. The intention may be, we presume, that he wanted to discourage the entry of foreigners to Muslim territory so that the society might remain immune from their influence.

The 'Irāqīs occasionally apply the term *Qiyās* to the strict literal sense of a word and call it *Istiḥsān* when they take it in a broader sense. This use of *Istiḥsān* is clear from the following illustration. If the inhabitants of a certain town or a fort seek protection from Muslims including the town or fort in the agreement, the protection, according to *Qiyās*, would apply only to the fort or town alone and not to their contents. But al-<u>Sh</u>aybānī holds that on the basis of *Istiḥsān* the protection will cover the fort or town along with their contents; for in its common usage (*'urf*) the term *qal'ah* or *madīnah*, for example, does not simply mean the building, but all its contents.[87]

Sometimes it happens that the end-results of *Qiyās* and

Istiḥsān are the same from the material point of view, but the decision is taken on the basis of *Istiḥsān* to validate something which has been declared invalid on the basis of *Qiyās*. Let us give an example. In the transaction of *salam* (pre-paid sale) a purchaser stipulates that the goods purchased should be supplied by the seller at the former's home after the stipulated time. This sort of transaction becomes invalid on the basis both of *Qiyās* and a *Ḥadīth* which prohibits all conditional sales. This decision, then, is based on *Qiyās*. But al-Shaybānī validates this particular form of transaction of *salam* on the basis of *Istiḥsān*. He argues that even if there were no express condition, the seller was expected to supply the goods at the purchaser's home. The condition, therefore, is adding nothing more to the transaction than what would have been naturally implied in an unconditional sale, since the seller would have, in any case, supplied the goods at the home of the buyer. Al-Shaybānī, therefore, treats the unconditional sale as *Qiyās* and conditional sale as *Istiḥsān*. The reason for treating the conditional sale as *Istiḥsān* seems to be that the whole transaction would have become void if it were treated on the basis of *Qiyās*.[88]

If the Muslim army attacks a cellar or a fort of the infidels, and some of them seek protection of their families and property on the express condition that they would open the gates to the Muslims, these people would be given protection for their own selves as well, although they had not made an express mention of themselves. When the inmates of the cellar or the fort come out and the people who were promised protection state that so-and-so are their family and property, pointing to the best property and skilful captives, their statement should not be accepted according to *Qiyās* (rule), except on the production of the evidence of the upright Muslims. But *Qiyās*, al-Shaybānī adds, is not feasible in this situation because they cannot find upright Muslim witnesses to testify to their statement before opening the gate of the cellar.

Further, he remarks that as the condition of being a male is waived in case of necessity, i.e. in cases where men cannot get proper (direct) information, similarly, the general rules of evidence will be suspended in the present situation for the sake of necessity. Hence, the principle of *Istiḥsān* must be applied. On this basis, he holds that if the captives whom they claim to be the members of their family testify to their statement, their testimony will be accepted, and they will be given protection along with them.[89] This example shows that even rules of fundamental nature can be waived in special circumstances for the sake of necessity.

These are a few instances of the 'Irāqī *Istiḥsān* out of many. These examples show the legal acumen and dexterity of the 'Irāqīs. From the use of *Istiḥsān* on different occasions by them we understand that it was, in fact, a method of deducing what the situation and the circumstances required, and *Qiyās* was the name of the established law.

The use of *Istiḥsān* is not peculiar to the 'Irāqīs but we find its traces in the Medinese reasoning too. The reason for its universal use is the frequent exercise of personal opinion by the early schools. Mālik himself does not use the term *Istiḥsān* in *al-Muwaṭṭa'*, but his sporadic remarks show that the concept of *Istiḥsān* was there. For example, he quotes the opinion of two Medinese jurists that if a widow, during her waiting period (*'iddah*), feels pain in her eye, she can anoint it with collyrium or cure it with a medicine which contains perfume (these being normally forbidden to a widow in her *'iddah*). Concluding he remarks: "(This is) when necessity arises, because God's religion makes for leniency.[90] This implies that he could depart from the binding rule for the sake of ease and leniency, if need be, by providing exception in a problem to the rule. That is why, on the question of compensating Ramaḍān fast, if a man grows aged and infirm, Mālik does not think feeding the poor obligatory. "It is more acceptable to me (*aḥabbu ilayya*)", he says, "that he feed the indigent, if he is capable of doing so."[91] There seems no serious difference between the expression *aḥabbu ilayya* (more acceptable to me) and *astaḥsinu* (I prefer) used by the 'Irāqīs. We, therefore, conclude that the same methodology of "preference" was at work in law in the early schools.

Ibn Qāsim, a disciple of Mālik, attributes even the term *Istiḥsān* to him. In *al-Mudawwanah* we come across cases where Mālik is reported to have used this term, and his reasoning appears quite similar to that of the 'Irāqīs. Such cases, however, reflect the influence of the 'Irāqīs on the Medinese at least in respect of the use of *Istiḥsān*. Saḥnūn asks Ibn Qāsim whether *kaffārah* (expiation) falls on a man if he hits the abdomen of a pregnant woman and causes abortion. Ibn Qāsim reports Mālik as saying that, according to the Qur'ān, *kaffārah* falls on a free man if he commits unintentional murder. But also in case of abortion, he reportedly says, he prefers (*astaḥsinu*) to impose *kaffārah* on the criminal.[92] We do not believe that the *concept* of *Istiḥsān* in Medina was taken from Iraq because the use of *ra'y* by the Medinese, as we pointed out before, was no less frequent than by the 'Irāqīs. Therefore, the idea of *Istiḥsān* must have co-existed in both the regions, but the term was borrowed from the 'Irāqīs.

We do not find the term *Istiḥsān* in al-Awzā'ī's writings or cases decided by him by "preferring" public interest to the established rule. Rather, his strict adherence to law is challenged by the 'Irāqīs on the basis of *Istiḥsān*. The following example throws light on this point. The problem under discussion is whether the Muslims can attack a fort of non-Muslims if they stand on its wall and shield themselves by the children of the Muslims. Abū Ḥanīfah holds that the Muslims may attack them aiming at the non-Muslims and not the children. Al-Awzā'ī maintains that the Muslims should not throw arrows at them, but in case any of the non-Muslims comes out, he may be attacked. Arguing on the basis of the Qur'ānic verse 48 : 25 he asks how it is possible to attack the infidels when the Muslims do not see them. Abū Yūsuf, defending his teacher, accuses al-Awzā'ī of misapplication of the Qur'ānic verse. Moreover, he brings forward a parallel that the Prophet prohibited to kill women and children in the battle; yet he invaded the forts and towns of Ṭā'if, Khyber, and of Banū Qurayẓah and Banu Naḍīr, which contained women, children and aged persons.[93] In this case, no doubt, Abū Yūsuf refutes the argument of al-Awzā'ī on the basis of *Qiyās*, although the parallel does not strictly resemble the point at issue. We, however, think this is a case of *Istiḥsān*, and not of *Qiyās*, because the children of the Muslims can be killed only when some serious social or religious interest is involved. It is remarkable that al-Awzā'ī does not take this sort of interest into consideration but simply follows the rule strictly.

NOTES

1. Mālik, *al-Muwaṭṭa'*, Cairo, 1951, vol. I, p. 303.
2. *Ibid.*, vol. II, pp. 853, 859.
3. *Ibid.*, p. 858.
4. *Ibid.*, pp. 455-56.
5. Al-Shaybānī, *al-Muwaṭṭa'*, Deoband, n.d. p. 294.
6. Ibn al-Nadīm, *al-Fihrist*, Cairo, 1348 A.H., p. 288.
7. Ibn Manẓūr, *Lisān al-'Arab* (s.v.).
8. *Ibid.*, (s.v.); cf. Ibn Sa'd, *al-Ṭabaqāt al-Kubrā*, Beirut, 1957, vol. V, pp. 292-93.
9. Qur'ān, 11 : 27.
10. Qur'ān, 47 : 24.
11. Ibn Hishām, *Sīrat al-Nabī*, Cairo, 1329 A.H., vol. II, 210-211.
12. Al-Shāfi'ī, *Kitāb al-Umm*, Cairo, 1324 A.H., vol. VII, p. 245.
13. Qur'ān, 9 : 60.
14. Al-Jaṣṣās, Abū Bakr al-Rāzī, *Aḥkām al-Qur'ān*, Constantinople, 1325 A.H., vol. III, pp. 123-24.
15. Ibn Sa'd, *op. cit.*, vol. v, p. 350.
16. Abū Yūsuf, *Kitāb al-Kharāj*, Cairo, 1302 A.H., pp. 13-15; cf. Fazlur Rahman, *Islamic Methodology in History*, Lahore, 1965, pp. 180-81.
17. Mālik, *op. cit.*, vol. II, p. 748.

18. Abū Yūsuf, *op. cit.*, p. 14.
19. Mālik, *op. cit.*, vol. II, p. 776; cf. Fazlur Rahman, *op. cit.*, p. 182.
20. *Ibid.*, pp. 742-43; cf. Fazlur Rahman, *op. cit.*, p. 185.
21. Al-Juwayanī, Imām al-Ḥaramayn, 'Abd al-Malik, *al-Waraqāt fī uṣūl al-Fiqh*, in *Majmū' Mutūn Uṣūliyah*, Damascus, n.d., p. 32.
22. Al-Shaybānī, Muḥammad b. al-Ḥasan, *al-Siyar al-Kabīr* (with commentary by al-Sarakhsī), Cairo, 1957, vol. I, pp. 252-53.
23. *Ibid.*, pp. 170, 253, 306, 328.
24. Al-Shāfi'ī, *op. cit.*, vol. VII, p. 271.
25. Al-Shāfi'ī, *al-Risālah*, Cairo, 1321 A.H., pp. 5, 7, 16, 50, 66.
26. *Ibid.*, pp. 21, 24, 63. It is deserving of note that *naṣṣ* in the late works on jurisprudence has been subdivided into four kinds, namely *'Ibārat al-naṣṣ*, *Ishārat al-naṣṣ*, *Dalālat al-naṣṣ*, and *Iqtiḍā' al-naṣṣ*. Further, to indicate the degree of clarity of the meaning of the text the late jurists suggested four degrees: *Ẓāhir*, *Naṣṣ*, *Mufassar*, and *Muḥkam*. These are not available in al-Shāfi'ī's works, and is apparently a further development in *naṣṣ* doctrine.
27. *Ibid.*, pp. 22-24.
28. Al-Shāfi'ī, *Kitāb al-Umm*, *op. cit.*. vol. VII, p. 256.
29. Ibn Qutaybah calls various theological sects *Ahl al-Kalām*. See *Tā'wīl Mukhtalif al-Ḥadīth*, Cairo, 1326 A.H., pp. 2-6f.
30. Al-Shāfi'ī, *Jimā' al-'Ilm*, Cairo, 1940, (ed. Shākir), pp. 13, 28, 46-47.
31. Al-Shāfi'ī, *Kitāb al-Umm*, *ed. cit.*, vol. VII, p. 273.
32. *Ibid.*, pp. 187, 221, 231, 240, 242; al-Shāfi'ī, *Ikhtilāf al-Ḥadīth*, on the margin of *K. al-Umm*, vol. VII, p. 115.
33. Al-Shaybānī, *al-Muwaṭṭa'*, n.d., Deoband, p. 319; al-Shāfi'ī, *Kitāb al-Umm*, *ed. cit.*, vol. VII, p. 291.
34. Al-Shāfi'ī, *Ikhtilāf al-Ḥadīth*, *ed. cit.*, p. 197.
35. Al-Shāfi'ī, *Kitāb al-Umm*, *ed. cit.*, vol. VII, p. 291.
36. Ibn Sa'd, *op. cit.*, vol. VI, p. 251; cf. al-Dārimī, Cairo, 1349 A.H., vol. I, pp. 46, 67f.

    It is remarkable that Ibn Ḥazm gives a number of reports in favour of *ra'y* where al-Sha'bī is one of the transmitters of these reports. See Ibn Ḥazm, *al-Iḥkām fī uṣul al-Aḥkām*, Cairo: 1347 A.H., vol. VI, p. 29. The contradiction in these reports makes them doubtful.
37. Abū Yūsuf, *op. cit.*, p. 25; cf. al-Shāfi'ī, *Kitāb al-Umm*, *ed. cit.*, vol. VII, pp. 162, 170.
38. Ibn Sa'd, *op. cit.*, vol. VI, p. 252.
39. In view of the *Ḥadīth-ra'y* situations prevalent towards the end of the first and the early second century of the Hijrah, we doubt the authenticity of the anti-*ra'y* and pro-*ra'y* reports attributed to al-Shā'bī and

others. Similar is the case with the appellation of *Rabī'at al-Ra'y*. But it is highly important to note that we do not deny the role played by them in the development of law in Kufa and Medina, like Prof. Schacht who has tried to portray them as legendary. (*The Origins of Muhammadan Jurisprudence*, Oxford, 1959, pp. 24, 230).

40. Ibn al-Muqaffa', *Risālah fi'l-Ṣaḥābah in Rasā'il al-Bulaghā'*, Cairo, 1954, p. 126.
41. Mālik, *op. cit.*, vol. II, pp. 861-62; cf. al-Shāfi'ī, *Kitāb al-Umm*, *ed. cit.*, vol. VII, p. 218.
42. Al-Shāfi'ī, *Kitāb al-Umm*, *ed. cit.*, vol. VII, p. 218.
43. *Ibid.*
44. *Ibid.*
45. Mālik, *op. cit.*, vol. II, p. 854.
46. *Ibid.*, p. 860.
47. Al-Shaybānī, *Kitāb al-Āthār*, Karachi, n.d., (Sa'īdī press), pp. 257-58; cf. al-Shāfi'ī, *Kitāb al-Umm*, *ed. cit.*, vol. VII, p. 282.
48. *Ibid.*, p. 282.
49. Mālik, *op. cit.*, vol. I, p. 144.
50. Al-Shāfi'ī, *Kitāb al-Umm*, *ed. cit.*, vol. VII, p. 192.
51. *Ibid.*, pp. 186, 233.
52. Al-Shāfi'ī, *Ikhtilāf al-Ḥadīth*, *ed. cit.*, pp. 336-342.
53. Abū Yūsuf, *Kitāb al-Kharāj*, *ed. cit.*, p. 11; cf. Abū Yūsuf, *al-Radd 'alā Siyar al-Awzā'ī*, Cairo, n.d. p. 21.
54. Al-Shaybānī, *al-Siyar al-Kabīr*, (with commentary by al-Sarakhsi), Hyderabad, Deccan, 1335 A.H., vol. II, p. 176.
55. Al-Shaybānī, *Kitāb al-Ḥujaj*, MS, p. 104.
56. Al-Shaybānī, *al-Siyar al-Kabīr*, *ed. cit.*, vol. II, p. 260.
57. Al-Shāfi'ī, *Kitāb al-Umm*, *ed. cit.*, vol. VII, p. 283.
58. Ibn al-Muqaffa', *op. cit.*, pp. 121, 122, 125 and 127.
59. Schacht, Joseph, *op. cit.*, p. 99.
60. Ibn Qayyim, *I'lām al-Muwaqqi'īn*, Delhi, 1313 A.H., vol. I, p. 23.
61. Ibn al-Muqaffa', *op cit.*, p. 127.
62. See Chapter VIII.
63. Mālik, *op. cit.*, vol. II, p. 862.

'Alī, the fourth Caliph, is reported to have suggested eighty lashes as punishment for drinking on the basis of the punishment for *qadhf* (false accusation of unlawful intercourse) prescribed by the Qur'ān. He argues that when a person drinks he is intoxicated and eventually falls into raving. When he raves, he commits slandering. (*Ibid.*, vol. II, p. 842). This sort of reasoning is more akin to the logical syllogism than to the simple method of *Qiyās*. Its sophisticated constructions in that early age puts the report in doubt.

64. Abū Yūsuf, *al-Radd 'alā Siyar-al-Awzā'ī* Cairo, n.d., pp. 99-100.
65. Mālik, *op. cit.*, vol. II, p. 841.
66. *Ibid.*, p. 528.
67. Al-Shāfi'ī, *Kitāb al-Umm. ed. cit.*, vol. VII, p. 207.
68. Al-Shaybānī, *al-Aṣl*, Cairo, 1954, vol. I, pp. 23, 181, 182, 218, 222.
69. *Ibid.*, p. 181.
70. *Ibid.*, p. 23.
71. *Ibid.*, p. 136.
72. *Ibid.*, p. 222.
73. Abū Yūsuf, *Kitāb al-Kharāj, ed. cit.*, pp. 50-51. Cf. Al-Shāfi'ī, *Kitāb al-Umm, ed. cit.*, vol. VII, pp. 101-102.
74. Al-Shāfi'ī, *Kitāb al-Umm, ed. cit.*, vol. VII, p. 147.
75. Al-Shāfi'ī, *Ikhtilāf al-Ḥadīth, ed. cit.*, p. 117.
76. Al-Shaybānī, *Kitāb al-Ḥujaj*, MS, p. 46. See also Abū Yūsuf, *Kitāb al-Āthār*, Cairo, 1355 A.H., p. 28.
77. Abū Yūsuf, *al-Radd 'alā Siyar al-Awzā'ī, ed. cit.*, pp. 23, 43, 51.
78. Abū Yūsuf, *Kitāb al-Kharāj, ed. cit.*, p. 106.
79. Saḥnūn, *al-Mudawwanat al-Kubrā*, Cairo, 1323 A.H., vol. XVI, p. 82.
80. Al-Shāfi'ī, *Jimā' al-'Ilm*, (ed. Shākir), Cairo, 1940, p. 50.
81. Schacht, Joseph, *op. cit.*, p. 112.
82. Al-Shaybānī, *al-Aṣl, ed. cit.*, vol. I, p. 298. See also his *al-Jāmi' al-Saghīr*, Lucknow, 1291 A.H., p. 84.
83. Abū Yūsuf, *Kitāb al-Kharāj, ed. cit.*, p. 109.
84. Al-Shāfi'ī, *Kitāb al-Umm, ed. cit.*, vol. VII, p. 134. See also al-Shaybānī, *al-Jamī', al-Saghīr, ed. cit.*, p. 31.
85. Al-Sarakhsi, *al-Mabsūṭ*, Cairo, 1324 A.H., vol. IV, p. 138. It is to be observed that Ibn Abī Laylā, Abū Yūsuf and al-Shaybānī recognize this custom on the basis of the traditions of the Prophet.
86. Abū Yūsuf, *Kitāb al-Kharaj, ed. cit.*, p. 117.
87. Al-Shaybānī, *al-Siyar al-Kabīr*, (with commentary by al-Sarakhsī), Hyderabad, Deccan, 1335 A.H., vol. I, p. 276. For more similar uses of *Istiḥsān* see pp. 208, 209, 219, 279.
88. Al-Shaybānī, *al-Aṣl, ed. cit.*, vol. I, p. 27.
89. Al-Shaybānī, *al-Siyar al-Kabīr*, (with commentary by al-Sarkhsi), Cairo, 1957, vol. I, pp. 308-9.
90. Mālik, *op. cit*; vol. II, p. 599. See also vol. I, p. 302.
91. *Ibid.*, vol. I, p. 307.
92. Saḥnūn, *al-Mudawwanat al-Kubrā, ed. cit.*, vol. XVI, p. 200. See also p. 228.
92. Abū Yūsuf, *al-Radd 'alā Siyar al-Awzā'ī, ed. cit.*, pp. 65-68.

Chapter VII

IJMĀ' IN THE EARLY SCHOOLS

We have already touched, in Chapter III, on some of the questions connected with the position of *Ijmā'* in the order of the four "foundations" of law, its relationship with *Qiyās* and its character. In this chapter we shall discuss the concept of *Ijmā'* in Islam with some elaboration of the points already discussed, particularly *Ijmā'* in the early phase.

Before we deal with the main problem, let us briefly mention the classical theory of *Ijmā'*. *Ijmā'* has been defined, in the classical *Fiqh*-literature, in different ways. One definition says: "*Ijmā'* is an agreement of the Islamic Community on a religious point." Another definition states: "'*Ijmā'* is a consensus of opinion of the persons competent for *Ijmā'* (*Ahl al-Ijmā'*), when a religious issue arises, whether rational or legal." A third definition runs: "*Ijmā'* is a unanimous agreement of the jurists of the Community of a particular age on a certain issue."[1] The first two definitions have been criticized by the later jurists themselves,[2] while the third has been accepted as the standard definition. This is no doubt only a theoretical definition agreed upon by the jurists, and it should be noted that it does not represent the actual historical process of *Ijmā'* in Islam. This definition does not allow difference of opinion of even one jurist of the generation in which an *Ijmā'* is supposed to have taken place. The reason is that, according to the classical theory, *Ijmā'* is not complete, if even one person competent for *ijtihād* (interpretation) and *naẓar* (thinking) remains opposed to the "agreed" decision.[3] Further, to substantiate 'total *Ijmā'*' it is said that *Ijmā'* is not subject to reason, but is the "privilege (*karāmah*)" of the Community. Infallibility, therefore, inheres in the total Community and not in the majority.[4] Now, the question arises: Is 'total *Ijmāʿ*' possible on points of detail? Apart from the essentials, we find a large number of points on which *Ijmāʿ* is said to have taken place, but there are still differences among the jurists with regard to these points. This shows that either the classical definition of *Ijmāʿ* is defective or *Ijmāʿ* is only a thoeretical concept.

Again, *Ijmāʿ*, according to the Ẓāhirīs and Aḥmad b. Ḥanbal, is the consensus of the Companions alone. Mālik validates only the practice of Medina, and the Shīʿah recognize only the agreement of the members of the Prophet's family.[5] These different opinions about the nature of *Ijmāʿ* themselves show that *Ijmāʿ* is not 'total', as the classical definition of *Ijmāʿ* suggests. Goldziher remarks that the scope of *Ijmāʿ* is extensive and cannot be strictly defined and limited. The jurists have given, he continues, many definitions of *Ijmāʿ*; but total *Ijmāʿ*, especially in respect of dogmatic issues, is difficult, without difference of opinion, because about a certain point what is held by one group is not held by the other.[6]

Ijmāʿ in actual Islamic history has been a natural process of solving problems through the gradual formation of majority opinion of the Community. After the death of the Prophet and the close of Revelation there arose the need for checking the fallibility of *Ijtihād*. The idea of *Ijmāʿ*, it seems to us, came into being as a socio-political necessity, approved of later on the basis of Qur'ānic verses and traditions from the Prophet. We do not think that the concept of *Ijmā'* as such was available during the lifetime of the Prophet. The reason is that the Revelation and the Prophet's word were the final answer to the problems that cropped up during his days. Therefore, it seems natural that its concept emerged when the Muslims were faced with fresh problems. It was then that the necessity must have been felt to ensure the veracity of their answers based on personal opinion. The first practical example of *Ijmāʿ* after the death of the Prophet is the incident of Saqīfah banī Sā'idah. In this assembly, the personal opinion of 'Umar regarding the selection of Abū Bakr for the caliphate was accepted by the Muslims present there and was recognized later by the Community. The idea no doubt found its expression in this event ; nevertheless, this, too, gave no technical basis or formulation to this concept. By and large, a number of problems arose and their answers were sought by the Muslims on the basis of *ra'y* guaranteed by the tacit approval of the *Ummah*. The personal opinions of the Companions, especially of 'Umar, in many legal problems, were accepted later as *Ijmā'* of the Companions. Thus, *Ijmā'* begins with the personal judgement of individuals (or *Ijtihād*) and culminates in universal acceptance of a certain opinion by the Community in the long run. *Ijmā'* emerges by itself and is not imposed upon the *Ummah*.

Later jurists justified the validity of *Ijmā'* on the basis of the Qur'ānic verses 3 : 103, and 4 : 115 and quoted a number of traditions from the Prophet that we shall discuss in the next chapter. It is remarkable that the Qur'ānic verses quoted in its support refer to the general behaviour of the Muslims and their unity and not to the consensus of the Muslims in the sphere of law, particularly in its technical sense. These verses were not originally understood either by the Prophet or by his Companions as an argument in favour of *Ijmā'*. It was only afterwards, when the theory of *Ijmā'* was propounded, that scholars sought to justify it by means of these verses. As regards the traditions about *Ijmā'*, the most outstanding of them is: "My community will never agree on an error."[7] This *Ḥadīth* is regarded by some Western critics as an invention to justify the principle of *Ijmā'*.[8] It may be pointed out that the Qur'ānic verses and the traditions quoted in this connection are of a general nature, although they have been construed by the jurists to justify the doctrine of *Ijmā'*. Moreover, it is most probable that the Prophet had uttered these words on a certain occasion in a particular context and he might have meant something more general than what is understood by the jurists. From the fact of seeking justification of *Ijmā'* on the basis of this *Ḥadīth* by the jurists it does not follow that the *Ḥadīth* in question is an invention. Further, to justify the idea of *Ijmā'* the jurists argue not only on the basis of traditions but also on the basis of the Qur'ānic verses. But, since the Qur'ānic verses cannot be invented, we criticize them by saying that their interpretation and application are not correct. The same is true of *Ḥadīth* which is not always coined, but might be motivatedly misinterpreted and applied. Therefore, the *Ḥadīth* in question might be genuine but applied subjectively. Shāh Walī Allāh interprets this *Ḥadīth* in a different way. He says that the Prophet might have meant that in the Community there will always remain people who will continue to perform their duty (search for truth), i.e. that never shall all community be in error. He also remarks that the Prophet did not mean *Ijmā'* by this *Ḥadīth*.[9]

The *Ḥadīth* under discussion can also be doubted from a different angle. Al-Shāfi'ī, in the second century of the Hijrah, quotes several traditions from the Prophet to justify the principle of *Ijmā'*, but about this *Ḥadīth* he is silent. He merely states, "We know that people will agree neither on what contradicts the *Sunnah* of the Prophet nor on an error."[10] It is difficult to say whether al-Shāfi'ī had the tradition in question in his mind and was referring by this statement to it. But had he known the *Ḥadīth*, he would certainly have quoted it together with other traditions. This shows that the tradition did not exist before al-Shāfi'ī, but it is possible that his statement might have appeared in the form of *Ḥadīth* in later ages. It may also be remarked that al-Shāfi'ī's ignorance of a certain *Ḥadīth* is not necessarily an indication of its spuriousness. He never claimed in his writings that he had known all traditions and no *Ḥadīth* escaped his knowledge. What is true is that this *Ḥadīth* was not quoted by his time to justify solely the principle of *Ijmā'*. It might have been in existence during al-Shāfi'ī's time but interpreted differently as Shāh Walī Allāh did later.

As to the concept of the infallibility of the *Ummah* in a general sense, it should be noted that this cannot be doubted for the obvious reason that the Community *in toto* never agreed on an error in the past; and should this prove false, the Community would almost cease to exist. For, if the entire Community agreed upon some error (*ḍalāl*), there would remain no righteousness and truth in the Community. It is true that the Muslims have suffered a number of eclipses in the past, but this does not jeopardize the rectitude of the *Ummah* as a whole. So long as some individuals or a group of Muslims have remained on the right path, it should not be said that an agreement of the entire Community on an error has taken place. The *Ḥadīth* in question may be taken as a prediction which has come true so far.

Prof. Schacht maintains that the concept of the consensus of the scholars corresponds to the *opinio prudentium*, (i.e. the opinions of the wise) of Roman law the authority of which was stated by the Emperor Severus (193-211 A.D.). He quotes Goldziher as having suggested that this is an influence of Roman law on Muhammadan law.[11] This view is not acceptable to us. It may be pointed out that the *Ijmā'* of the learned in Islam has nothing to do with the *opinio prudentium* of Roman law; rather, it is quite different in several aspects. Firstly, in Islam, neither the Community nor any other known authority has ever vested scholars with such authority as was vested by the Emperor in the "Opinions of the Wise." In other words, there is no hierarchy in Islam. It is true that the '*ulamā'* have claimed the right of *Ijmā'* for themselves, but this was grounded in the Qur'ānic verse which says that among Muslims there should be a group who should have a deep understanding of the Faith (9 : 122). Secondly, every Muslim who possesses the ability of interpreting law has the right to rethink and reinterpret law. Besides, one can challenge the decisions taken by the learned, if one thinks that they are not in consonance with the teachings of Islam. This sort of liberty for interpreting law and for criticizing the consensus of the scholars, which is available in Islam, is not found in Roman law. To clarify further the idea of *Ijmāʿ* it may be remarked that *Ijtihād* and *Ijmāʿ* are two instruments interlinked in a continuous process. During the course of *Ijtihād* activity it happens that the opinion of some individual in a certain case is so appealing that it is recognized by the Community in general, and eventually culminates in the universal practice. But still there remains room for difference of opinion and for re-interpretation of this practice reached as a result of *Ijmāʿ*, if the conditions require change in future. Thus, *Ijmāʿ*, in Islam, is an on-going process and a continuous activity, and changes with the changing circumstances. In any case there is and there has been no locatable body in Islam whose opinions can be claimed as *opinio prudentium* simply because Islam has set up no such institution.

Ijmāʿ plays a most crucial role in the development of Islamic law. The existing body of *Fiqh* is the result of the age-long *Ijtihād* and *Ijmāʿ* process. This process is still operative and can add to the body of law. The idea that *Ijmāʿ* was confined to the early three generations seems to have developed in the period when the door of *Ijtihād* was closed. The traces of this idea are to be found in al-Shāfiʿī, but he is not categorical on this point. As *Ijtihād* and *Ijmāʿ* are interlinked, it appears that *Ijmāʿ* was deemed invalid when the possibility of original interpretation of law was discarded. The Medieval view that *Ijmāʿ* after the early three generations is invalid, is, in fact, a later concept and cannot be accepted. The major function of *Ijmāʿ* is to unite the divergent opinions on a problem progressively and to ascertain the truth of a *Qiyās*. Its other important functions may be summed up in the words of Snouck Hurgronje: "The consensus guarantees the authenticity and correct interpretation of the Koran, the faithful transmission of the *Sunnah* of the Prophet, the legitimate use of analogy and its results; it covers, in short, every detail of the law, including the recognized differences of the several schools."[12]

Let us now turn to *Ijmā'* in the early schools. As a result of the difference of opinion on a host of problems in the various regions of legal activity, the need for a mainstay was acutely felt by the jurists themselves. In Chapter VI we saw how Ibn al-Muqaffa' was dissatisfied with divergent views of the lawyers and, therefore, wanted to assign the whole authority to the Caliph. Unlike Ibn al-Muqaffā', Abū Yūsuf does not want to ban the exercise of *ra'y* in law by the jurists, but he suggests that the Caliph may adopt any one opinion out of the different opinions on a problem which he thinks best in the interests of the Muslims and in harmony with Islam. In his *Kitāb al-Kharāj* he recounts in several places different views of the legists on a problem, then concludes with the following remarks: "Adopt, O Commander of the Faithful, any of the two (or more) opinions which you like, and follow the one that you think better for the Muslims. This is because you are allowed to do so in this respect."[13] These suggestions of Ibn al-Muqaffa' and Abū Yūsuf reflect the trend of eliminating chaos in law and bringing about integrity through the executive authority. However, this end was not achieved through state machinery but through a process of gradual agreement and recognition of the individual opinion by the Muslims themselves.

The early concept of *Ijmā'*, as we pointed out in Chapter III, is quite distinct from the one developed in al-Shāfi'ī's period and since. The classical theory of *Ijmā'* depicts it as something formal and static and not as a living process of the *Ijtihād-Ijmā'* activity. That is why the *Ijmā'* that took place in the past cannot be changed by another *Ijma'* according to the classical view.[14] The early idea of *Ijma'* was a forward-looking process using the *Qiyās-Ijmā'* complex as a living instrument for the revision and creation of fresh law for new needs.

We give below the views of an opponent of al-Shāfi'ī, which show the attitude of the early schools towards *Ijmā'* developed till al-Shāfi'ī's time. He says that legal knowledge has several avenues:

(1) the knowledge which is transmitted by the people at large (*'āmmah*) from the past generations of people at large (*'ammah*), like the knowledge of the fundamental duties, as prayer, etc.;

(2) the Qur'ānic commands which allow interpretation and hence differences of opinion. In case of difference, he adds, they would be interpreted in their obvious (*ẓāhir*) and general sense (*'āmm*) except where the consensus of people dictates otherwise;

(3) knowledge on which the Muslims are agreed, and have reported agreement of those who preceded them. This sort of agreement, he says, although it is not based on the Qur'ān or the *Sunnah*, stands, according to him, on the same level as the agreed *Sunnah* (*al-Sunnat al-mujtama' 'alayhā*). For this he gives the reason that *Ijmā'* of the Muslims is not based on (pure) *ra'y*, for *ra'y* is subject to difference of opinion;

(4) the agreement of the learned (*Ijmā' al-'ulamā'*), which cannot be an absolute authority (*ḥujjah*) unless transmitted in a manner wherein there is no possibility of error;

(5) *Qiyās*. Two things cannot be compared analogically, according to him, unless strict resemblance is found among them.

He goes on to say that matters stand in their original state unless people are agreed upon their removal from their origins. He believes that *Ijmāʿ* is an authority (*ḥujjah*) over everything, because it is not subject to error. He places *Ijmāʿ* of the people and *Ijmāʿ* of the learned on the same footing in respect of their importance and validity. Since al-Shafiʿī had raised serious objections to the latter, he elaborates it. He says that the *Ijmāʿ* of the learned on points of detail must be followed, because they alone have the requisite knowledge and are agreed upon an opinion. When they (the learned) are agreed, it stands as an authority (*ḥujjah*) for those who do not know. But if the *ʿulamāʾ* differ, their opinions do not constitute binding authority.

Again, al-Shafiʿī's antagonist speaks of the *Qiyās-Ijmāʿ* process. He says that the unsettled points on which there is difference of opinion should be referred back to *Qiyās* on the basis of their agreed points. He does not think it necessary that an actual report should exist in respect of the *Ijmāʿ* of the learned of the past generation on a given point; he regards the agreement and disagreement of the existing generation as an indication of the agreement and disagreement of the previous generation. He takes into consideration only those reports of *Ijmāʿ* which are agreed upon.[15]

As a basis for *Ijmāʿ*, the opponent of al-*Shāfiʿī* considers it necessary that a person be regarded as authority by his town or his region which accepts his opinion as verdict. Nothing stands, according to him, as an authority, except what is agreed upon by the jurists in all towns. Despite differences among them, he accepts the opinion generally agreed by their unanimous consent. By "unanimous consent" he explicitly states that he means the majority opinion and not 'total *Ijmāʿ*'.[16]

We find also that the concept of the *Ijmāʿ* of the Companions had already developed at the stage of these early schools. These early schools took the tacit approval of the Companions and absence of any difference of opinion among them as sufficient proof of the validity of *Ijmāʿ*. Al-Shāfiʿī asks his opponent whether by *Ijmā'* of the Companions he means that all the Companions (*en masse*) say the same thing and perform the same deed or whether he means their majority. The opponent replies that he does not intend total agreement, nor did such an *Ijmā'* ever exist; but he means that if a certain Companion reports a *Ḥadīth* from the Prophet and none of them opposes it, this indicates their unanimous consent and that they agreed that the report had come from the Prophet in the same form as it was transmitted to them. From this, he concludes that silence of the Companions over a *Ḥadīth* stood as their *Ijmā'*. But al-Shāfi'ī is not convinced by this argument and further raises objections against this assumption. This is indeed a controversy over the problem of *Ijmā' sukūtī* (tacit agreement) which is not accepted by al-Shāfi'ī.[17] We shall come to this question in the chapter on al-Shāfi'ī.

The *Ijmā'* of the Companions represents the established practice during the time of the first four Caliphs. These Caliphs, especially 'Umar, the second Caliph, consulted the Companions on fresh cases and announced their decisions in public meetings.[18] For instance, 'Umar is reported to have consulted the Companions on the problem of the punishment of a thief. They reportedly agreed (*ajma'ū*) on cutting his hand if he commits theft (for the first time), and his foot, if he repeats it, and to put him in prison if he does so for the third time.[19] There are cases in which the Companions are said to have differed and later agreed on a decision. We are told, for example, that people after the death of the Prophet diverged with regard to the apportioning of the two shares of booty (*khumus*), namely, the share of the Prophet and that of his kinsmen. Some opined that the Prophet's share and that of his kinsmen should go to the public treasury (*bayt al-māl*). Others held that the share of the Prophet's kinsmen should be given to them. A third group maintained that the share of the Prophet's kinsmen should go to the kinsmen of the Caliph. Finally, it was agreed (*ajma'ū*) that both these shares should be reserved for defence purposes (*al-Kurā' wa'l- silāḥ*).[20] According to al-Ṭaḥāwī (d. 321 A.H.), this *Ijmā'* was arrived at during the caliphate of Abū Bakr.[21] The first four Caliphs are also reported to have apportioned the *khumus* into three shares, and the shares of the Prophet and his kinsmen were dropped. But it should be pointed out that 'Umar b. 'Abd al-'Azīz is said to have given the share of the Prophet and his kinsmen to Banū Hāshim.[22] We do not know exactly the reason for the infringement of the established practice of the Companions by 'Umar b. 'Abd al-'Azīz. But this, in any case, shows that one can differ from the *Ijmā'* of the Companions on the basis of reasoning. From these examples we also gather that there is no difference between the *Ijmā'* of the Companions and their *Sunnah*. We believe that the phrase *maḍat al-Sunnah,* which was so commonly used by the early jurists,[23] and even by al-Shāfi'ī,[24] contained the element of the *Sunnah* of the Companions, putative or actual.

Let us now discuss *Ijmā'* according to the early schools severally. The 'Irāqīs are generally known to put reliance in their belief in universal *Ijmā'*. But circumstantial evidence shows that this was not actually the fact. Apart from the essentials, the actual *Ijmā'* in Iraq as well as in Syria on points of detail was more or less regional as distinguished from the claim made.

In the writings of the 'Irāqīs we find phrases *al-amr al-mujtama' 'alayhi* (agreed practice), and *'alayhi amr al-nās 'āmmatan* (practice of the people in general).[25] These phrases lead one to think that they refer to the consensus of the whole Community. But this is not so, because the cases where they occur are disputed between the 'Irāqīs and jurists of other regions. Therefore we think that they refer to the consensus of the lawyers of Iraq and not to all the Muslims. The 'Irāqīs rely mostly on their own jurists and criticize others. In a number of cases al-Awzā'ī categorically claims that his view is based on the consensus of the scholars (*ahl al-ʻilm*), but this is not accepted by Abū Yūsuf. He asks al-Awzāʻī to let him know whether these scholars were reliable or not. Occasionally, he doubts even their basic knowledge of law.[26] This shows the parochial attitude of the ʻIrāqīs towards their *Ijmāʻ*. This proposition is corroborated by the use of certain phrases which beyond doubt refer to their local *Ijmāʻ*. They are: "This is on which our scholars are agreed," or "I found our masters agreed on it".[27] Towards the end of each chapter in his *al-Muwaṭṭa'*, al-Shaybānī generally remarks: "This is the opinion of Abū Ḥanīfah and our scholars in general".[28] Such phrases clearly speak of the local *Ijmāʻ* of the ʻIrāqīs.

It is important to note that a certain *Ḥadīth* in Syria is well known and agreed upon by the scholars but it is held to be solitary in Iraq. Al-Awzāʻī says that the Prophet had given share from the *ghanīmah* (booty) to those Muslims who were killed in the battle of Khyber.[29] Further, he remarks that it is the agreed practice of the *rightly-guided leaders* to give share to those who died or were killed in the battle. But Abū Yūsuf disagrees with him and describes the Prophet's action in the battle of Khyber as an exception.[30] It is remarkable that in several other cases also, Abū Yūsuf rejects the evidence produced by al-Awzāʻī by saying that it is an exception, and, therefore, irrelevant. Besides, Abū Yūsuf insists on accepting the *Ḥadīth* known to people in general (*al-ʻāmmah*) and to beware of the solitary *Ḥadīth*. This means that he treats the *Ḥadīth* presented by al-Awzāʻī as solitary.[31] Likewise, in many other cases he neglects a *Ḥadīth* because it is solitary.[32] In Chapter V we explained the meaning of solitary (*shādhdh*) *Ḥadīth* according to Abū Yūsuf. His emphasis on the well-known *Ḥadīth* does not refer necessarily to the universally known traditions but to those accepted by the scholars of Iraq in general; otherwise he would not have rejected the traditions known to the scholars of Syria

— rather, agreed upon by them. Therefore, we conclude that the ʿIrāqī concept of *Ijmāʿ* on points of detail was regional like that of the Medinese.

In support of the concept of *Ijmāʿ* al-Shaybānī reports a *Ḥadīth* from the Prophet which states: "Whatever the Muslims consider good is also good in the eyes of Allāh, and whatever they consider bad is also bad in His eyes."[33] In the preceding paragraphs we have pointed out that no idea of *Ijmāʿ* seems to have existed in its technical sense during the time of the Prophet. If this *Ḥadīth* is genuine, the Prophet might have meant something specific in a particular context and not of the *Ijmāʿ* because the idea developed later. Moreover, there is a difference of opinion among later traditionists whether the *Ḥadīth* in question is the saying of the Prophet or of Ibn Masʿūd. It is generally taken to be a saying of Ibn Masʿūd quoted by the jurists in justification of *Istiḥsān* in the later works of jurisprudence. In any case, the *Ḥadīth* is an expression of the ʿIrāqī concept of *Ijmāʿ*. This shows that ʿIrāqīs had a concept of universal *Ijmāʿ* in their minds, although in practice their *Ijmāʿ* was regional and not universal, as has been conclusively shown by previous examples. It is also clear from al-Shāfiʿī's controversies against the ʿIrāqīs.[34]

The Medinese take the practice (*ʿamal*) of Medina as one of the strongest source of law. This is evident from the phrases like the 'agreed practice with us' used by Mālik in *al-Muwaṭṭa'*. It appears that he refers to three types of *Ijmāʿ*: (1) the practice of the people of Medina, (2) the consensus of the scholars of Medina, and (3) the practice of the political authorities. Below we support this claim with relevant evidence.

Mālik allows *musāqāh* ('the lease of a plantation of fruit trees'), provided two-thirds or more of the land is covered by trees. Conversely, he validates the renting of land (*kirā' al-arḍ*) when two-thirds of it is vacant and one-third is covered by trees. He gives as the reason for this principle the fact that people practised (*amr al-nās*) *musāqāh* when a (minor) portion of land was vacant, and rented it when trees were comparatively few in number. Similarly, he allows for a *dirham* the sale of a copy of the Qur'ān or a sword which is decorated with silver, and for a *dīnār* the sale of a necklace or a ring embellished with gold. These transactions have been declared permissible since people used to practise them commonly. He adds that nothing definite has been reported to him about this issue. The agreed practice (*al-amr*) with him, therefore, is what people had practised and allowed among themselves.[35] The phrase *sunnat al-Muslimīn* used by Mālik in connection with the transaction of *qirāḍ* (i.e. transaction of investment loans), and the phrase *'amal al-nās* used in *qasāmah*[36] (collective oaths and fines) refer to the same kind of *Ijmā'* of people at large.

A number of questions have been answered by Mālik on the basis of the consensus of the learned of Medina. Of course, he mentions their consensus often as a corroborating evidence, while he originally bases himself on some *Ḥadīth* or a tradition from the Companions. But we find cases where he has no basis except what he found the learned say so or their agreement. About keeping six fasts during the month of Shawwāl he remarks that he never witnessed anyone of the learned and the jurists (*ahl al-'ilm wa'l-fiqh*) keeping these fasts, nor was it reported to him from the early generations (*salaf*). Rather the learned, he goes on to say, disapproved of this practice and feared that it was an innovation (*bid'ah*).[37] Here it is worthy of note that the whole basis of Mālik's disapproval of these fasts is the practice and the unanimous agreement of the learned of Medina.

On the question of saying funeral prayers for martyrs, Mālik observes that it was reported to him from the learned (*ahl al-'ilm*) that neither are martyrs washed nor prayers are said for them. They are buried in the clothes in which they were killed. Further, he remarks that this *Sunnah* (practice) is applicable only to those who die in the battlefield and are not shifted from there until their death.[38] The 'Irāqīs differ from the Medinese on this issue. They maintain that the martyrs who die in the battlefield will not be washed but funeral prayers will be said for them. They argue on the basis of the action of the Prophet with the martyrs of Uḥud.[39] It is remarkable that Mālik calls the practice and the agreements of the learned of Medina *Sunnah* but this is not *Sunnah* for the 'Irāqīs, who differ from the Medinese. Moreover, Mālik gives so much weight to the idea of the agreement of the learned of Medina that he does not base himself on the precedent of the martyrs of Uḥud but on the local consensus. These examples show that *Sunnah* and local *Ijmā'* were identified in various localities. We have pointed out previously that in *Sunnah* also there were as many differences among them as were in *Ijmā'*.

Let us now discuss the third type of *Ijmā'* according to Mālik. In many places we find Mālik say: "The authorities (*a'immah*) agreed on so-and-so in the past and in the present (*fi'l qadīm wa'l ḥadīth*)." We do not know for certain what he means by *qadīm* and *ḥadīth*. *Qadīm* might sometimes refer to the practice of the first four Caliphs and the Companions, but sometimes it refers later governors also, whose adherence is not obligatory on Muslims[40] according to al-Shāfi'ī. We find, however, numerous[41] cases where Mālik argues on the basis of the agreed decision of the political authorities. For example, on the issue of administering an oath in the case of *qasāmah* he observes: "The agreed practice with us, and what I heard those whom I like (*arḍā*) on *qasāmah* say, and what is agreed upon by the authorities (*a'immah*) in the past and present that taking oaths will begin from the plaintiffs."[42] From these remarks of Mālik and from the controversies of al-Shāfi'ī, it appears that *Ijmā'* of the people of Medina was tremendously influenced by the personal opinions of the jurists and the judges appointed in Medina from time to time and by the administrative practice of the political authorities.[43]

According to the Medinese, the doctrines reportedly agreed upon and practised in Medina were more authentic and stronger than those based on traditions transmitted by a single reporter. On the basis of this principle the Medinese rejected, as we mentioned before, a number of the traditions of the Prophet, and opinions of the Companions and the Successors. They followed this principle so strictly that al-Shāfi'ī accused them of being the arch-enemies of the tradition of the early authorities of Medina (i.e. generations before Mālik).[44] They believed that there was no *Sunnah* of the Prophet which was not practised by the *a'immah* (i.e. first four Caliphs) after him.[45] Hence, the traditions not practised in Medina were not followed by them. In support of their stand they adduced the argument that 'Umar always decided cases in the gathering of the Companions of Medina and he consulted them on many issues. Hence, the decisions of 'Umar at Medina stand for the consensus of the Companions in general (*min 'āmmatihim*).[46] In the chapter on *Sunnah*, we elaborated their contention that knowledge in Medina became visible and patent to people, as the first four Caliphs were questioned about various issues in public—on pulpit, in the gathering of *Ḥajj*, and in the mosques. Therefore, what was unknown became well known to the people.[47] All these positions were challenged by al-Shāfi'ī.

We believe that the concept of the preference of the practice prevalent in Medina emerged in Mālik's generation and it appears not to have existed in the generation before him. The reason is that the authorities of Medina before Mālik like Sa'īd b. al-Musayyib, al-Zuhrī, Sālim, 'Urwah and others had different opinions on several issues. Medina was as good in respect of differences in law as other localities. It follows that there was hardly such a thing as the agreed practice of Medina. Al-Shāfi'ī points out that the issues which were controversial in Medina were also controversial in other places, and those which were agreed upon in Medina were also agreed upon outside Medina.[48] According to al-Shāfi'ī, there have been differences of opinion in every generation in Medina and complete *Ijmā'* never existed there. He believes that the Medinese might have meant *Ijmā'* on some special points (*khāṣṣ al-aḥkām*). But nothing should be attributed, he adds, to those who were silent and did not give expression to their opinion.[49]

The most outstanding example for the criticism of Mālik's opponents on the 'agreed practice of Medina' is the 'doctrine of the evidence of one witness together with the oath of the plaintiff'. To establish this doctrine, Mālik quotes traditions from the Prophet, some *āthār* (sayings of the Companions) and the fact that it had been the practice (*Sunnah*) in the past. But his 'Irāqī opponent raises objection to this doctrine on the ground that it goes against the Qur'ānic verse[50] which stipulates two witnesses as necessary for the settlement of disputes. Mālik replies to this objection not on the basis of the *Ḥadīth* or *āthār* quoted by him, but on the basis of *Qiyās*. He adduces a parallel that in case of the absence of witnesses in a dispute, the defendant is asked to take an oath; if he refuses to do so the plaintiff is administered an oath and the case is decided in his favour. This is the doctrine, Mālik says, in which there is no difference of opinion among jurists of any place. Where, he asks his opponents, is this doctrine mentioned in the Qur'ān? If this doctrine is recognized by all, he continues, the doctrine of the evidence of one witness together with the oath of the plaintiff must also be recognized. He further contends that, although it is not mentioned in the Qur'ān, the practice in the past (*mā maḍā min al-Sunnah*) is sufficient for its validity.[51] This shows the importance of the *Ijmā'* of Medina according to Mālik. It is worthy of note that he does not base himself on the tradition of the Prophet and the sayings of the Companions but on the agreed practice. Al-Shāfi'ī, on the contrary, follows this doctrine not because it is agreed upon in Medina, but because it is established by an authoritative tradition.

Al-Shaybānī tells us on the authority of al-Zuhrī that the doctrine of evidence of one witness together with the oath of the plaintiff is an innovation (*bid'ah*) and the man who first decided cases on this basis was Mu'āwiyah. Of all the learned in Medina, he continues, al-Zuhrī was the greatest authority on *Ḥadīth*. Besides, he quotes Ibn Jurayj on the authority of 'Aṭā saying that cases in the earliest days of Islam used to be settled with two witnesses, and 'Abd al-Malik b. Marwān first introduced this doctrine.[52] Since al-Shāfi'ī is himself an advocate of this doctrine, he refutes these objections stating that the sayings of al-Zuhrī and 'Aṭā are not worth consideration when the *Sunnah* of the Prophet is established through a tradition. Moreover, to prove this doctrine he also adduces a parallel which is agreed upon by jurists of all places. He says that the evidence of a woman is valid in the affairs of women, although it is not authorized by the Qur'ān or the *Sunnah*. To all these arguments al-Shāfi'ī's 'Irāqī opponent replies that the Muslims are more aware of the meaning of the Qur'ān and the *Sunnah*.[53] By 'the Muslims' the 'Irāqī opponent might have meant the Muslims of Iraq; for the majority of the Muslims outside Iraq accepted the doctrine of the evidence of one witness together with the oath of the plaintiff. This also shows the regional character of *Ijmā'* of the 'Irāqīs.

We do not think that the practice of Medina had any preference in Mālik's time over the tradition of other regions. It might have had this preference during the period of the first four Caliphs when the practice of the Muslims was pure and continuous. The Prophet no doubt had lived in Medina and a large number of the Companions settled there. Other regions were devoid of this distinction during the lifetime of the Prophet. This position of Medina could have survived, if the political authorities, after the death of the first four Caliphs, strictly adhered to their practice. But conditions had changed during the Umayyad rule and the continuity of the practice was shaken. We have just stated that the doctrine of the evidence of one witness together with the oath of the plaintiff is alleged to have been introduced by Mu'āwiyah or 'Abd al-Malik. Besides, it is a fact that after the death of the first four Caliphs law was enforced on the basis of the opinions of the jurisconsults. The public was but to abide by the laws executed by the political authorities. Thus, the later practice of Medina was not necessarily based on the *Sunnah* of the Prophet or on the practice of the Companions. We are told that there was no rapprochement between the political authorities (*wulāt*) and the jurists (*fuqahā'*) in Medina; the authorities used to decide cases by their own opinion.[54] In these circumstances, how can one claim that the practice of Medina had superiority over that of other provinces?

The Syrian al-Awzā'ī refers mostly to the practice of the Muslims (*lamyazal al-muslimūna 'alā dhālika*) as a supporting evidence to his original basis, the *Sunnah* of the Prophet. Occasionally, he refers to the *Ijmā'* of the political authorities and the learned. Phrases like practice of the 'Muslims', '*a'immah*', '*jamā'ah*', and '*salaf*', which recur in his writings, apparently indicate the universal consensus of the Muslims, as we find in the 'Irāqīs. But when the 'Irāqīs differ from al-Awzā'ī on those very issues where these phrases occur, it becomes plain that he refers to the local *Ijmā'* and not to an *Ijmā'* of the whole Community. This is evident from the controversies of al-Awzā'ī and Abū Yūsuf in *al-Radd 'alā Siyar al-Awzā'ī*. Here we discuss a problem which reflects the attitude of al-Awzā'ī towards *Ijmā'*. Abū Ḥanīfah thinks that it is permissible for the Muslims to own the *Kharāj* lands, and he does not consider it a disagrace for them. Al-Awzā'ī disapproves of this practice and quotes a *Ḥadīth* from the Prophet and a tradition (*athar*) from Ibn 'Umar. He further confirms his opinion by saying: "The scholars in general (*al-'āmmah min ahl al-'ilm*) are agreed upon its disapproval." In support of his master's point of view Abū Yūsuf quotes a number of the Companions who held the *Kharāj*-lands.[55] In this example it is important to note that al-Awzā'ī refers to the scholars in general which apparently indicates the universal agreement of the scholars of the Muslim world. He nowhere says that he means the scholars of Syria alone. A similar phrase is also used by al-Shaybānī in *al-Muwaṭṭa'*, but there he explicitly adds 'our scholars' by which he means the lawyers of Iraq alone. Mālik is more explicit than the Syrians and 'Irāqīs in this respect. He often says, "I found the learned in our town say so-and-so," which refers to the learned of Medina. Thus, it should be noted that although al-Awzā'ī, like the 'Irāqīs, lays claim to the universal *Ijmā*,' this *Ijmā*' does not necessarily go beyond Syria. In Chapter V we stated that Abū Yūsuf construes al-Awza'i's reference to *Sunnah* as the opinion of Syrian scholars.

From the above analysis we conclude that *Ijmā*' in various provinces meant only the average opinion of the lawyers of each province and not the universal *Ijmā*' of all regions. In each region, *Ijmā*' was crystallizing progressively as a consolidated opinion emerging from the individual opinion of jurists. Hence, *Ijmā*' was anonymous in each region, as no meeting was ever held to reach this agreement nor did there ever exist any such institution in Islam. *Ijmā*' in this phase was so much influenced by the regional character that even reference to *Ijmā*' of the Companions by the early schools does not go beyond their particular region. Abū Yūsuf, for instance, claims that the Companions of the Prophet had not agreed on any point with regard to prayer so strongly as they did on the fact that the morning prayer should be offered until it had become fairly light.[56] This prima facie means that he was referring to the practice in Iraq or to the Companions who had lived there; otherwise the problem arises as to why Mālik and al-Shāfi'ī do not follow this alleged *Ijmā'* of the Companions on this point if it was universal. Mālik and al-Shāfi'ī, it may be remarked, prefer to say *Fajr* prayer in the darkness of dawn (*ghalas*) and not in the morning light. This is a disputed issue, but Abū Yūsuf pretends to stamp it with the universal *Ijmā'* of the Companions. It seems that, for the Irāqīs, the real reason for adopting *isfār* (light) in *Fajr* prayer is other than *Ijmā'* of the Companions. About this point, the 'Irāqī opponent states that two different traditions have been reported from the Prophet. He then describes the *Ḥadīth* on *isfār* reported by Rāfi' b. Khadīj and remarks: "We followed this because it was more lenient for people (*arfaqv bi'l-nās*)".[57] This shows that they adopted the *Ḥadīth* in question on grounds of practical expediency and not because of the *Ijmā'* of the Companions. The 'Irāqī asks al-Shāfi'ī why the latter followed the tradition of *taghlīs*, to which the latter replied : "Of these two traditions, the tradition of *taghlīs* is nearer to the general spirit (*ma'na*) of the Qur'ān, more genuine according to the doctors of *Ḥadīth*, more akin to the *Sunnahs* of the Prophet on the whole, and more known to the scholars."[58]

NOTES

1. 'Abd al-'Azīz al-Bukhārī, *Kashf al-Asrār 'alā Uṣūl al-Bazdawī*, Stanbul, 1308 A.H., vol. III, p. 227.
2. *Ibid.*
3. Al-Bazdawī, 'Alī b. Muḥammad, *Uṣūl al-Bazdawī* (on the margin of *Kashf al-Asrār*), Stanbul, 1308 A.H., vol. III, p. 245.
4. *Ibid.*, pp. 242, 243, 245.
5. 'Abd al-'Aziz al-Bukhārī, *op. cit.*, vol. III, pp. 240-41. For different points of view on *Ijmā'* see Ibn Ḥazm, *al-Iḥkām fī Uṣūl al-Aḥkām*, Cairo, 1345 A.H., vol. IV, pp. 143-47.
6. Goldziher, Ignaz, *Le Dogme et La Loi de l'Islam*, Paris, 1958, p. 152.

7. This tradition has been reported in the classical collections of *Ḥadīth* as detailed below:
   (i) Al-Bukhārī, *al-Jāmi' al-Ṣaḥīḥ*, (*Kitāb al-Fitan*).
   (ii) *Jāmi' al-Tirmidhī* (*Fitan*).
   (iii) *Sunan b. Mājah*, (*Manāsik Fitan*).
   (iv) Ahmad b. Ḥanbal, *Musnad*, Cairo, n.d. (old edition), vol. IV, p. 101, and vol. V, p. 145.
8. Watt, W. Montgomery, *Islam and the Integration of Society*, London 1961, p. 204.
9. Shāh Walī Allāh, *al-Tafhīmāt al-Ilāhiyah*, Bijnor, 1936, vol. II, p. 118.
10. Al-Shāfi'ī, *al-Risālah*, Cairo, 1321 A.H., p. 65.
11. Schacht, Joseph, *The Origins of Muhammadan Jurisprudence*, Oxford, 1959, p. 83.
12. *Ibid.*, p. 2; cf. Coulson, N. J., *Conflicts and Tensions in Islamic Jurisprudence*, Chicago, 1969, pp. 22-24.
13. Abū Yūsuf, *Kitāb al-Kharāj*, Cairo, 1302 A.H., pp. 11, 31, 34, 39, 54.
فخذ يا امير المؤمنين باى القولين رأيت ، و اعمل بما ترى انه افضل و اخير للمسلمين ، فان ذلك موسع عليك ان شاء الله تعالى
14. Among the classical scholars al-Bazdawī (d. 482) is an exception. He holds that one *Ijmā'* can be changed by a subsequent *Ijmā'*. See al-Bazdawī, *op. cit.*, vol. III, p. 262.
15. Al-Shāfi'ī, *Jimā' al-'Ilm*, (ed. Shākir), Cairo, 1940, pp. 49-53.
16. *Ibid.*, pp. 53, 56, 58, 64 f.
17. *Ibid.*, pp. 88-90.
18. Al-Shāfi'ī, *Kitāb al-Umm*, Cairo, 1325 A.H., vol. VII, p. 242; Abū Yūsuf, *Kitāb al-Āthār*, Cairo, n.d., p. 192.
19. Abū Yūsuf, *Kitāb al-Kharāj*, *ed. cit.*, p. 106.
20. *Ibid.*, p. 12.
21. Al-Ṭaḥāwī, *Sharḥ Ma'āni'l-Āthār*, Deoband, n.d., vol. II, pp. 133, 148.
22. Abū Yūsuf, *Kitāb al-Kharāj*, *ed. cit.*, pp. 11, 12.
23. Mālik, *al-Muwaṭṭa'*, Cairo, 1951, vol. II, p. 792; Abū Yūsuf, *Kitāb al-Kharāj ed. cit.*, p. 33; *idem.*, *al-Radd 'alā Siyar al-Awzā'ī*, Cairo, n.d. p. 46 *passim.*
24. Al-Shāfi'ī, *Kitāb al-Umm. ed. cit.*, vol. VII, p. 163.
25. Al-Shaybānī, Muḥammad b. al-Ḥasan, *Kitāb al-Ḥujāj*, MS. fols. 188, 241.
26. Abū Yūsuf, *al-Radd 'alā Siyar al-Awzā'ī*, *ed. cit.*, pp. 21, 41 *passim.*
27. Abū Yūsūf, *Kitāb al-Kharāj*, *ed. cit.*, pp. 29, 43, 92 *passim.*
28. Al-Shaybānī, *al-Muwaṭṭa'*, Deoband, n.d., pp. 71, 78 *passim.*
29. Abū Yūsuf mentions only أئمة الهدى *in al-Radd 'alā Siyar al-Awazā'ī* p. 23, but al-Ṭabarī mentions أهل العلم too. See *Ikhtilāf al-Fuqahā'* (s.v.).

30. Abū Yūsuf, *al-Radd ʿalā Siyar al-Awazāʿī, ed. cit.*, pp. 24, 34, 134, 135.
31. *Ibid.*, p. 24 *passim.*
32. *Ibid.*, p. 41.
33. Al-Shaybānī, *al-Muwaṭṭa'*, *ed. cit.*, p. 144.
See comments on this *Ḥadīth* by the traditionists in the annotations on the margin of al-Shaybānī's *al-Muwaṭṭa'*, *ed. cit.*, p. 144.
34. Al-Shāfiʿī, *Kitāb al-Umm, ed. cit.*; vol. VII, p. 244.
35. Mālik, *op. cit.*, vol. II, pp. 708-09.
36. *Ibid.*, pp. 690, 693, 879 *passim.*
37. *Ibid.*, vol. I, p. 311.
38. *Ibid.*, vol. II, p. 463.
39. Al-Shaybānī, *Kitāb al-Ḥujaj*, MS. fol. 91.
40. Mālik, *op. cit.*, vol. II, p. 879.
41. Al-Shāfiʿī, *Kitāb al-Umm, ed. cit.*, vol. VII, p. 297.
42. Mālik, *op. cit.*, vol. II, p. 879.
43. Al-Shāfiʿī, *Kitāb al-Umm, ed. cit.*, vol. VII, p. 242; cf. *idem.*, ***al-Risālah***, Cairo, 1321 A.H., p. 73.
44. Al-Shāfiʿī, *Kitāb al-Umm, ed. cit.*, vol. VII, pp. 193, 248.
45. *Ibid.*, p. 243.
46. *Ibid.*, p. 215.
47. *Ibid.*, p. 242.
48. *Ibid.*, pp. 188, 218.
49. Al-Shāfiʿī, *Ikhtilāf al-Ḥadīth* (on the margin of *Kiātb al-Umm, ed. cit.*, vol. VII, pp. 141-143; cf. *Kitāb al-Umm, ed. cit.*, vol. VII, p. 249.
50. Qur'ān, 2: 282.
51. Mālik, *op. cit.*, vol. II, p. 724.
52. Al-Shaybānī, *al-Muwaṭṭa'*, *ed. cit.*, p. 363.
53. Al-Shāfiʿī, *Kitāb al-Umm, ed. cit.*, vol. VII, p. 10.
54. *Ibid.*, p. 240.
55. Abū Yūsuf, *al-Radd ʿalā Siyar al-Awzāʿī, ed. cit.*, p. 91.
56. Abū Yūsuf, *Kitāb al-Āthār*, Cairo, 1355, A.H., p. 20.
57. Al-Shāfiʿī, *Ikhtilāf al-Ḥadīth, ed. cit.*, p. 210.
58. *Ibid.*, 210.

Chapter VIII

AL-SHĀFI'Ī'S ROLE IN THE DEVELOPMENT OF ISLAMIC JURISPRUDENCE

Al-Shāfi'ī stands at the turning point in the history of Islamic jurisprudence. With him begins a new phase of the development of legal theory. He did not strictly belong to any particular region of legal activity which might make him prejudiced or restricted in outlook on the principles of law. We noticed in the previous chapters that the early schools were already systematizing the law, each in the particular milieu of its own region. They had no doubt differences among them, but their differences were not basic. These differences were mostly in the details of legal problems, while their basic reasoning and approach to problems, apart from certain sharp distinctions here and there, seem to have been more or less uniform. But al-Shāfi'ī's differences from the early schools are of fundamental nature and, therefore, he cannot be placed on a par with them. The reason for his disagreement with the early schools is that by his extensive study of law and debates with the jurists of different regions he formulated certain new principles of law and strictly followed them. These principles are spread out in his writings, especially in *al-Risālah*. The doctrines of his predecessors which conflicted with his self-formulated theories and principles were rejected by him. Thus, in a way he was pioneer of a system in law which was adopted by the jurists of the later ages.

Here a question arises whether there had existed some explicit and concrete principles of law before al-Shāfi'ī or he was the first legal thinker to have formulated these principles. It is generally alleged that al-Shāfi'ī laid down for the first time the theory of law in a systematic form. His contribution to jurisprudence is claimed by his biographers to resemble the work of Aristotle in logic and that of al-Khalīl b. Aḥmad in prosody.[1] We think that al-Shāfiʿī has been accepted as the unique pioneer in the field of jurisprudence because no works on the theory of law produced by his predecessors are extant now. We find reports, however, which show that there did exist some works on *Uṣūl al-Fiqh* before him. The earliest evidence of Abū Yūsuf's criticism on the scholars of Syria for their ignorance of *Uṣūl al-Fiqh*[2]. Here Abū Yūsuf's use of the term *Uṣūl al-Fiqh* clearly shows that it embodies a definite enough concept. Besides, Ibn al-Nadīm (d. ca. 385 A.H.) while giving the list of al-Shaybānī's works mentions one work on *Uṣūl al-Fiqh*.[3] Of Abū Yūsuf he remarks that he had a work on *Uṣūl* and a collection of lectures (*'amālī*).[4] We are also told that the Muʿtazilah produced major works on jurisprudence opposed to those produced by the *Ahl al-Sunnah*.[5] Wāṣil b. 'Aṭā' (d. 131 A.H.) is said to have produced the first book on the principles of law. These reports show that al-Shāfiʿī's predecessors and some of his contemporary jurists had formulated the principles of law before him. The works of Mālik, Abū Yūsuf and al-Shaybānī on *Fiqh* and al-Shāfiʿī's controversies with *Ahl al-Kalām* indicate that they must have had some consistent theory and a system of reasoning in law before him. In the early *Fiqh* literature we find the key-terms of the theory of law, viz. *Kitāb*, *Sunnah*, *Ijmāʿ*, *Qiyās*, *Ra'y*, *'Amal*, *Istiḥsān*, *Naskh*, *Ḥadīth* and *Shādhdh* etc. These terms indicate that the early jurists in general had some sort of principles of law which were present in their minds but not in writing.[6] Al-Shāfiʿī developed his own system and gave it a defined shape. Except certain additions, the key-terms used by al-Shāfiʿī were the same as those of his predecessors, but their application and interpretation differed in his system. Thus, the claim that al-Shāfiʿī was the first legal thinker who introduced the principles of law would not seem to be correct.

I

Let us now examine al-Shāfi'ī's views on various doctrines in law. In the opening chapter of *al-Risālah* he discusses the position of the Qur'ān in law and proves that it is the basis of all legal knowledge. He thinks that the Qur'ān is the basic repository of all basic knowledge about law. He says that the Qur'ān contains guidance for any occurrence (*nāzilah*) which might befall a Muslim. He adduces a number of Qur'ānic verses[7] in justification of his statement.[8] He takes the commands of the Qur'ān as explicit statements (*al-bayān*) on all matters. He wrote a chapter on *al-bayān* and divided it into several categories in order to show that the commands of the Qur'ān are clear in their meaning, though some are more clear than others. The first category consists of specific legal provisions such as prayer, *zakāh*, pilgrimage, and fasting and clear prohibitions from certain evils like adultery, drinking, and eating blood, carrion, and swine flesh. The second class includes certain duties whose details were explained by the *Sunnah* of the Prophet like the number of prayers, amount on which *zakāh* falls due, and the time-limit for the payment of *zakāh*. The third consists of the legal provisions established by the Prophet and not provided by the Qur'ānic text. This is based on the principle that the Qur'ān made the obedience of the Prophet obligatory on Muslims. The fourth comprises rules derived through *Ijtihād*.[9]

Al-Shāfi'ī studied the Qur'ān deeply and classified the Qur'ānic statements into general (*'āmm*) and particular (*khāṣṣ*). He says that there are certain statements which are absolutely general, and intended to be general; there are other statements which are general, and are intended to be so, and yet refer to certain particular situation or events as well; again, there are statements which are apparently general, but whose meaning does not become definite unless they are applied to particulars. He wrote three chapters on these three categories and discussed them giving examples.[10]

He then divides the Qur'ānic statements according to a different classification. There are certain verses whose meaning is determined by their context, while others whose wordings indicate their inward meaning (*bāṭin*) and not their external or literal sense (*ẓāhir*). Further, he states that the Qur'ān contains a set of verses which are apparently general but the *Sunnah* indicates that they are intended to be particular and not as general. He illustrates all these divisions by examples from the Qur'ān.[11] Al-Shāfi'ī's classification of the Qur'ānic verses was a truly great contribution towards an adequate understanding of the Book. The Qur'ān undoubtedly differs in its expressions in different places. If the distinction between the general and the particular is not made as is done by al-Shāfi'ī, great confusion may arise by a literal interpretation of the Qur'ānic words. This division of general (*'āmm*) and particular (*khāṣṣ*) was adopted by the later jurists in their works.

II

The most controversial point between the early schools and al-Shāfi'ī is the concept of the *Sunnah*. In Chapter V we stated that the early schools took the established usage of the Muslims and the practised traditions as *Sunnah*. We also analysed the reasons for their standpoint. Al-Shāfi'ī launched a movement to eliminate this "practice". He validated solitary traditions from the Prophet and sought to prove that *Ḥadīth* was the only channel for knowing the *Sunnah* of the Prophet. The bone of contention between him and the early schools was the solitary traditions (*khabar al-wāḥid*). He did not attach any significance to the practice of the Community.

Al-Shāfi'ī appears to be the first jurist who advocated the validity of *khabar al-wāḥid*. In *al-Risālah* he devotes two chapters to *khabar al-wāḥid* and in *Kitāb al-Umm* he writes a lengthy chapter to prove its authoritativeness and refutes the arguments advanced by his opponents. He seeks to establish his thesis by traditions from the Prophet.[12] We think that the traditions adduced by him at best support the authority of *Ḥadīth* as such and not necessarily that of *khabar al-wāḥid*; for there is all the difference between accepting the authority of *Hadīth* and between accepting something as authenticated. Moreover, he mentions a large number of instances where a report of a single person was accepted during the Prophet's lifetime. It should be pointed out that this analogy of the Companions' reports in certain circumstances during the lifetime of the Prophet cannot be necessarily extended to later generations. That is why we find some Companions and most early jurists rejecting this principle. From his controversies on this problem it appears that the early schools recognized a tradition genuine if it was narrated at least by two transmitters. They did not make any distinction between legal evidence and the report of a tradition from the Prophet. But al-Shāfi'ī draws a distinction between the report of *Ḥadīth* and legal evidence. He refutes the notion of his opponents that the two are parallel. He asserts that *Ḥadīth* is *sui generis* (*aṣlun fi nafsihī*) and cannot be regarded as analogous to any other discipline. He mentions several aspects of distinction between transmission of *Ḥadīth* and legal evidence. He points out that even the standard of legal evidence is not always two witnesses. He quotes 'Uthmān and Zayd b. Thābit who had accepted the evidence of one woman in a case relating exclusively to women's affairs.[13] He further points out that a legal witness is not himself affected by his evidence, e.g. the payment of debt or punishment falls on others and not on him. But a narrator of a *Ḥadīth* and other Muslims stand on the same footing in relation to obligations and rights that arise from a particular *Ḥadīth*. The *Ḥadīth* is equally applicable to him as to others. Further, he says that the conditions of a narrator of *Ḥadīth* never change, while the conditions of a legal witness may change. He argues that in special circumstances like fear of death caused by disease or journey, an unreliable person may speak the truth temporarily and he is taken into confidence by people. But it is possible that with the change of the circumstances he may tell a lie or become uncautious in his reports. When people can rely on such an unreliable person, the reporters of *Ḥadīth* are more worthy to be trusted because of their piety and scrupulous trustworthiness. Again, legal *Ḥadīth* stands beyond suspicion because it holds the most important position in law. Therefore, according to him, there is no resemblance between a narrator of *Ḥadīth* and a legal witness.[14] The opponent asks him why he occasionally accepts the legal evidence of a person whom he rejects in case of the transmission of *Ḥadīth*. Al-Shāfi'ī replies that he does so because of the importance of *Ḥadīth* and its eminent position among Muslims. He rejects a *Ḥadīth* reported even by a reliable and upright (*'adl*) person if he does not memorize its words and understand its meaning.[15]

To establish the validity of *khabar al-wāḥid al-Shāfi'ī* quotes, among other things, the instances where 'Umar, the second Caliph, had changed his opinion when a tradition from the Prophet reached him. From this he draws two conclusions, namely, the authenticity of solitary tradition, whether accompanied by practice or not, and renunciation of earlier practice when the tradition from the Prophet is established as genuine.[16] When it was pointed out to him that 'Umar demanded at least two persons for the acceptability of a *Ḥadīth*, he replied that there might be one of the following three reasons. Firstly, he might have done so for his own satisfaction, for sometimes in a legal case a third witness is demanded for confirmation and satisfaction; secondly, he might not have known a reporter, hence asked for another person who would be known to him; or, a transmitter might not have been acceptable to him. Al-Shāfi'ī tries to prove on the basis of some reports that 'Umar might have done so as a precautionary measure and not as a rule.[17] He quotes Ibn 'Umar as having given up the practice of *mukhābarah* (the lease of agricultural land for a share of its produce) when he was informed that the Prophet had forbidden it. He contends that Ibn 'Umar did not employ his *ra'y* when the *Ḥadīth* reached him, nor did he say: "This is the practice to which none objected to us so far, and we have been practising it until today"[18]—the oft-repeated argument of the Medinese. He insists that the practice of reasoning on the basis of *khabar al-wāḥid* has been followed by the early generations (*salaf*) and all the subsequent generations up till his time. Finally, he contends that if it is lawful to recognize a *khabar al-wāḥid* which claims to embody a universal *Ijmā'* of the learned (*'ilm al-Khāṣṣah*), he should, *a fortiori*, be allowed to validate isolated traditions because he remembers no difference of opinion among (early?) jurists about their acceptability.[19] He gives an example by which he seeks to prove that the early schools themselves recognize solitary traditions. He asks his opponent whether taking the life of an innocent person and his property is prohibited. The opponent says: "Yes." Again, al-Shāfi'ī enquires of him if two witnesses give evidence that he killed a man and misappropriated his property, what would be his opinion on the same point? The opponent replies that the accused should be killed and his property taken from him and given to the heirs of the deceased. Further, he asks him whether witnesses can give false evidence. He says: "Yes". Thereupon he remarks that he allows the taking of life and property of a man on the basis of the report of two persons which may not be certain (*ghayr iḥāṭah*), while the prohibition of taking the life of a man stands on a much more emphatic basis (*iḥāṭah*). The opponent replies that they had been ordered (by the Qur'ān) to accept the evidence of two persons in case of murder, and, although this has not been explicitly mentioned in the Qur'ān, the Muslims have unanimously deduced it from the Qur'ān. Further, he says that the Qur'ān bears the meaning which is agreed upon by the Muslims and real meaning of the Qur'ān cannot escape the Community in general (*'āmmatuhum*), although it may escape individuals. From this al-Shāfi'ī belabours to draw the conclusion that the opponent has resorted to the principle of the recognition of solitary traditions from the Prophet because *Ijmā'* is something lower than reports from the Prophet.[20] It may be remarked that al-Shāfi'ī's argument is not sound because *Ijmā'*, according to the early schools, as we pointed out in Chapter VII, was not based on a report as maintained by him, but was something universally handed down from one generation to another, and thus, according to them, the present state of "practice" was an index of the *Ijmā'* of the previous generations.[21]

Al-Shāfi'ī, however, does not accept *khabar al-wāḥid* unconditionally, but lays down certain conditions for its acceptance. The reporter, according to him, must be reliable in his faith, and known for his trustworthiness in transmission of traditions. He must comprehend what he transmits and be conversant with the correct wordings, since different wordings might change the meaning of the tradition. He must be capable of reporting a *Ḥadīth* word for word, not merely of conveying its meaning and sense. He lays down this condition because if the reporter transmits the meaning and sense of a tradition, he might unconsciously change what is lawful into unlawful and vice versa. But if he transmits a tradition literally, there is no such apprehension. Further, he says that he must learn the tradition by heart if he relates it orally, and should memorize the written text if he relates it from a writing. If the tradition is compared with that of other transmitters who have preserved the *Ḥadīth* (*ahl al-ḥifẓ*), it must agree with their report. Again, the reporter must not be an interpolator (*mudallis*), i.e. reporting something from a person 'A' whom he did meet, but did not actually hear the particular tradition from 'A' and yet insinuating that the tradition in question should be taken to have been actually reported from 'A'. He will thus be attributing to the Prophet a report different from that related by reliable authorities from him. Al-S͟hāfiʿī regards these qualifications as necessary for all the transmitters of the chain.[22] He, however, does not recognize *k͟habar al-wāḥid* on a par with the unanimously agreed *Sunnah.* He says that there may occur a mistake in reporting a *Ḥadīt͟h* by the narrator; hence the decision taken on its basis is right only prima facie (*ẓāhiran*) and not both really and prima facie (*ẓāhiran wa bāṭinan*) as in the case of the recognized *Sunnah.*[23]

The K͟hawārij and the Muʿtazillah (*Ahl al-Kalām*) in al-S͟hāfiʿī's time raised serious objections to *Ḥadīt͟h* on grounds of its contradictions. But al-S͟hāfiʿī does not regard contradictions as a serious defect in *Ḥadīt͟h* and does not reject traditions from the Prophet because of their contradictions. He tries to reconcile them, as far as possible, either by interpretation or by mentioning different circumstances in which the Prophet behaved differently. Sometimes he takes one *Ḥadīt͟h* as repealed by another. He wrote several sub-chapters in *al-Risālah* to provide illustrations for harmonizing contradictory traditions. As regards the traditions which contain prayer (*duʿā*) like *tas͟hahhud,* he takes a broad-minded view about their different versions. He says that if all the versions of a prayer indicate the same meaning, any version can be accepted. Out of different versions of *tas͟hahhud* he adopts the one reported to have been recited by ʿUmar on a pulpit among a congregation. But of the other versions he says that all of them portray the majesty of God; hence any of them can be adopted. He quotes a Successor as saying that traditions of different wordings can be accepted if their meanings are not changed.[24]

If the traditions vary on the same subject, al-S͟hāfiʿī has laid down certain definite rules to make a selection from among them. Out of these variant traditions he recommends the choice of the one more in keeping with the Qur'ān, for consistency with the Qur'ān is an indication of its authenticity.

If this condition is not apparently fulfilled, the other criteria for judging the authenticity of traditions are applied, the foremost of these being that the chain of transmission should contain an authority well known as a specialist of the traditions, or someone having good reputation for a strong memory. If this is not available, al-Shāfi'i prefers the tradition transmitted through two or more chains; or follows the tradition which is more in consonance with the general meaning (spirit) of the Qur'ān, or with some other known *Sunnah* of the Prophet. If none of these conditions is available, he chooses the tradition best known to the scholars or that which is acceptable to reason (*Qiyās*). Finally, he selects the tradition followed by a majority of the Companions.[25]

Al-Shāfi'ī believes that no authentic *Ḥadīth* goes against the Qur'ān. His opponent presents a number of cases where traditions are contradictory to the Qur'ān. Al-Shāfi'ī reconciles them and explains that they are supplementary to the Qur'ān and shows how they clarify its meaning.[26] He does not agree with Abū Yūsuf who regards the Qur'ān as a criterion for the authenticity of *Ḥadīth*. To him he replies that no *Ḥadīth* is contradictory to the Qur'ān, but it clarifies its meaning. Moreover, he contends that the criterion of Abū Yūsuf contradicts Abū Yūsuf's own position. On the basis of his criterion, he contends, Abū Yūsuf should not validate *masḥ* on socks, prohibition of marrying a woman together with her aunt (*'ammah*), and prohibition of eating the flesh of the beasts of prey having canine teeth.[27] These *Hadīth* cases, however, do not represent contradiction of the Qur'ānic injunctions as al-Shāfi'ī seems to think.

III

As to the chain of transmission, al-Shāfi'ī is very careful about its perfectness. He generally rejects a tradition if some reporter is missing in the middle or at the end. He does not generally accept the *mursal* or *munqaṭi'* traditions

(traditions with broken chains) as valid. In the early days of Islam, even in Mālik's generation and prior to him, little emphasis was laid on the chain of transmission. Hence, the early jurists argued frequently on the basis of *mursal* and *munqaṭi'* traditions and sometimes without quoting any chain at all.

Mālik and the Medinese validate *mursal* traditions. A large number of traditions quoted in *al-Muwaṭṭa'* and al-Shāfi'ī's controversies with the Medinese bear testimony to this statement. The well-known tradition containing the doctrine of one witness together with the oath of plaintiff is reported as a *mursal* in *al-Muwaṭṭa'* and hence objected to by al-Shāfi'ī. Among the 'Irāqīs, *mursal* and *munqaṭi'* traditions are no less current than among the Medinese. The *Āthār* of Abū Yūsuf and of al-Shaybānī are full of such traditions. Al-Shaybānī regards a tradition with a perfect chain as having been repealed by a *mursal* tradition.[28]

Al-Shāfi'ī laid down certain strict rules for the validity of *munqaṭi'* (broken) traditions. His opponent questions him about the authority (*ḥujjah*) of *munqaṭi'* tradition and whether it stands on a par with other traditions. He replies that such traditions (*munqati'*) are of various types. If a Successor, who witnessed the Companions, reports a tradition from the Prophet with the broken chain (*munqaṭi'an*) it should be examined from various angles: Firstly, the transmission should be examined. If the narrator of the tradition is corroborated by traditions of other trustworthy reporters who transmit from the Prophet tradition conveying the same meaning, this indicates the trustworthiness of the narrator. Secondly, if this is not the case and the *mursal* tradition is reported only by a single reporter, it will be accepted provided it is supported by some other *mursal* tradition transmitted by authoritative transmitters. Al-Shāfi'ī accepts it, but regards it as weaker than the former. Thirdly, if no supporting tradition from the Prophet is available, corroboratory evidence on the subject from some of his Companions may be examined. If this is in keeping with the *mursal* tradition in question reported from the Prophet, this means that the narrator took the tradition from a sound source. Finally, if the scholars' opinion in general is in consonance with the contents of a *mursal* tradition, provided the narrator cites the authorities who are not obscure and objectionable, the tradition should be taken as sound.

Despite the aforesaid rules laid down by him for accepting *munqaṭi'* and *mursal* traditions, al-Shāfi'ī does feel their weakness. *Mursal* traditions, according to him, do not stand on a par with traditions having perfect chains. For this he gives the reason that a *munqaṭi'* tradition could be reported by a person who might have been objectionable if his name were to come to light.' Further, if a *mursal* tradition is supported by another *mursal* tradition, the source in both the cases might have been the same and not acceptable to the authorities. Again, if the opinion of a Companion agrees with the *mursal* tradition, it never indicates that the *Ḥadīth* is perfectly sound and beyond doubt. The narrator might have mistakenly thought the opinion of the Companion as agreeing with the tradition; and the same thing is possible in the case of the jurists' opinion.

The above rules are meant for the *mursal* traditions reported by the leading Successors who frequently witnessed the Companions of the Prophet. As for those who came after them, al-Shāfi'ī is not willing to accept their *mursal* traditions in any case. For this he gives some reasons. Firstly, they were not very careful about those from whom they reported traditions. Secondly, indications were found of several shortcomings in the source from where they took the traditions; and this provides possibility of misunderstanding and lack of reliability of those from whom they reported the *mursal* tradition. The reason for his scepticism about *mursal* traditions is, as he states himself, that he had scrutinized a number of such traditions and found them defective. He found that these traditions were accepted from narrators whose similar or even better traditions had been rejected by the late Successors. Moreover, traditions, if they agreed with the opinions of the scholars, were generally accepted even if there had been suspicion of interpolation; on the other hand, such traditions as were not in harmony with the accepted opinions of the scholars were rejected, even when their source was reliable.[29]

It is astonishing to note, however, that, despite al-Shāfi'ī's over-emphasis on the perfectness of *isnād*, he himself could not escape adducing traditions with broken chains in his reasoning. At times he says that "a trustworthy person" reported to him such-and-such but does not mention the reporter's name.[30] This shows that his criterion of the perfection of *isnād* was a formal one.

Al-Shāfi'ī formulated these detailed rules for judging the validity of isolated and broken (*munqaṭi'*) traditions because it was the first venture of departure from the continuous practice of their non-acceptance. Thus, he revolutionized the early standard of judging the authenticity of *Ḥadīth*. It is important, however, to note that the perfection of *isnād* is not, in fact, enough to establish the authenticity of a tradition. Traditions must be examined in the light of historical background and other internal evidence should be taken into consideration. The stand of the early schools, therefore, that a *Hadīth* should be generally known and practised was more sound than the essentially formal criteria of al-Shāfi'ī. We do not, however, underestimate the importance of *isnād* in *Ḥadīth*—a distinctive feature developed by Islamic tradition.

IV

Al-Shāfi'ī is uncompromisingly opposed to the view that the opinion of a Companion or of a Successor may be preferred to a tradition from the Prophet if the latter be authenticated.

It was pointed out to him that some mistake might occur in the *Ḥadīth* during the course of its transmission, and, therefore, it can never be perfectly authenticated. Al-Shāfi'ī argues that a *Ḥadīth* from the Prophet is reported by his Companions, while the opinions of the Companions are reported by the Successors. He, therefore, asks why the report of a higher source (i.e. the Companions) should be regarded as less weighty than the report from the inferior source (i.e. the Successors). Hence, he thinks that the final authority (*ḥujjah*) is the tradition from the Prophet and not of anyone else.[31] He holds that the tradition of the Prophet is self-sufficient and independent authority and does not require any reinforcement from "the practice" as held by the early schools. He accuses his opponents of acquiring their knowledge from the lower source, while he prefers to take it from the higher source (Prophetic traditions).[32]

With the free acceptance of solitary traditions in law by al-Shāfi'ī', he vehemently attacked unrestricted exercise of *ra'y* which was a simple and natural instrument of solving problems before him. He was not in favour of the long standing *Ḥadīth* - *ra'y* phenomenon prevalent in various centres. His controversies with his opponents indicate that he was fed up with the early modes of reasoning which were characterized by frequent employment of *ra'y* and criticism of *Ḥadīth*. He disliked the critical attitude of the early schools towards *Ḥadīth*, and introduced a basis for following *Ḥadīth* unquestioningly as far as possible. He blamed the Medinese saying: "I do not understand why you transmit *Ḥadīth* when you follow whatever part you wish and reject whatever (part) you wish. You narrate (traditions) from the Prophet but do not place reliance on that which is known to you."[33] He held that the "practice" of Medina was meaningless, because the Medinese called "their own opinions" '*amal* (practice) and *Ijmā'* (consensus). He invalidated the decisions taken and the rulings given by the authorities of Medina because they were based on their own opinions and differed from the early Medinese legists.[34] Since *Ḥadīth* was mixed with *ra'y* and it was not taken literally by the early schools, this phenomenon aroused in al-Shāfi'ī a fervour of sympathy with *Ḥadīth*. It was, in fact, the reaction against *ra'y* which moved him to accuse the lawyers constantly: "You neglect much of the little (*Ḥadīth*) you transmit."[35]

Now so far as law is concerned, *Hadīth* cannot be followed in its strictly literal sense as the Ẓāhirīs hold. *Ra'y* and reason will certainly be employed in its interpretation and application. That is why al-Shāfi'ī, despite his denunciation of the exercise of *ra'y*, could not escape employing reason in his arguments. The phrases *'arayta* (what do you think?), *alā tara* (do you not think?) recur in his writings. He constantly criticizes the arguments of his opponents stating that their doctrine is against *Sunnah*, *āthār* and *ma'qūl* (i.e. reason).[36] He raises many rational objections to the view of the ritual purity of water held by the 'Irāqīs and his 'Irāqī opponents is forced to confess that the opinion of the Ḥijāzīs on the question of purity of water is better than theirs.[37] On the question of the validity of the sale of a dog he compares, on rational grounds, the views of the Medinese and the 'Irāqī lawyers. The Medinese report a *Ḥadīth* from the Prophet which prohibits the sale of a dog. But they hold the view that if a man kills a dog owned by someone, he should pay its price. The 'Irāqīs do not accept the *Ḥadīth* which prohibits the sale of a dog. They treat its sale on a par with that of other animals. Comparing both these views al-Shāfi'ī remarks that the 'Irāqīs understand what they say; they can be blamed only for the rejection of the *Ḥadīth* reported by the Medinese. But he accuses the Medinese of rejecting the *Ḥadīth* which they themselves transmit. He criticizes the Medinese by saying that they invalidate the price (*thaman*) of the dog when it is alive and has its utility but validate its price when it is dead and loses its utility.[38] These examples show that al-Shāfi'ī is not against the use of reason in law absolutely. It seems, however, that, according to him, a *Ḥadīth* must be accepted literally when its authenticity is established. His views on this point are unequivocally set out in the following statement: "What is established as authentic from the Prophet, there is no alternative but to submit to it. Your talk and the talk of others as to 'why' and 'how' in this respect are meaningless. God ordained (*ta'abbada*) for His creatures in His Book and through the Prophet as he wished and there is none to question His command. Therefore, people should obey what they are commanded, and to this they are but to yield. 'How' can apply only to the opinion of people which is secondary (*tābi'*) and not primary (*matbū'*). If 'how' is permitted to be applied to the binding command so that it can be measured by analogy and reason, there will be no end of exercising opinion. When there is no end of exercising opinion, *Qiyās* would become corrupt."[39]

Al-Shāfi'ī, however, could not follow the rule of strict adherence to *Ḥādīth*. We find instances where he employs *Qiyās* to judge the authenticity of traditions themselves in case they are contradictory. For example, there is a difference of opinion whether a Muslim can be killed for a non-Muslim in retaliation. The traditions in this connection are contradictory. Al-Shāfi'ī argues on the basis of a *Ḥadīth* which says that a Muslim should not be killed in retaliation for a non-Muslim. He rejects, on the basis of reason, the *Ḥadīth* adduced by the 'Irāqīs, and contends that a non-Muslim is separated from a Muslim in several respects. Firstly, a non-Muslim is deprived of a share from booty, even if he fights alongside of the Muslims. Secondly, *jizyah* (poll-tax) is levied on a non-Muslim as a disgrace, while *Zakāh* is levied on a Muslim by which God purifies him. Thirdly, a non-Muslim is not allowed to marry a Muslim woman, while a Muslim can marry a woman of the *Ahl al-*

Kitāb.[40] Similarly, in another case he says: "Our *Ḥadīth* is more worthy to be followed because it is supported by *Qiyās* (reason) and opinion of people in general (*qawl al-'āmmah*)."[41] Al-Shāfi'ī no doubt claims to show unquestioning adherence (*ittibā'*) to the traditions of the Prophet and accepts them generally without any criticism. The *Ḥadīth* of *muṣarrāh* (i.e. a case where the seller of an animal deceives the purchaser by not milking the animal for a time prior to the sale in order to show the quantity of the yield of milk greater than it actually is), as is shown in Chapter VI, is not followed literally by the 'Irāqīs because it is irrational. But al-Shāfi'ī follows it literally and replies to them that he adheres to this tradition because of the obedience to the Prophet (*ittibā'*) and rejects *Qiyās* in this case.[42] We have, however, seen above that in a number of cases he rejects the traditions adduced by his opponents on rational grounds. Thus, his claim of unquestioning literal adherence to the traditions of the Prophet seems to be based on the formal requirements of his theory rather than on genuine grounds.

V

Al-Shāfi'ī refutes arbitrary *ra'y* to pave the way for *Qiyās*. He divides legal knowledge into two kinds, viz. *'ittibā'* (adherence) and *istinbāṭ* (inference). Under *ittibā'*, he says, one should primarily follow the Qur'ān then the *Sunnah*, and, finally, the unanimously agreed opinions of the early generations (*'āmmat salafinā*). If *ittibā'* is not possible in a case, he allows the exercise of *Qiyās* on the basis of the Qur'ān, then on *Sunnah* and lastly on *Ijmā'* of the early generations. He regards *Qiyās* as the last basis of law and distinguishes it from *ra'y* and other allied terms.[43] In Chapter VI, we pointed out that the early schools exercised *Qiyās* in a more liberal manner and it was closer to *ra'y* than to *naṣṣ*. With the restrictions that al-Shāfi'ī placed on *Qiyās* it became a *quasi-naṣṣ* and lost its efficacy for the development of law. By limiting the scope of *Qiyās*, he wants to bring about systematic reasoning in law and to eliminate chaos, which resulted from the free use of *ra'y*. That is why he justifies the validity of *Qiyās* on the basis of the Qur'ān and regards its exercise as an obligatory duty of Muslims. We come across the justification of *Qiyās* on the basis of the Qur'ān for the first time in al-Shāfi'ī. We have already pointed out, in Chapter III, that *Qiyās* and *Ijtihād* in the first place must have been a social necessity for solving fresh problems, but that later they were justified on the basis of the Qur'ān. Moreover, the verses which al-Shāfi'ī quotes from the Qur'ān do not speak of *Qiyās*. In any case, he narrowed *Qiyās* and made it so technical that it became virtually ineffective. About him Margoliouth says: "Although not many Greek books can have been rendered into Arabic before the end of the second century, Shāfi'ī displays some acquaintance with the Aristotelian logic, and is clear about the meaning of the words 'genus' and 'species'.[44] We do not, however, think that al-Shāfi'ī was influenced in his views of *Qiyās* by Greek logic. Our conclusion is that his narrow view of *Qiyās* was a reaction against the free interpretation of law by the early schools. This free flow he sought to restrict in two ways. Firstly, he laid stress on *naṣṣ* and on adherence to the traditions of the Prophet. Secondly, he rejected *ra'y* and limited the scope of *Qiyās*. In the following paragraphs we shall examine a few problems which involve *Qiyās* and will show the distinction between al-Shāfi'ī and his opponents on this principle.

Al-Shāfi'ī quotes a *Ḥadīth* from the Prophet which says that if a person sells a pollinated palm-tree, the fruit belongs to the seller unless the purchaser expressly stipulated that it is also covered by the sale transaction. From this he infers that the fruit of an unpollinated palm-tree belongs to the purchaser. The 'Irāqīs differ from him on this point. They hold the view that the fruit of an unpollinated tree belongs to the seller like that of the pollinated tree. The *Sharī'ah*-

value (*'illah*) in this case, according to them, is the separation of fruit from the tree. They contend that in the case of the sale of a pregnant slave-girl the child during the period of pregnancy belongs to the purchaser, but when it is born and is separated from her mother belongs to the seller. Similarly, when a tree is pollinated, the fruit ceases to remain hidden in it, but may be assumed as separated from it. Therefore, they do not see any difference between a pollinated tree and a tree bearing fruit without pollination. Al-Shāfi'ī's approach to this *Ḥadīth* is quite literal. He argues that the *Ḥadīth* in question distinguishes the fruit born without pollination from those born after pollination. Therefore, these two cases are not parallel as the 'Irāqīs think. His following remarks indicate how he avoids *Qiyās* and adheres to the *Ḥadīth* literally. He says: "We follow the command of the Prophet in the way he ordered, and do not extend the analogy of one to the other to make them equal; nor do we base these two cases on the (analogy of the) sale of the child of the slave-mother. We do not compare (*naqīs*) one *Sunnah* with another *Sunnah*, but implement each *Sunnah* properly as far as possible; and we do not belittle this *Ḥadīth* by *Qiyās*".[45]

Qiyās, according to the Medinese, was akin to *ra'y*; hence it was not strictly consistent and formal. Their argument involving *Qiyās* fall short of al-Shāfi'ī's yard-stick of *Qiyās*. Let us give an example. According to the Medinese, performance of *Ḥajj* by proxy is unlawful in the lifetime of a person. It is lawful only in case he dies or leaves a will to that effect. They derive this doctrine from the saying of Ibn 'Umar that one should not say prayer or keep fast on behalf of another person by the same logic; but this is not allowed by them. Besides, he argues that if a man leaves a will to say prayers and to keep fasts on his behalf, it would not be valid according to them.[46] By such criticism al-Shāfi'ī intends to show that the Medinese themselves distinguish *Ḥajj* from prayer and fast. Therefore, their *Qiyās* is inconsistent. In the previous case al-Shāfiʿī laid down the principle not to compare one *Sunnah* with another *Sunnah*, and in the present case he prohibits comparison between two institutions (*sharīʿah*). We pointed out earlier, in Chapter VI, that *Qiyās*, according to the early schools, was nothing but the presentation of border-line parallels which had no strict resemblance with each other, whereas al-Shāfiʿī understands by *Qiyās* identical or quasi-identical cases. Al-Shāfiʿī does not approve of the procedure of the early jurists. He wants perfect resemblance in both the cases. From the above examples, it is evident that he intends to avoid *Qiyās* as far as possible and to follow the traditions literally as they stand.

In Chapter VI, we established that a *Qiyās*, according to the early schools, could be based on the result of another *Qiyās*. We gave an illustration of the contract of *muzāraʿah* (lease of agricultural land). Al-Shāfiʿī is opposed to this view. According to him, *Qiyās* must stand on some original and independent basis and not on a derivative and analogical conclusion. He discusses in detail the problem of *muzāraʿah* and refutes the *Qiyās* of some of the ʿIrāqī scholars. Ibn Abī Laylā validates the contract of *muzāraʿah* on the basis that the Prophet had concluded a similar contract with the Jews of Khyber. Secondly, he argues, it corresponds to the contract of *muḍārabah* (sleeping partnership) which was practised by ʿUmar, Ibn Musʿūd and ʿUthmān. He says that *muzāraʿah* is based on *Qiyās* together with a tradition (*athar*). Moreover, he refers to Saʿd b. Abī Waqqāṣ and Ibn Masʿūd as having practised *muzāraʿah*. Al-Shāfiʿī invalidates *muzāraʿah* because the Prophet prohibited it like *muḥāqalah* (barter in corn) and *mukhābarah* (lease of agricultural land for a share of its produce) but he validates *musāqāh* (lease of a plantation of fruit trees) on the basis of the Prophet's contract with the Jews of Khyber. He does not regard *muzāraʿah* as a parallel to *musāqāh*. Further, he does not allow analogical comparison between a tradition from the Prophet and a tradition from the Companions. This is also a new idea of al-Shāfi'ī in respect of *Qiyās*. Thus, there remains the problem of *muḍārabah* which he himself validates on the basis of *Qiyās*, i.e. contract of the Prophet with the Jews of Khyber. He says that *muḍārabah* is valid derivatively and analogically (*taba'an* and *qiyāsan*) and not originally and independently (*matbū'an* and *maqīsan 'alayhā*). He, therefore, accuses Ibn Abī Laylā of performing incorrect *Qiyās* in the case of *muzāra'ah* because it is based on *muḍārabah* which is itself based on *musāqāh*.[47] This example shows al-Shāfi'ī's narrow view of *Qiyās*.

Al-Shāfi'ī has a peculiar kind of *Qiyās* which is not traceable in the early schools nor even in the classical theory of *Qiyās*. According to him, if a little of anything is declared unlawful by God or by the Prophet, the greater quantity of it should also be taken as unlawful. Similarly, if a small act of obedience is praised, the greater of it deserves also to be praiseworthy. This is due to the superiority of 'much' over 'little'. Similarly, he holds the view that if much of anything is permitted, the little of it should equally be taken to be so. He regards this sort of *Qiyās* as the strongest of all. Al-Shāfi'ī elaborates it by giving several illustrations. Here we mention one of them. He says that, according to a tradition, it has been prohibited to shed the blood of a believer, to insult him, and to take away his property. The *Ḥadīth* also requires to have good faith about him. Now, something more contrary to his good, say, speaking ill of him, should be all the more unlawful. The degree of prohibition will increase in proportion to the increase in the evil done to him. Besides, he says that some scholars do not regard it as *Qiyās*, because 'little' and 'much' of a thing in respect of appreciation or condemnation are one and the same thing and not two things which make *Qiyās* possible. They allow the only usual form of *Qiyās* as *Qiyās*.[48]

There are certain injunctions where al-Shāfi'ī does not allow the application of human reason. Hence, those injunctions cannot be extended analogically. He says that if there is some general rule in the Qur'ān or the *Sunnah* on some point, but the Prophet made an exception from that rule, that exception should not be generalized. He gives the illustration of performing *masḥ* on shoes which he regards as an exception from the general rule of washing feet in ablution. But one should not perform *masḥ* on the head-wear, according to him, on the basis of the *masḥ* on shoes. He gives similar other examples from *Ḥadīth* where the Prophet made exceptions from general rules. Al-Shāfi'ī describes this sort of exception as *ta'abbud*.[49] We find the concept of *ta'abbud* in Abū Yūsuf too, but the term is not available there.[50]

Al-Shāfi'ī does not permit any person to exercise *Qiyās* unless he is well-equipped with the knowledge of the injunctions of the Qur'ān, its prescribed duties, its ethical principles, its abrogating and abrogated verses, its general and particular rules, and in general, its right guidance. Further, he suggests that the ambiguous verses of the Qur'ān should be interpreted in the light of the *Sunnah* of the Prophet; if no such *Sunnah* is available, they should be interpreted on the basis of the *Ijmā'* of the Muslims; and if this is also not possible, recourse may be had to *Qiyās*. According to him, a person who exercises *Qiyās* must be conversant with the established *Sunnah*, the opinions of his predecessors, the agreement and disagreement of the people, and he must have sufficient knowledge of the Arabic language. Moreover, he must be sound in mind, able to distinguish between closely parallel precedents; he should not be hasty in expressing an opinion unless he is confident of its correctness.

He does not allow the exercise of *Qiyās* to a man who is perfect in reason but lacks other qualities mentioned above. For this he gives the reason that he might be ignorant of the original precedeht to which he applies *Qiyās*; just as a jurist having sound mind may not be permitted to assess the price of a *dirham* if he is unaware of the market prices. Further, a person who possesses legal knowledge through memory, but does not understand it, should not be allowed to exercise *Qiyās* because he may be mistaken in understanding the meaning of a precedent.

Again, according to him, a person who is good in memory, but is not mature in mind, or is wanting in knowledge of the Arabic language, should not be allowed to exercise *Qiyās*. Lack of these two qualities is very serious. Al-Shāfi'ī regards them as fundamental, being an instrument (*ālah*) for the application of *Qiyās*. Despite all these restrictions and conditions suggested by him for the application of *Qiyās*, he says that it may not be maintained that one should always show adherence (*ittibā'*) and not make use of *Qiyās*.[51]

By prescribing the qualifications and limits for application of *Qiyās* al-Shāfi'ī tends to restrict free use of personal opinion in law. This limited scope of *Qiyās* kept the answers to the problems tied closely to the literal text of the Qur'ān and the *Sunnah*. He divides *Qiyās* into two kinds: (1) that wherein the parallel is close, or, indeed, nearly identical in its essence with the original; (2) that wherein a case has resemblances to several original models. In this latter case that which is more close in resemblance shall be taken as the model for the question in hand.[52] This division shows that even in analogical deductions he wants to keep the parallel nearest to the original.

According to al-Shāfi'ī, *Qiyās* and *Ijtihād* are two terms conveying the same meaning. Defining *Ijtihād* he says that if a Muslim is faced with a given situation, he should follow the express binding injunction if available; otherwise he should try to seek by *Ijtihād* the indications which lead him to truth. He says that *Ijtihād* is nothing but *Qiyās*. Further, he remarks that *Ijtihād* is always intended for searching something which cannot be found without indications and such indications (*dalā'il*) constitute *Qiyās*. In other words, the endeavour which a person makes in seeking an answer to a question is

Ijtihād, while the indications on which he bases his search, i.e. the method of search, is *Qiyās.* He does not allow anyone to take any decision on the basis of his liking (*mustaḥsinan*) without *Ijtihād,* because, he contends, no one is permissible to say one's prayer facing any direction one likes in case the direction of the *Ka'bah* is not known, but one should try to face the direction of the *Ka'bah.*[53] We give an example which throws light on his view of *Ijtihād.* While discussing the question of allotting spoils to a killer of an ememy in battle, al-Shāfi'ī refutes his opponent's argument that the matter depends on the discretion of the *Imām* (political authority). On the occasion of the battle of Ḥunayn, he (al-Shāfi'ī) contends, the Prophet had announced that the spoils belong to the killer provided he produces evidence. He regards this announcement of the Prophet as a general principle and not an *Ijtihād* without proof (*dalālah*). Further, he asks, if the spoils do not belong to the killer but to those who are present in the battle, how would the *Imām* exercise *Ijtihād* about giving the spoils sometimes to the killer and sometimes to some other person. Again, when an *Imām* neglects the *Sunnah,* on what basis will he exercise *Ijtihād*? *Ijtihād,* he asserts, is, in fact, *Qiyās* on the *Sunnah* and therefore when *Ijtihād* which is subservient to the *Sunnah* is binding, the *Sunnah* should be all the more binding on him[54]. This example again shows that al-Shāfi'ī wants to follow the *Sunnah* literally as far as possible, and wants to resort to *Ijtihād* only when the literal *Sunnah* becomes utterly unacceptable.

To establish the validity of *Itjihād,* al-Shāfi'ī seeks justification from the Qur'ān. He quotes the same verses which he quotes in support of *Qiyās.* Moreover, he justifies *Ijtihād* by quoting two traditions from the Prophet, namely, the well-known tradition of *Mu'ādh* b. Jabal[55] and the tradition which speaks of different degrees of reward for a *mujtahid* depending whether his *Ijtihād* is correct or not. It should be noted that the idea of *Ijtihād* emerged among the Muslims when they were faced with new conditions. Therefore, it does not seem historically correct to seek its justification from *Ḥadīth*.

According to al-Shāfiʻī, every person is allowed to hold what he concludes on the basis of his *Ijtihād* and is not required to follow others against his findings. He remarks that if two persons exercise *Ijtihād* and differ in their conclusions, each of them thereby discharges his duty to God and each is right in so far as his *Ijtihād* is concerned.[56] That is why he thinks that the decisions taken on the basis of *Ijtihād* are all correct ostensibly (*ẓāhiran*) and not really (*bāṭinan*). He argues that, for instance, what is obligatory on Muslims is to face the direction of the Kaʻbah and not the Kaʻbah itself.[57] Since *Qiyās* and *Ijtihād*, according to him, are justified on the authority of the Qur'ān, although inferentially, he holds that the decisions taken on their basis should be accepted as being from God, like the Qur'ān and the *Sunnah*. The difference between them is that the former is *jumlah* (ambiguous), as he puts it, and the latter is *iḥāṭah* (certain).[58]

VI

With his emphasis on *Qiyās* and *Ijtihād* which are based on the Qur'ān, *Sunnah*, or *Ijmāʻ*, al-Shāfiʻī nevertheless condemns reasoning by *Istiḥsān*. He regards it as arbitrary opinion and subjective decision. He validates reasoning in law on the basis of the Qur'ān, *Sunnah*, *Ijmāʻ* and *Qiyās*. *Istiḥsān*, according to him, is neither essential (*wāʻjib*), nor does it fall under any one of the four sources.[59] He thinks that while exercising *Istiḥsān*, a jurist does not base himself on any of the four sources but he behaves arbitrarily. He, therefore, attacks it vehemently by describing it sometimes as "pleasing onself (*taladhudh*)",[60] and sometimes "presumptive law-making in religion (*sharaʻ fiʻl-Dīn*)".[61] He advances numerous arguments in refutation of *Istiḥsān* which we discuss presently.

He quotes the Qur'ānic verse which says: "Doth man think that he is to be left unbridled?"[62] He interprets the word '*sudan*' (unbridled) which occurs in the verse as the man who is neither commanded nor prohibited. Further, he quotes the Prophet as having said that he had conveyed to the people everything which God commanded, and prohibited all those things which God prohibited. Again, he argues that the Prophet asked the Muslims to adhere to the Community which he interprets as the adherence to the opinions of the Community, i.e. *Ijmā'*. From the above Qur'ānic verse and the traditions of the Prophet he infers that people have not been left unguided in life. Everything has been described explicitly or implicitly. From this he concludes that no *Ijtihād* is valid except on the basis of *naṣṣ* or *Qiyās*.[63]

He repeatedly argues on the basis of the Qur'ānic verse which asks Muslims to face the direction of the Ka'bah while saying prayer. He says that it is reasonable to believe that God has ordered people to face the direction of the Ka'bah by seeking indications, while he made the *Ka'bah* itself concealed from their eyes. Therefore, people should face it on the basis of indications and not as they like (*istaḥsanū*) or what occurs to their mind. By this he seeks to condemn the use of arbitrary opinion which he describes as *Istiḥsān*.[64]"

Further, he argues that even the Prophet did not exercise *Istiḥsān* in cases where revelation was not available. In support of this point he gives several examples, namely, the story of the people of the Cave, and of the injunctions about *ẓihār* (calling one's wife as unlawful as one's mother) and *qadhf* (accusation of adultery). He contends that the Prophet, when asked about these points, did not reply by his own opinion but waited for revelation.[65]

Again, he adds that if a ruler or a jurisconsult uses *Istiḥsān* in a fresh problem without *naṣṣ* or *Qiyās*, another jurisconsult may take a different decision in the same case.

Consequently, divergent decisions will be taken on the same point by the jurisconsults even of the same town.[66] Here al-Shāfi'ī, it should be noted, contradicts himself. In applying the principle of *Istiḥsān* he is afraid of chaos, but he takes no notice of the divergence of opinion which results from exercising *Qiyās* and *Ijtihād* so strongly advocated by him, In fact, we have seen in *Ijmā' al-khāṣṣah* that al-Shāfi'ī, by not recognizing any possibility of *Ijmā'*, recognizes a perpetual difference of opinion.

Al-Shāfi'ī brings forward another logical argument to refute *Istiḥsān*. He says that even the rationalists (*ahl al- 'uqūl*) who are superior to the learned in respect of intelligence and reason are not allowed to decide cases on the basis of reason, how will then the learned, who are inferior to these rationalists in reason, be allowed to do so? His opponent replies that the rationalists are not conversant with the original examples (*uṣūl*), while the learned are. Al-Shāfi'ī asks him whether their knowledge of *uṣūl* requires them to exercise *Qiyās* or asks them to abandon it. If with their knowledge the learned are allowed to abandon *Qiyās*, the rationalists, too, should be allowed. Rather, he continues, the rationalists are worthy of praise if they are correct in their decisions because they have no knowledge of precedents. Similarly, they should be more excused for abandoning *Qiyās* or committing mistakes because of their ignorance of precedents (*mithāl*) than the learned who are conversant with them. Thus, al-Shāfi'ī does not make any distinction between the rationalists and the learned in case the learned abandon *Qiyās*.[67] It should be pointed out that al-Shāfi'ī's argument here appears to rest on a fallacy. A man who knows the precedent will never neglect it while solving a problem. On the supposition that he does so in the public interest, he still does so while he knows the situation, spirit and the purpose of the precedent better than the man who is entirely ignorant of it and bases himself on pure reason. Can both be equal?

Al-Shāfi'ī recognizes only that mode of *Ijtihād* which is based on the Qur'ān and the *Sunnah*. He substantiates this point by quoting the famous *Ḥadīth* of Mu'ādh b. Jabal and contends that people have been ordered to adhere to the Qur'ān and the *Sunnah* and not to their personal opinions. One's arguing on the basis of *Istiḥsān* without any textual basis in the Qur'ān and the *Sunnah*, according to him, amounts to the fact that one brings his personal opinion on a par with the Qur'ān and the *Sunnah*, and regards it as the third source of law as if people were ordered to follow it, too. But this is against the Qur'ān because it asks people to be obedient to God and His Prophet only (i.e. without resorting to reason).[68] Thus, he invalidates *Istiḥsān* as a principle of law on the basis of the Qur'ān.

To justify *Istiḥsān* it is argued by his opponent that the Prophet had ordered Sa'd to decide the matter of Banū Qurayẓah and therein he took the decision on the basis of his personal opinion. Thereupon the Prophet said that his decision coincided with God's decision in that matter. This shows, the argument goes, that his personal opinion having no basis on an original precedent from the Prophet ("*'alā ghayri aṣlin*"), stood approved. Secondly, it is contended that, during the time of the Prophet, once a dead fish was thrown out of the sea and some Muslims who were on journey had eaten of it. They carried the remnant with them to the Prophet who himself took a little. From this incident it is inferred that the Muslims had eaten the fish through their personal opinion which had no basis in any directive of the Qur'ān or the *Sunnah*. Thirdly, to support the validity of *Istiḥsān* it is said that the Prophet used to send groups of the Companions for preaching Islam to tribes and had asked people to obey their leaders so long as they obeyed God. But some leaders ordered, on occasions, certain things which were not lawful, e.g. they asked a man to throw himself into fire. These leaders had done so on the basis of their personal opinions, although it was disapproved of by the Prophet later.[69]

Al-Shāfi'ī refutes all these arguments one by one. On the first he comments that the Prophet had allowed Sa'd's decision because it was right. For, he asserts, an opinion of the man-of-opinion may be sometimes right and at others wrong. But people are not required to follow a man whose opinion is subject to error. The Prophet, on the other hand, was protected by God Himself from falling into error. Further, a man who asks people to follow a person who exercises *Ijtihād* by his individual opinion and prefers it without any reason, in fact, asks people to follow a man whose opinion is subject to mistake and he is putting such a man in place of the Prophet whose obedience is obligatory. To the second he replies that the Companions had eaten the dead fish out of necessity, although they were not confident whether their action was lawful. That is why on their return they had asked the Prophet about this matter. On the third point he rejoins that the argument itself goes against the exercise of personal opinion and not in favour of it. The Prophet had asked the people to obey their leaders so long as they remained obedient to God. Further, the Prophet himself disapproved of the acts which they had done on their personal opinion.[70]

After examining al-Shāfi'ī's arguments in refutation of *Istiḥsān* we think there was some misunderstanding on the part of al-Shāfi'ī about *Istiḥsān* as exercised by the early schools. It is not correct to say, as al-Shāfi'ī does, that *Istiḥsān* was arbitrary opinion based on one's whims, wishes and fancy influenced by passion. He himself confesses that the Companions had eaten the dead fish out of necessity. It should be noted that necessity is the basic factor of *Istiḥsān*. There is no evidence to believe that *Istiḥsān* in the early schools was based on one's pure reason and whim and had no basis in the Qur'ān and the *Sunnah.* It is true that the basis and the reason for departure from *Qiyās* were often latent and not explicit at first glance. Nevertheless, the jurists must have had some basis in their minds which could be covered under any of the sources of law—so vehemently emphasized by al-Shāfi'ī himself. This is why all decisions taken on the basis of *Istiḥsān* can be related by a chain of reasoning to some decision in the Qur'ān or the *Sunnah.*[71]

Al-Shāfi'ī himself uses the terms *Istiḥsān* and *Istiḥbāb* in his writings, but they are used in a non-technical sense. In the case of the sale of *'arāyā* (sing. *'ariyyah*—assigning a palm-tree to a poor man to eat its fruit, then exchanging dried dates for fruit on the tree to avoid inconvenience caused by his frequent visits) he himself departs from *Qiyās* due to a tradition from the Prophet which allows this kind of barter as an exception; otherwise *muzābanah* (the exchange of dry fruit for that on a tree) is forbidden by the Prophet as a general rule.[72] It is true that al-Shāfi'ī does not use the term *Istiḥsān* in this case, but the method he adopts is the same known as *Istiḥsān* among the 'Irāqīs. We pointed out, in Chapter VI, that *Istiḥsān* was sometimes used by the 'Irāqīs as an exception from a general principle because of a tradition. Therefore, in our view al-Shāfi'ī's sweeping condemnation of *Istiḥsān* is not justified, although it must be admitted that in this case he accepts *Istiḥsān* on the basis of a tradition only.

VII

Let us now turn to the principle of *Ijmā'* in al-Shāfi'ī. In several places in his writings he divides legal knowledge (*al-'ilm*) into two kinds, viz. *'ilm al-'āmmah* and *'ilm al-khāṣṣah.* By the former he means the knowledge which cannot be ignored in any case by a mature and a sane Muslim; rather it is obligatory on him to be familiar with it. The reason is that this kind of knowledge is fundamental in Islam. This covers the obligatory commands and prohibitions like five prayers, Ramaḍān fast, *Ḥajj* pilgrimage, *Zakāh*, prohibition of adultery, homicide, theft, and drinking. The Qur'ān mentioned these essentials explicitly and Muslims at large possess their knowledge. It reached them through the transmission of the people at large ultimately who acquired it from the Prophet. There was no dispute among them on its universal transmission and its obligatoriness. This is the only kind of knowledge where there is no possibility of committing an error in its transmission or interpretation and, therefore, no disputation is allowed. By the latter kind of knowledge, he means the knowledge relating to the details of essentials (*furū' al-farā'iḍ*) which are not plainly mentioned in the Qur'ān or in the *Sunnah*. Although this kind of knowledge is found in the *Sunnah*, it is transmitted by individuals (*akhbār al-khāṣṣah*) and not by the people at large (*akhbār al-'āmmah*). There is room for interpretation in this sort of knowledge which can be acquired by exercising *Qiyās*. According to him, the acquisition of this knowledge is binding neither on the common nor on all the learned but on the sufficient number of the learned (*man fī hi'l-kifāyah*).[73] He conceives that *Ijmā'* is possible only in the former and not in the latter. He establishes this proposition by adducing several arguments which we analyse in the following paragraphs.

Al-Shāfi'ī thinks there is a basic difference between *'ilm al-'āmmah* and *'ilm al-khāṣṣah*; the former is found with every Muslim and no one doubts its existence. He gives the example of the essential obligations as, for example, the number of prayers and that there are four *raka'āt* in *Zuhr* prayer.[74] He maintains that there are two possibilities with regard to the *Ijmā'* of the Community: either it is based on a report from the Prophet or it is not. In the first case, *Ijmā'* would be "certain," while it would not be so in the second case. None the less, he takes the latter as *Ijmā'* in conformity with the people in general, because, he argues, the *Sunnahs* of the Prophet cannot escape the Community at large (*ʻāmmatihim*), while they can escape individuals. Again, he contends that it is well known that people at large cannot gather on what contradicts the *Sunnah* of the Prophet nor on an error. He substantiates this by quoting two traditions from the Prophet. The first reads: "May God grant prosperity to the man who hears my words, remembers them, guards them, and transmits them! Many a transmitter of law is not intelligent himself; and many transmit law to another who is more intelligent than them. There are three things which should not be hated by a Muslim: sincerity in working for God, faithfulness to Muslims, and adherence to the Community of the Muslims—their call shall protect them from behind." The second *Ḥadīth* says: "Addressing the people at Jābiyah (a place in Syria) ʻUmar b. al-Khaṭṭāb said: "The Prophet stood among us as I am standing among you and said: Respect my Companions, then those who follow them and then those who follow them. After them lie will spread so much that a man will swear without being asked to swear and will bear witness without being asked to do so. Beware! One who is pleased to live in the expanse of the Paradise should follow the Community, because the devil is with a solitary man but keeps away from two."[75] In these traditions adherence to the Community has been emphasized by the Prophet. Al-Shāfiʻī says that this means adherence to the agreement of the Community on a certain point relating to what is lawful or unlawful, and not to its physical unity which is meaningless. From this he concludes that one who holds what the Community holds will be regarded as following the Community; and one who holds differently shall be regarded as opposing it. He thinks that error comes from isolation but the Community at large cannot commit an error concerning the meaning of the Qur'ān, the *Sunnah* and *Qiyās*.[76]

These are al-Shāfiʿī's arguments regarding the validity of the *Ijmāʿ* of the Community. It is remarkable that he does not quote any verse from the Qur'ān[77] as quoted later to justify *Ijmāʿ*. This shows that justification of *Ijmāʿ* on the basis of the Qur'ān had not started up to al-Shāfiʿī. As to the traditions adduced by al-Shāfiʿī, it is noteworthy that they do not contain any specific and clear-cut sanction from the Prophet for *Ijmāʿ* in its technical sense. These traditions, if genuine, are as general as there are several other Qur'ānic verses which signify the unity of Muslims. Moreover, al-Shāfiʿī argues inferentially to prove the validity of the *Ijmāʿ* of the Community. These traditions do not speak specifically of the principle of *Ijmāʿ*. In the preceding chapter we pointed out that the idea of *Ijmāʿ* emerged as a socio-political necessity. It was later justified on the basis of the Qur'ān and the traditions of the Prophet. From the above analysis it is evident that no Qur'ānic verse was adduced to justify the principle of *Ijmāʿ* during the period closing with al-Shāfiʿī. Secondly, the traditions on *Ijmāʿ* brought forward by al-Shaybānī and al-Shāfiʿī were not generally known because al-Shaybānī apparently is ignorant of the traditions presented by al-Shāfiʿī while al-Shāfiʿī does not seem to know the tradition quoted by al-Shaybānī. It follows that there was no universal agreement on any *Ḥadīth* to justify the principle of *Ijmāʿ* during the first two centuries of the Hijrah.

From the second tradition quoted by al-Shāfiʿī it appears that he confines the absolute *Ijmāʿ* to the first three generations. This idea seems to have emerged for the first time in al-Shāfiʿī. During the course of his controversies, his opponents do not refer to such a concept. Instead, the traditions quoted by al-Shaybānī on *Ijmāʿ* indicate that there is no limited period for the validity of *Ijmāʿ*. Al-Shaybānī himself does not make any comment on the *Ḥadīth* quoted by him. It follows that he was himself unaware of this notion. We may take the tradition quoted by al-Shāfiʿī, in case it is genuine, as a prediction by the Prophet and not the condemnation of the good works of the later generations. Further, it is worthy of note that the idea of limiting *Ijmā'* to the first three generations contradicts al-Shāfi'ī's statement that the Community will never agree on an error and it also contradicts the famous *Ḥadīth*: 'My community will never agree on an error.' We believe that this sort of tradition has no concern with the principle of *Ijmā'* and its implications but they are interpreted in this manner by the jurists themselves.

We may now discuss al-Shāfi'ī's views on *Ijmā'* in respect of *'Ilm al-khāṣṣah*. We pointed out earlier that he does not validate the *Ijmā'* of the learned. In the following paragraphs we shall analyse his position on this issue.

Al-Shāfi'ī's opponent thinks that certainty (*iḥāṭah*) is necessary in both kinds of knowledge, namely, *'āmmah* and *khāṣṣah*. But al-Shāfi'ī refutes this point of view. He maintains that certainty is found only in the former and not in the latter. He contends that the early generations had divergent opinions on the problems not clearly answered in the Qur'ān. Therefore, they exercised *Qiyās* which resulted in differences. Moreover, there is a possibility of slipping into error in performing *Qiyās* and one can regard ones opponent as erroneous on a question answered on the basis of *Qiyās*. Hence, how can certainty (*iḥāṭah*) be found in *'ilm al-khāṣṣah*?[78]

Again, the opponent holds that the *Ijmā'* of the learned is authoritative provided there is no difference among them. But if they differ, their *Ijmā'* does not constitute authority because it may involve error. In case of disagreement, he suggests that matters should be referred back to their origins (*al-ashyā 'alā uṣūlihā*) unless people at large agree on their displacement from their origins. Further, he maintains that the agreement of the learned in the existing generation is an indication of their agreement in the past and so in the case of disagreement, whether the report of their agreement or disagreement is available or not. To all these arguments al-Shāfi'ī replies that this presupposes the refutation of traditions (*akhbār*) in favour of *Ijmā'*. He holds that a report is necessary to indicate agreement or disagreement of the jurists in the past, for he does not find any *Ijmā'* of the learned in his generation. Thus, al-Shāfi'ī discards the standard of knowing the *Ijmā'* in the past as suggested by his opponent. He disagrees with his opponent on the point that issues should be referred back to their origins in case of difference of opinion. Al-Shāfi'ī tells his opponent that on the latter's view of *Ijmā'*, he has no right to stone a married adulterer since no universal *Ijmā'* exists on the point. He asks his opponent why he maintains the punishment of stoning and does not refer the problem to its origin, that is, executing a person is unlawful unless people universally agree on his execution. Thus the opponent, according to him, breaks his principle himself.[79]

Al-Shāfi'ī begins his inquiry by raising the question of the learned sufficient to validate an *Ijmā'*. He asks his disputant if one out of ten is absent or does not speak, or if one of them dies or turns insane, will the *Ijmā'* of nine be valid? If five or nine die, can one of them give the verdict, and will that be regarded as *Ijmā'*? To all these questions the interlocutor replies that he will follow the majority opinion. Al-Shāfi'ī inquires about the exact number of the majority—would ten, for example, constitute such majority or nine? The opponent replies that both are nearly equal. He does not mention any fixed number constituting majority. Al-Shāfi'ī remarks that he leaves the number absolute and unlimited because if he follows one specific opinion, he wants to be able to say that this carries the approval of the majority; but if he rejects an opinion, he simply be able to say that this is the minority opinion. Further, he asks him if six out of ten agree on a point and four differ from them, whom will he follow? The opponent replies: "Six". On this al-Shāfi'ī retorts that only for the difference of "two" he might follow the wrong and depart from the right opinion; but according to his own principle, he should not follow the erroneous opinion. With this kind of argumentation based on a numerical and mechanical majority, al-Shāfi'ī attempts to prove the absurdity of the concept of the *Ijmā'* of the learned and that majority is not the criterion of right.[80]

Further, he contends that it is well-nigh impossible to meet every jurist in various towns and ask him whether on a certain point he agrees with a given opinion or not; nor is there any possibility to transmit their consent by the people at large from the people at large. Hence, he will have to rely on the solitary report (*khabar al-khāṣṣah*) or *Ḥadīth*. Al-Shāfi'ī, in fact, wants to assert that there is no escape from following the solitary report, whether in *Ijmā'* or in *Ḥadīth*. Thus, there is no reason to reject it in case of *Ḥadīth* when it is accepted in case of the *Ijmā'* by the opponent himself.

Besides, al-Shāfi'ī quotes concrete examples of difference among jurists of various towns. He recounts the names of the lawyers of Mecca, Medina, Kufa and Basra and says that there is no agreement among them in any town. Moreover, he contends that some jurisconsults are held inefficient because of their little knowledge and want of intelligence, while others are regarded as highly competent for giving verdicts on legal problems. When each finds fault with the other, how can they agree universally on any point? Being dismayed by the endless objections raised by al-Shāfi'ī on the *Ijmā'* of the learned, the interlocutor asks him whether there is *Ijmā'* on any problem. Al-Shāfi'ī replies that *Ijmā'* is confined to the obligatory duties (*farā'iḍ*) alone.[81]

Finally, al-Shāfi'ī argues that what the opponent describes as *Ijmā'* is, in fact, the consensus of Ibn al-Musayyib, 'Aṭā', al-Ḥasan, and al-Shā'bī, i.e. jurists of different towns, but the fact is that they never got together in a meeting to his knowledge. He speaks of their *Ijmā'* only on the basis of reports. Moreover, he says that questions on which the Qur'ān and the *Sunnah* are silent, it is *presumed* that these early authorities had exercised *Qiyās*. But al-Shāfi'ī remarks that this is merely a conjecture (*tawahhum*), because, he thinks, they probably employed *ra'y* rather than *Qiyās*. Therefore, he says that his opponent recognized mere conjecture as an authority (*ḥujjah*). Again, he adds that the opinions of these early authorities on several problems were not accepted universally by the Muslims in their lifetime. They died while the Muslims had divergent opinions about their views and no *Ijmā'* ever took place. Besides, he contends that differing laws (*sunnan*) are reported from these authorities by the opponent himself. In respect of these laws the early generations (before Mālik) based themselves on solitary report (*khabar al-infrād*) and on their accommodating attitude towards disagreement (*tawassu'hum fi'l-ikhtilāf*). Further he maintains that criticism on solitary reports began in his own generation while the preceding generations had agreed on their recognition. He refutes his opponent's view that the authorities on law in the earlier generations (before Mālik) had never kept silent on anything they knew. Al-Shāfi'ī argues that the earlier generations passed away and none of them uttered a word about *Ijmā'*. He thinks that after the death of the Prophet none professed *Ijmā'* except in those problems which involved no difference of opinion. He reiterates that it is only the people of the contemporary generation who assert the validity of *Ijmā'* in disputed problems. Al-Shāfi'ī regards this argument as sufficient for the weakness of the concept of the *Ijmā'* of the learned.[82] According to him, the Companions of the Prophet and the Successors of the second and third generations never insisted on *Ijmā'* on any problem with the exception of obligatory duties which are binding on all and sundry; nor had any scholar done so, so far as he knows, on the surface of the earth.[83] These are the arguments advanced by al-Shāfi'ī to refute the *Ijmā'* of the learned claimed by the Medinese and the 'Irāqīs both. It should be pointed out, however, that if the earlier generations had never insisted on *Ijmā'* as al-Shāfi'ī asserts, then it becomes difficult to assign meaning to the *Ḥadīth* on *Ijmā'* quoted by al-Shāfi'ī himself.

From the above controversies of al-Shāfi'ī on *Ijmā'* it is evident that *Ijmā'* of the learned is not valid according to him. However, from *al-Risālah* it appears that his concept of *Ijmā'* is in consonance with that of the early schools. In this work he refers in various places to the *Ijmā'* of the learned and bases his argument on this principle. For instance, he says that the learned (*ahl al-'ilm*) are agreed on the point that *'āqilah* (clan of the murderer) should pay one-third or more of the blood-money (*diyah*) in the case of the accidental murder.[84] In another place, he says that the learned of the Muslims will never agree (*Ijmā' 'ulama' al-Muslimīn*) on a matter which contradicts the *Sunnah* of the Prophet.[85] This statement is obviously very different from his statement that "we know that people at large (*'āmmatahum*) will never agree on a point which contradicts the *Sunnah* of the Prophet or on an error.[86] It is indeed, puzzling that when he confines *Ijmā'* to the obligatory duties and to the people at large (*'āmmah*), how can his former statement about the infallibility of the agreement of the learned stand, particularly in view of the fact that he spent so much force in refuting the possibility of the *Ijmā'* of the learned? It is, therefore, likely that al-Shāfi'ī's theory of the *Ijmā'* of the learned represents a later development from his earlier position. Prof. Schacht puts forward a different thesis that "Shāfi'ī's doctrine of consensus shows a continuous development throughout his writings". Further, he remarks that al-Shāfi'ī started by recognizing the *Ijmā'* of the learned, but "finally he reached the stage of refusing it any authority and even denying its existence". Nevertheless, he went on using it, Prof. Schacht adds, as a subsidiary argument and as an argument *ad hominem*, since the idea was deeply ingrained in him.[87]

Towards the end of *al-Risālah*, al-Shāfi'ī wrote a chapter on disagreement (*ikhtilāf*). He divides disagreement into two kinds, viz. prohibited and permitted. He thinks that on questions for which textual evidence is available in the Qur'ān or the *Sunnah*, disagreement is unlawful for those who are conversant with it. He adduces the Qur'ānic verses 3 : 105 and 98 : 4 which condemn disagreement. He allows disagreement with regard to those problems which provide room for different interpretations by analogy. He discusses a large number of problems in which difference of opinion is reported to have come down since the earliest days of Islam.[88] We pointed out previously, however, that disagreement results from interpretation and application of a text, whether explicit or implicit. However explicit a Qur'ānic passage or a *Ḥadīth* may be, one can differ on its application to a given situation. Therefore, the sharp division of disagreement into lawful and unlawful as done by al-Shāfi'ī does not rest on a sound basis.

Al-Shāfi'ī's formulation of principles no doubt gave a systematic form to Islamic jurisprudence. It brought about consistency in the principles of law and synthesized the stray and isolated opinions of his predecessors. By substituting solitary traditions for *Ijmā'* he discontinued the *ray-ijmā'* process—and this paved the way for closing the door of *Ijtihād*. The principles of law enunciated by him fundamentally influenced the succeeding generations which are under his direct and obvious impact. He introduced a methodology which produced an integrated legal system and brought about its stability. But this formalization arrested the freedom of *Ijtihād* and subsequently contributed to the annihilation of the spirit of originality and creativity. He laid great stress on *Ḥadīth* and its literal implementation in order to wipe out chaos from law. But *Ḥadīth*, too, could not solve the problem because differences in *Ḥadīth* were no less than the differences in *ra'y*.

NOTES

1. Al-Rāzī, Fakhr al-Dīn, *Manāqib al-Imām al-Shāfi'ī*, Cairo, n.d., pp. 56, 57.
2. Abū Yūsuf, *al-Radd 'alā Siyar al-Awzā'ī* Cairo, 1357 A.H., p. 21.
3. Ibn al-Nadīm, *al-Fihrist*, Cairo, 1348 A.H., p. 288.
4. *Ibid.*, p. 286.
5. Ḥājjī Khalīfah, Muṣṭafā b. 'Abd Allāh, *Kashf al-Ẓunūn 'an Asāmī al-Kutub wa'l-Funūn*, Istanbul, 1360 A.H., vol. I, p. 110.
6. Abū Hilāl al-'Askarī, *Kitāb al-Awā'il*, quoted by Shabbīr Aḥmad Khān Ghawrī, 'Islam mayn 'ilm wa ḥikmat kā āghāz', *Ma'ārif*, Azamgarh, vol. LXXXIX, No. 4, April, 1962, p. 278.

   Muḥammad al-Bāqir (d. 114 A.H.) and Ja'far al-Ṣādiq (d. 148 A.H.) are reported to have formulated the principles of law for the first time and dictated them to their disciples. Muḥammad Abū Zahrā, criticizing this view, says that they might have had certain principles in rudimentary form like the 'Irāqīs and the Medinese, but they left no systematic work as al-Shāfi'ī did. See Muḥammad Abū Zahrā', *Uṣul al-Fiqh*, Cairo, 1957, pp. 14-15.
7. Qur'ān, 14:1; 16:44, 89; 42:52.
8. Al-Shāfi'ī, *al-Risālah*, Cairo, 1321 A.H., p. 4.
9. *Ibid.*, pp. 5-10.
10. *Ibid.*, pp. 10-11.
11. *Ibid.*, pp. 11-12.
12. *Ibid.*, pp. 55 f.
13. *Ibid.*, pp. 52, 60.
14. *Ibid.*, p. 54.
15. *Ibid.*, p. 53.
16. *Ibid.*, pp. 58-59.
17. *Ibid.*, pp. 59-60.
18. *Ibid.*, p. 61.
19. *Ibid.*, p. 63.
20. Al-Shāfi'ī, *Kitāb al-Umm*, Cairo, 1325 A.H., vol. VII, p. 252.
21. *Ibid.*, p. 255.
22. Al-Shāfi'ī, *al-Risālah*, *ed. cit.*, p. 51.
23. *Ibid.*, p. 82.
24. *Ibid.*, p. 39.
25. *Ibid.*, pp. 40-41.
26. *Ibid.*, pp. 30, 32, 33 f.
27. *Ibid.*, pp. 32-33. Cf. *Kitāb al-Umm*, *ed. cit.*, vol. VII, pp. 308-10.
28. Al-Shaybānī, *al-Muwaṭṭa'*, Deoband, n.d., pp. 115-117.

29. Al-Shāfi'ī, *al-Risālah, ed. cit.*, pp. 63-64.
30. Al-Shāfi'ī, *Kitāb al-Umm, ed. cit.*, vol. VII, pp. 249, 297. See also his *Ikhtilāf al-Ḥadīth*, on the margin of *al-Umm*, vol. VII, pp. 61, 88, 90, 95, 175 *passim.*
31. Al-Shāfi'ī, *Kitāb al-Umm, ed. cit.*, vol. VII, p. 179.
32. *Ibid.*, p. 246.
33. *Ibid.*, p. 242.
34. *Ibid.*, p. 240.
35. *Ibid.*
36. *Ibid.*, p. 190 *passim.*
37. Al-Shāfi'ī, *Ikhtilāf al-Ḥadīth, ed. cit.*, pp. 116-21.
38. Al-Shāfi'ī, *Kitāb al-Umm, ed. cit.*, vol. VII, pp. 205-6.
39. Al-Shāfi'ī, *Ikhtilāf al-Ḥadīth, ed. cit.*, pp. 339-40.
40. Al-Shāfi'ī, *Kitāb al-Umm, ed. cit.*, vol. VII, p. 291-92.
41. Al-Shāfi'ī, *Ikhtilāf al-Ḥadīth, ed. cit.*, pp. 218-21.
42. Al-Shāfi'ī, *al-Risālah, ed. cit.*, pp. 76-77.
43. Al-Shāfi'ī, *Ikhtilāf al-Ḥadīth, ed. cit.*, p. 148.
44. Margoliouth, D. S., *The Early Development of Mohammedanism*, London, 1914, p. 97.
45. Al-Shāfi'ī, *Kitāb al-Umm, ed. cit.*, vol. VII, p.. 181; cf. *idem, al-Risālah*, Cairo, 1321 A.H., p. 48.
46. Al-Shāfi'ī, *Kitāb al-Umm, ed. cit.*, vol. VII, p. 197.
47. *Ibid.*, p. 101-2.
48. Al-Shāfi'ī, *al-Risālah, ed. cit.*, pp. 70-71.
49. *Ibid.*, pp. 75-76.
50. Abū Yūsuf, *al-Radd 'alā Siyar al-Awzā'ī, ed. cit.*, pp. 24, 135.
51. Al-Shāfi'ī, *al-Risālah, ed. cit.*, p. 70; cf. Majid Khadduri, *Islamic Jurisprudence*, Baltimore, 1961, pp. 306-7.
52. *Ibid.*, p. 66.
53. *Ibid.*, pp. 66, 70. Cf. *Kitāb al-Umm*, vol. VII, p. 85.
54. Al-Shāfi'ī, *Kitāb al-Umm, ed. cit.*, vol. VII, p. 211.
55. *Ibid.*, pp. 273, 275.

The tradition of Mu'ādh regarding *Ijtihād al-ra'y* has been reported by the following authorities:

1. Abū Dā'ūd, *Sunan* (*Bāb Ijtihād al-ra'y fi'l-qaḍā*).
2. Al-Tirmidhī, *Jāmi'* (*Bāb mā Jā'a fi'l Qāḍī kayfa yaqḍī*). After reporting this tradition al-Tirmidhī says: We know this *Hadīth* through this chain alone, which is not continued (*muttaṣil*).
3. Ibn Sa'd, *al-Ṭabaqāt al-Kubrā*, Beirut, 1376 A.H., vol. III, p. 584.
4. Aḥmad b. Ḥanbal, *Musnad*, Cairo, n.d., (old edition), vol. V, p. 230.

Ibn Mājah reports this tradition with a version different from the well-known one. It goes :

قال معاذ : لمابعثنى رسول الله صلى الله عليه وسلم الى اليمن
قال : لا تقضين و لا تفصلن الابما تعلم ، و ان اشكل عليك امر فقف
حتى تبينه ، اوتكتب الى فيه -

(Do not decide anything but by what you know; if you are doubtful in a case, you should wait until it becomes clear to you; otherwise write it to me). Commenting on this tradition Ibn Qayyim al-Jawziyah remarks that the chain of this version is better than that of the well-known version. (Ibn Qayyim, *Tahdhīb*, Cairo, 1949, vol. V, p. 212). According to Ibn Ḥazm, this *Ḥadīth* is a fabrication. He says that al-Ḥārith b. 'Amr, a reporter in the chain, is obscure. Besides, he also rationally criticizes the tradition. (Ibn Ḥazm, *al-Iḥkām fi Uṣūl al-Aḥkām*, Cairo, 1347 A.H., vol. VI, p. 35f). It is important to note that al-Bukhārī and Muslim report, in their collections, the instructions given by the Prophet to Mu'ādh b. Jabal, but they do not mention anything about *Ijtihād*. The doctors of *Ḥadith*, however, themselves are not certain about the authenticity of this *Ḥadith*. It is, therefore, open to question. Cf. Fazlur Rahman, review on Kemal A. Faruki, *Islamic Jurisprudence*, *Islamic Studies*, vol. II, No. 2 (June, 1963), pp. 288-89, under 'Book Reviews.'

It is astonishing that al-Shāfi'ī quotes the *Ḥadīth* of Mu'ādh which favours the use of *ra'y*, although he condemns it vehemently.

56. Al-Shāfi'ī, *Kitāb al-Umm*, *ed. cit.*, vol. VII, pp. 261, 274.

فاذا اجتهد من له أن يجتهد وسعه أن يقول بما وجد الدلالة بان
يكون فى معنى كتاب ، اوسنة اواجماع -

57. *Ibid.*, p. 272. Cf. al-Shāfi'ī, *al-Risālah*, *ed. cit.*, p. 69.
58. *Ibid.*, p. 272.
59. *Ibid.*, p. 271.
60. Al-Shāfi'ī, *al-Risālah*, *ed. cit.*, p. 70.
61. Al-Shāfi'ī, *Kitāb al-Umm*, *ed. cit.*, vol. VI, p. 207.

ويحرم عليه أن يعمل هذا من قوله استحسنت لانه اذا اجاز لنفسه
استحسنت اجاز لنفسه ان يشرع فى الدين -

62. Qur'ān, 75 : 36.
63. Al-Shāfi'ī, *Kitāb al-Umm*, *ed. cit.* vol. VII, p. 271.
64. *Ibid.*, p. 272.
65. *Ibid.*, p. 271.
66. *Ibid.*, p. 273.
67. *Ibid.*, p. 273.

68. *Ibid.*, vol. VI, p. 203.
69. *Ibid.*, p. 205.
70. *Ibid.*, p. 205-6.
71. *Ibid.*, vol. VII, pp. 190, 239.
72. *Ibid.*, p. 182.
73. Al-Shāfi'ī, *al-Risālah*, *ed. cit.*, p. 50.
74. Al-Shāfi'ī, *Kitāb al-Umm*, *ed. cit.*, vol. VII, p. 255.
75. Al-Shāfi'ī, *al-Risālah*, *ed. cit.*, pp. 55, 65. Cf. Fazlur Rahman, *Islamic Methodology in History*, Lahore, 1965, pp. 45-53.
76. Al-Shāfi'ī *al-Risālah*, *ed. cit.*, p. 65.
77. It is reported that al-Shāfi'ī, when he was asked about the justification of *Ijmā'* from the Qur'ān, had pondered over this point for three days and then quoted the verse 4: 115. Tāj al-Dīn al-Subkī, *Ṭabaqāt al-Shāfi'īyat al-Kubrā*, Cairo n.d., vol. II, pp. 19-20. We doubt the authenticity of this report because al-Shāfi'ī does not quote any Qur'ānic verse in justification of *Ijmā'* in his works.
78. Al-Shāfi'ī, *Kitāb al-Umm*, *ed. cit.*, vol. VII, p. 255.
79. *Ibid.*, pp. 255-56.
80. *Ibid.*, p. 256.
81. *Ibid.*, p. 257.

قل فهل من اجماع ؟ قلت : نعم بحمدالله ، كثير فى جملة الفرائض التى لا يسع جهلها -

82. *Ibid.*, p. 258.
83. Al-Shāfi'ī, *Ikhtilāf al-Ḥadīth*, *ed. cit.*, p. 147.
84. Al-Shāfi'ī, *al-Risālah*, *ed. cit.*, p. 73.
85. *Ibid.*, p. 46.
86. *Ibid.*, p. 65.
87. Joseph Schacht, *The Origins of Muhammadan Jurisprudence*, Oxford, 1959, pp. 88-89.
88. Al-Shāfi'ī, *al-Risālah*, *ed. cit.*, p. 77 f.

CONCLUSION

The phase of the Islamic jurisprudence we have dealt with in the preceding chapters is characterized by a freedom of interpretation in the field of law. It has certain features which distinguish it from the later periods. In the light of the foregoing detailed discussion and analysis of the history or the principles of law, we have arrived at certain conclusions which we have already stated in the previous chapters separately. Here we recapitulate briefly the salient points.

We have shown that *fiqh* and other allied terms now used in their restricted sense originally had wider meaning. Their meaning was changed and restricted in course of time. The terms *ra'y* and *riwāyah* were used in opposition to each other in the early stages. *Ra'y* was developed into law (*Fiqh*) and *riwāyah* into *Ḥadīth*. While *ra'y* and *Ḥadīth* were together in the early period, they began to separate from each other in al-Shāfi'ī's time.

Earlier, the four 'roots' of law were interlinked and united with their natural organic ties. The Qur'ān and *Sunnah* constituted one source and *Qiyās* and *Ijmā'* were its forward reaches. The strict technical order of priority in the four sources is found in al-Shāfi'ī's works; such a formal procedure was not there in the early schools. The *ra'y-Ijmā'* process was changed by al-Shāfi'ī which marred the efficacy of *ra'y* and *Ijmā'*; *Ijmā'* was restricted by him to the early generations and it became something like a tradition known through a report.

We then analysed the classical theory of *naskh* and concluded that no verse of the Qur'ān has been abrogated. The theory of *naskh* does not go back to the Prophet. All the verses in the Qur'ān can be shown to be operative if they are interpreted in the light of their historical perspective.

Sunnah was a wider concept, and *Ḥadīth* and *Sunnah* were two separate terms in the pre-Shāfi'ī period. Al-Shāfi'ī removed the distinction between the *Sunnah* and *Ḥadīth* by his emphasis on documenting the *Sunnah* by *Ḥadīth* only. The necessity of introducing *Ḥadīth* into law was felt when the continuous normative practice was threatened with break up through acute differences of legal opinion. The concept "*Sunnah* of the Prophet" had its origin in the Prophet's time when the Qur'ān made his obedience obligatory on the Muslims; but as the *Ḥadīth* was introduced as a universal principle in law, the contents of the *Sunnah* became much larger, as was bound to happen.

The concept of *naṣṣ* was not dominating in the pre-Shāfi'ī period. As a result of al-Shāfi'ī's emphasis on textual evidence, it acquired a dominant position in legal reasoning and became a substitute for the *ra'y-Ijmā'* phenomenon. Unrestricted *ra'y* was violently attacked by al-Shāfi'ī, and, therefore, *Qiyās* was naturally narrowed down to *naṣṣ*. The concept of *naṣṣ* grew progressively rigorous and culminated into a comprehensive term being subdivided into several kinds covering even allusion and implication.

The modern age has raised a large number of new problems for the Islamic *Ummah*. The Qur'ān and the *Sunnah* provide the concrete bases on which answers to these problems can be found. The early phase shows us a natural practical way for interpreting law in the context of new conditions. Now, while exercising *Ijtihād*, the scope of *Qiyās* should be widened, making it more practicable and efficacious in solving the problems. The *ra'y-Ijmā'* process should be resurrected to check the fallibility of new decisions.

To open the gate of *Ijtihād*, which is the crying need of the day, the question arises as to who should exercise *Ijtihād*, the competent scholars or the Government authorities? Besides, what method would be employed to ascertain that *Ijmā'* has been arrived at on a certain point? This question is important because *Ijmā‘* in the early period seems to be so informal that it is difficult to know whether on a certain point there was *Ijmā‘* or not. We are of the opinion that *Ijtihād* should be exercised by the competent scholars in cooperation with the Government so that it can be enacted into legislation; otherwise it would remain purely theoretical and the conflict between the scholars and the Government will continue. Because *Ijmā‘* establishes itself only gradually and almost imperceptibly with the passage of time, there should be some precise and formal machinery to ascertain the agreement on the immediate questions.

Bibliography

(Works referred to in this Book)

Abū Ḥanīfah, Nu'mān b. Thābit, *Kitāb al-'Ālim wa'l-Mut-a 'allim*, Hyderabad, Deccan, 1349 A.H.

idem, *al-Fiqh al-Akbar*, Hyderabad, Deccan, 1953.

idem, *al-Fiqh al-Absaṭ*, quoted by al-Bayāḍī in his *Ishārāt al-Marām min 'Ibārāt al-Imām*, Cairo, 1949.

Abū Yūsuf, Ya'qūb, *Kitāb al-Kharāj*, Cairo, 1302 A.H.

idem, *Kitāb al-Athār*, Cairo, 1335 A.H.

idem, *al-Radd 'alā Siyar al-Awzā'ī*, Cairo, n.d. (ed. Abu'l Wafā al-Afghānī).

Abū Hilāl al-'Askarī *Kitāb al-Awā'il*, quoted by Shabbīr Aḥmad Khān Ghawrī in his article *Islām mayn 'ilmu ḥikmat kā āghāz*, *Ma'ārif*, Azamgarh, volume LXXXIX, No. 4, April, 1962.

Abū Dā'ūd, Sulaymān b. Ash'ath, *Sunan*, Kanpur, 1928, 2 Vols.

Aḥmad b. Ḥanbal, *Musnad*, Cairo, 1313 A.H., 6 vols.

'Alī Ḥasan 'Abd al-Qādir, *Naẓrah 'Āmmah fī Tā'rīkh al-Fiqh al-Islāmī*, Cairo, 1956.

Al-Āmidī, Abu'l-Ḥasan 'Alī, *al-Iḥkām fī Uṣūl al-Aḥkām*, Cairo, 1914, 4 vols.

Al-Ash'arī, Abu'l-Ḥasan, *Maqālāt al-Islāmiyyīn wa Ikhtilāf al-Muṣallīn*, Cairo, 1950, 2 vols.

Baljon, J. M. S., *Modern Muslim Koran Interpretation*, Leiden, 1961.

Al-Bayhaqī, Abu'l-Ḥasan, *al-Sunan al-Kubrā*, Hyderabad, Deccan, 1354, A.H. 10 vols.

Al-Bukhārī, Muḥammad b. Ismā'īl, *al-Jāmi' al-Ṣaḥiḥ*, Leiden, 1862, 4 vols.

Al-Bukhārī, 'Abd al-'Azīz, *Kashf al-Asrār 'alā Uṣūl al-Bazdawī*, Stanbul, 1308 A.H., 4 vols.

Al-Bazdawī, *Uṣūl al-Bazdawī*, published on the margin of *Kashf al-Asrār, ed. cit.*

Coulson, N. J., *A History of Islamic Law*, Edinburgh, 1964.

idem, *Conflicts and Tensions in Islamic Jurisprudence*, Chicago/London, 1969.

Al-Dārimī, 'Abd Allāh, *Sunnan*, Damascus, 1349 A.H., 2 vols.

Al-Dhahabī, Shams al-Dīn, *Tadhkirat al-Ḥuffāẓ*, Hyderabad, Deccan, n.d., 4 vols.

Donaldson, D. M., *Studies in Muslim Ethics*, London, 1953.

Fayzee, Asaf, A. A., *Outlines of Muhammadan Law*, London, 1960.

Fazlur Rahman, *Islamic Methodology in History*, Lahore, 1965.

Al-Ghazālī, Muḥammad, *Iḥyā' 'ulūm al-Dīn*, Cairo, 1939, 4 vols.

Goldziher, Ignaz, *Le Dogme et la Loi de l'Islam*, Paris, 1958.

Von Grunebaum, G. E., *Islam*, London, 1961.

Guillaume, Alfred, *New Light on the Life of Muhammad*, Cambridge, n.d. *idem*, *Islam*, Edinburgh, 1962.

Ḥājjī Khalīfah, Muṣṭafā b. 'Abd Allāh, *Kashf al-Ẓunūn 'an Asāmi'l-Kutub wa'l-Funūn*, Stanbul, 1360 A.H., 2 vols.

Ḥassān b. Thābit, *Dīwān*, ed. 'Abd al-Raḥmān al-Barqūqī, Cairo, 1926.

Haykal, Muḥammad Husayn, *al-Fārūq, 'Umar*, Cairo, 1346 A.H., 2 vols.

Ibn 'Abd al-Barr, Yūsuf, *Jāmi' Byān al-'Ilm wa Faḍlihī*, Cairo, n.d. 2 vols.

Ibn Ḥazm, Abū Muḥammad 'Alī, *al-Iḥkām fī Uṣūl al-Aḥkām*, Cairo, 1947, 4 vols.

Ibn Hishām, 'Abd al-Malik, *Sīrat al-Nabi*, (1) Cairo, 1329 A.H., 3 vols., (2) Cairo, n.d. ed. Muhammad Muḥi al-Dīn 'Abd al-Ḥamīd, 4 vols.

Ibn Isḥāq, *Maghāzī*, MS. quoted by Alfred Guillaume, in his *New Light on the Life of Muhammad*, Cambridge, n.d.

Ibn Khaldūn, 'Abd al-Raḥmān, *Muqaddimah*, Beirut, 1900.

Ibn Khuzaymah, al-Muẓaffar, *al-Mūjaz fi'l-Nāsikh wa'l Mansūkh*, Cairo, 1323 A.H.

Ibn Manẓūr, Muḥammad b. Mukarram, *Lisān al-'Arab*, Beirut, 1956, 15 vols.

Ibn Mājah, Muḥammad b. Yazīd, *Sunan*, Lucknow, n.d. 2 vols.

Ibn al-Muqaffa', 'Abd Allāh, *Risālah fi'l-Ṣaḥābah* in *Rasā'il al-Bulaghā'*, Cairo, 1954.

Ibn al-Murtaḍā, Aḥmad b. Yaḥyā, *Kitāb Ṭabaqāt al-Mu'tazilah*, Beirut, 1961.

Ibn al-Nadīm, Muḥammad, *al-Fihrist*, Cairo, 1348 A.H.

Ibn Qayyim al-Jawziyah, Muḥammad, *I'lām al Muwaqqi'īn* Delhi, 1313 A.H., 2 vols.

idem, *Tahdhīb, Sharḥ Sunan Abī Dā'ūd*, Cairo, 1949, 8 vols.

Ibn Qutaybah, 'Abd Allāh b. Muslim, *Tā'wīl Mukhtalif al-Ḥadīth*, Cairo, 1326 A.H.

idem, *al-Imāmah wa'l-Siyāsah*, Cairo, n.d.

Ibn Sa'd, Muḥammad, *al-Ṭabaqāt al-Kubrā*, Beirut, 1957, 3 vols.

Al-Iṣfahānī, Abū Nu'aym Aḥmad, *Ḥilyat al-Awliyā'*, Cairo, 1936, 10 vols.

Imām al-Ḥaramayn, 'Abd al-Malik, *al-Waraqāt fī Uṣūl al-Fiqh* in *Majmū' Mutūn uṣūliyah*, Damascus, n.d.

Al-Jabarī, 'Abd al-Muta'āl Muḥammad, *al-Naskh fi'l Shar'iat al-Islāmiyah*, Cairo, 1961.

Al-Jāḥiẓ, 'Amr b. Baḥr, *al-Bayān wa'l-Tabyīn*, Cairo, 1949, 4 vols.

Al-Jaṣṣāṣ, Abū Bakr Aḥmad b. 'Alī, *Kitāb Aḥkām al-Qur'ān*, Constantinople, 1325 A.H., 3 vols.

Al-Jawharī, Ismā'īl b. Ḥammād, al-Ṣiḥāḥ, Cairo, n.d. ed. Aḥmad 'Abd al-Ghafūr 'Aṭṭār, 6 vols.

Al-Khuḍarī, Muḥammad, *Uṣūl al-Fiqh*, Cairo, 1938.

Lane, Edward William, *Arabic-English Lexicon*, London, 1863, 8 parts.

Majid Khadduri, *Law in the Middle East*, Washington, 1955.

idem, *Islamic Jurisprudence*, Baltimore, 1961.

Mālik, *al-Muwaṭṭa'*, Cairo, 1951, 2 vols.

Margoliouth, D. S., *The Early Development of Muhammedanism*, London, 1914.

Al-Mubarrad, Muḥammad b. Yazīd, *Kāmil*, Cairo, 1936, 3 vols.

Muḥammad 'Abduh, *Tafsīr al-Manār*, Cairo, 1954, 12 vols.

Al-Naḥḥās, Muḥammad b. Aḥmad, *Kitāb al-Nāsikh wa'l-Mansūkh fi'l-Qur'ān al-Karīm*, Cairo, 1323 A.H.

New Testament, in *the Holy Bible*, London, n.d.

Noldeke, Theodor, *Geschichte des Qorans*, Hildesheim, 1961.

Qur'ān.

Al-Rāzī, Fakhr al-Dīn Muhammad b. 'Umar, *Mafātīḥ al-Ghayb*, Cairo, 1307 A.H. 8 vols.

idem, *Manāqib al-Imām al-Shafi'ī*, Cairo, n.d.

Ritter, Von H., article Studien zur Geschichte der islamischen Frömmigkeit—Ḥasan al-Baṣrī, *Der Islam*, Band 21,—— The epistle of al-Ḥasan al-Baṣrī to 'Abd al-Malik b. Marwān, pp. 67-82.

Saḥnūn b. Sa'īd al-Tanūkhī, *al-Mudawwant al-Kubrā*, Cairo, 1323 A.H., 16 vols.

Al-Sarakhsī, Muḥammad b. Aḥmad, *al-Mabsūṭ*, Cairo, 1324 A.H., 30 vols.

Sayyid Aḥmad Khān, *Tafsīr al-Qur'ān*, Lahore, n.d., 6 vols.

Shabbīr Aḥmad Khān Ghawrī, article *Islām mayn 'ilm wa ḥikmat ka āghāz*, *Ma'ārif*, Azamgarh, vol. LXXXIX, No. 4, April, 1962.

Al-Shāfi'ī, Muḥammad b. Idrīs, *Kitāb al-Umm*, Cairo, 1325 A.H., 7 vols.

idem, *Jimā' al-'Ilm*, ed. Shākir, Cairo, 1940.

idem, *al-Risālah*, Cairo, 1321 A.H.

idem, *Ikhtilāf al-Ḥadīth*, published on the margin of *Kitāb al-Umm*, vol. VII.

Shāh Waliy Allāh, *al-Fawz al-Kabīr* (Urdu translation), Karachi, 1960.

idem, *al-Tafhīmāt al-Ilāhiyah*, Bijnor, 1936, 2 vols.

Al-Sharistānī, Muḥammad b. 'Abd al-Karīm, *Kitāb al-Milal wa'l-Niḥal*, Cairo, 1317 A.H., 4 vols.

idem, *Kitāb Nihāyat al-Iqdām fī 'Ilm al-Kalām*, Oxford, 1934.

Al-Shāṭibi, Abū Isḥāq Ibrāhīm b. Mūsā, *al-Muwafaqāt*, Cairo, n.d. 4 vols.

idem, al-I'tiṣām, Cairo, n.d., 4 vols.

Al-Shaybānī, Muḥammad b. al-Ḥasan, *al-Muwaṭṭa'*, Deoband, n.d.

idem, *Kitāb al-Ḥujaj al-Mubīnah fī radd 'alā Ahl al-Madīnah*, MS.

idem, *al-Aṣl*, Cairo, 1954.

idem, *al-Jāmi' al-Ṣaghīr*, Lucknow, 1291 A.H.

idem, *al-Siyar al-Kabīr*, with Commentary by al-Sarakhsī (1) Cairo, 1957, (2) Hyderabad, Deccan, 1335 A.H., 4 vols.

Shiblī Nu'mānī, *Sīrat al-Nabī*, Azamgarh, n.d., 6th edition, 6 vols.

Schacht, Joseph, *The Origins of Muhammadan Jurisprudence*, Oxford, 1959.

idem, *An Introduction to Islamic Law*, Oxford, 1964.

idem, Article 'Mālik b. Anas,' *Shorter Encyclopaedia of Islam*, Leiden, 1961, pp. 320-24.

Al-Suyūṭī, Jalāl al-Dīn, *al-Muzhir*, Cairo, n.d., 2 vols.

idem, *al-Itqān fī 'Ulūm al-Qur'ān*, Cairo, 1317, A.H., 2 vols.

Al-Ṭabarī, Muḥammad b. Jarīr, *Jāmi' al-Bayān fi Tafsir al-Qur'ān*, Cairo, 1328 A.H., 30 vols.

idem, *Ikhtilāf al-Fuqahā'*, Leiden, 1933.

Al-Ṭaḥawī, Aḥmad b. Muḥammad, *Mushkil al-Āthār*, Hyderabad, Deccan, 1333 A.H., 4 vols.

idem, *Sharḥ Ma'āni'l-Āthār*, Deoband, n.d., 2 vols.

Al-Tirmidhī, Muḥammad b. 'Īsā, *al-Jāmi'*, Kanpur, n.d., 2 vols.

Watt, W. Montgomery, *Islam and the Integration of Society*, London, 1961.

Yāqūt, *Kitāb Mu'jam al-Buldān*, Cairo, 1906, 10 vols.

Yūsuf, S. M. article '*The Sunnah*—its transmission, development and revision', *Islamic Culture*, vol. XXXVII October, 1963, No. 4, and vol. XXXVIII January, 1964, No. 1.

Al-Zawzanī, Ḥusayn b. Aḥmad, *Sharḥ al-Mu'allaqāt al-Sab'ah*, Cairo, 1315 A.H.

Al-Zurqānī, Muḥammad b. 'Abd al-Bāqī, *Sharḥ al-Zurqānī 'ala'l Mawāhib al-laduniyah*, Cairo, 1291 A.H., 8 vols.

INDEX